ESKIMO
OF THE
CANADIAN
ARCTIC

ESKIMO
OF THE
CANADIAN
ARCTIC

EDITED AND WITH AN INTRODUCTION BY

VICTOR F. VALENTINE

AND

FRANK G. VALLEE

The Carleton Library No. 41 / McClelland and Stewart Limited

The Canadian Publishers
McClelland and Stewart Limited
25 Hollinger Road, Toronto 16

PRINTED AND BOUND IN CANADA
BY
T. H. BEST PRINTING COMPANY LIMITED

THE CARLETON LIBRARY

A series of Canadian reprints and new collections of source material relating to Canada, issued under the editorial supervision of the Institute of Canadian Studies of Carleton University, Ottawa.

CONTENTS

Introduction

There are approximately 60,000 Eskimo in the world, the largest number of them living in Greenland and Alaska, 30,000 and 16,000 respectively, the smallest in Siberia, 1,300. About one quarter of the world's Eskimo population lives in Canadian territory. Despite a death rate which is high when compared with that of other ethnic groups in the country, Canada's Eskimo population is growing at a rate faster than that of the country as a whole. In the Canadian arctic and sub-arctic there were, in 1966, about 1,200 Eskimo in Labrador, about 2,000 in arctic Quebec, and about 10,000 in the Northwest Territories. Precise figures on migration are lacking, but the evidence suggests that only a very small number of Eskimo have taken up residence south of parallel 60 in the provinces. This trickle of migration has been of the sponsored kind: the federal government and private employers invite selected Eskimo to take advantage of specific employment and training opportunities.

Three major stages can be distinguished in the socio-economy of the Eskimo of the Canadian Arctic. The earliest stage was that of hunting and gathering; the next, that of trapping or whaling combined with hunting and gathering; and the most recent, that in which one of these activities is combined with wage labour in service occupations, dependence on statutory grants, and relief. A few hundred depend exclusively on wage employment; a few hundred are virtually dependent on wild-life harvesting; but the majority derive income and sustenance from a variety of sources such as hunting, fishing, trapping, casual wage employment, carving, and the manufacturing of handicrafts. Few Eskimo are identified with one specific occupational category. In social class terms and in the setting of the country as a whole, they form a frontier, non-agricultural proletariat sharing with Canada's Indians the lowest average income per family head of any group in the country.

In the literature of social science, Eskimo culture and society very often appear as an example of the classical hunting and gathering way of life. The Eskimo in this literature have the distinction of occupying a position at the extreme end of various continua. For example, they are often represented as having the least complex social organization, the most flexible normative system, the most rigorous and limiting habitat, and so on. The tendency, particularly in textbooks, is to present an over-simplified view of the Eskimo and to attribute to them much more uniformity than exists in fact.

Anthropologists often refer to the Arctic in terms of a single Eskimo culture area. However, we can talk in only the most general and abstract way of a single Eskimo culture and society: that is, by defining them in terms of certain shared features of material culture, custom, language, and expressive styles rather than in terms of one inclusive society and culture embracing the Eskimo in all northern regions. In effect, the Eskimo lived in small societies, the members of each of which shared certain sub-cultural patterns. Each of these small societies and sub-cultures was known by a name which, when translated into English, would be rendered as "the people of . . ." (Eskimo suffix, -miut). For example, to those inland from them, the people in the regions around Coppermine are *Kilinemiut*, "the people on the edge of the land"; those on the north shore of the Ungava Peninsula are the *Taqaqmiut*, "the people of the dark side, where the moon shines."

In the literature, these groups are frequently referred to as tribes. The Eskimo, however, did not have tribes in the anthropological sense, according to which the term tribe applies to a group of people linked together in a corporate structure. It is best to refer to these named Eskimo groupings as sub-cultures.

We tried to include a sample of Eskimo groups from each of the major regions in the north but were not as successful in this as we would have liked due to a paucity of contemporary published material dealing with some areas, particularly the western Arctic. This regional gap in the selections is more than compensated for by the ready availability in paper-back form of Diamond Jenness' classic, *The People of the Twilight*, and of

Raymond de Coccola's and Paul King's, *Ayorama*, both of which provide worthy accounts of traditional Eskimo culture in the western Arctic and are recommended as supplementary reading.

Two themes course through the selections: the flexibility of Eskimo social organization, and modernization. To illustrate these, the papers have been grouped into two parts. In the first, we present papers which focus on the traditional elements of Eskimo culture, even though most of the research upon which the papers are based was undertaken during the past decade, a period when the process of acculturation was becoming intense. The subjects covered in this part include prehistory, ecology, physical anthropology, world-view, religion, art, and aspects of social organization such as kinship and law.

In the second, we present papers dealing with trends and issues in modernization covering such topics as new forms of social organization, economic and educational trends, urbanization and the learning of new social skills, emergence of pan-Eskimoism, as well as the influence of a world market for Eskimo art on current Eskimo art-forms and world-view.

Most of the papers in the first part deal with those aspects of culture which are materialized or objectified in things or sounds which can be perceived directly by an observer: implements, carvings, dwellings, words, and social behaviour. One can make fairly precise statements about survival or loss of items of Eskimo culture which are so materialized and objectified, and several contributors do this, specifying changes in material culture, carving styles, kinship practices, residential patterns, and the like.

However, it is another matter to assess survival or loss in beliefs and the meanings with which people imbue reality. These elusive features of culture are not amenable to direct observation; they must be inferred from the oral tradition, reports on dreams, responses to projective tests, and other sources which observers who are fortunate and skilled enough have had transmitted to them by their Eskimo informants. The papers by Carpenter on mythology and by Frederiksen and Turquetil on religion are of this order, and are cast in terms of the "ethnographic present." The authors do not specify if or to what extent the beliefs and world-views they describe were prevalent among the Eskimo they studied. We are told simply that they occurred.

In his overview of Canadian Eskimo prehistory, Taylor makes economic, technological, and residential adaptation a focal concept in his interpretation of archaeological studies. There can be no dispute over the flexibility of the traditional Eskimo way of life in so far as these kinds of adaptation are concerned.

Other contributors are especially impressed with the flexibility of the traditional Eskimo culture and social organization. Gagné illustrates the suppleness of the Eskimo language in dealing with spatial concepts. Implicit in Martijn's account of the trends in carving techniques and styles is the Eskimo readiness to change as a result of outside pressures and demands. Van den Steenhoven's case histories on reactions to deviance reveal a strong tendency to "ride along" with situations and choose courses of action in an *ad hoc* manner rather than depend on a rigid normative code. Finally, Damas calls attention to the element of "electiveness" in traditional Eskimo kinship terminology and behaviour and emphasizes the influence of ecology and the seasonal cycle in determining which kinship usages prevail.

The adaptive responses of the Eskimo are also featured in the papers in the second part. Since the end of World War II, all Eskimo groups have been under mounting pressure to modernize. Previous to that time, changes introduced by whalers, fur traders, missionaries, and others wrought comparatively piecemeal and often gradual adjustments on the part of the Eskimo. Contact was as a rule sporadic and localized because of poorly developed methods of transportation and communication, and it occurred mainly in those areas of the north accessible by sea or inland waterways. The recent expansion northward of modern methods of transportation and communication and the massive intervention by the Canadian government in Eskimo affairs, coupled with the construction of the DEW line, defence bases, and administrative centres have intensified the pace of change. Almost every facet of Eskimo life has been affected. A growing number of Eskimo have abandoned life on the land for the security offered in the new, relatively large, government-administered towns. This has necessitated the learning of new social and occupational skills to deal with what in effect is a new environment for them.

The papers by Vallee on social differentiation, along with those by Willmott and Balikci on flexibility and adaptability in Eskimo community organization, touch on this point. They can be regarded as a bridge between parts one and two, at least as far as social organization is concerned, for they contrast the highlights of the traditional forms of organization with those emerging in today's settlements.

The resilient qualities and adaptive abilities of the Eskimo are not the central issue for Jenness. For him, the central issue is a chronic lack of employment opportunities and industrial development in the Arctic capable of providing steady work for a growing, youthful labour force. He suggests that industrial development will probably never come to the Arctic because of its limited natural resource base, remoteness from world markets, and rigorous climate. The Eskimo, in his view, must be educated and trained to find jobs in the cities of the south. Failing this he sees their progressive demoralization through government relief and "make work" projects.

We suggest that Jenness' analysis is rooted in the classical conception of an industrial society in which the making of marketable goods takes precedence over the provision of social services in the definition of what constitutes meaningful or productive work. He is skeptical about the possibility of the Eskimo being employed in service-type occupations because these do not generate capital and, for him, amount to having the Eskimo "take in one another's washing" at the expense of the southern taxpayer.

The Honigmanns, on the other hand, in both their papers, make a different kind of analysis and come to more optimistic conclusions. They tacitly accept the fact that new towns like Frobisher Bay are economically dependent on the "outside" and not on the arctic hinterland. For them Frobisher Bay can be viewed as providing practical learning experiences for the Eskimo. By living in the town and by participating in all its daily activities the Eskimo acquire new information about how our social system works, and in the process are drawn into a consideration of the larger world environment. This message is implicit in their paper dealing with Eskimo drinking behaviour, and is the central theme of their paper dealing with tutelage.

We suggest that the Honigmann's conceptual framework is more closely related to Daniel Bell's concept of the post-industrial society than to the classical model of an industrial society employed by Jenness. Frobisher Bay, a product of modern science and engineering, exhibits many of the features which Bell characterizes as post-industrial. It may well be one of the ironies of history that the Eskimo, commonly thought to be one of the least culturally advanced groups in the world, are experiencing the effects of the post-industrial period at a more intensive and perhaps faster rate than those of us living in the cities of the south. We also suggest that the Honigmanns are attempting to take a fresh look at acculturation theory – a look which should raise serious questions about the usefulness, at least in the Canadian Arctic, of the two-party transactional model of older acculturation studies.

Brant and Hobart, in their paper, draw attention to the social and psychological effects for the Eskimo of an educational system directed toward "cultural replacement" rather than "cultural continuity" or "synthesis." They are concerned about the efficiency of an educational programme which seems to regard the Eskimo as a "resource" to be processed through schools and other training programmes designed to turn them into a technically competent, mobile work force. Vallee's paper on co-operatives takes up this issue but from a different point of view. He suggests that more than any other government-sponsored programme, the cooperative movement provides a special kind of learning experience for the Eskimo, one in which the ties of unilateral dependency between adminis-trator and Eskimo are less restrictive, allowing the Eskimo flexibility to pursue goals which may be either traditional or modern. The spread of the cooperative movement, he thinks, provides a link between Eskimo of different regions and makes possible the emergence of a pan-Eskimo movement. Finally, the paper by Swinton on Eskimo art once again illustrates the themes of flexibility and modernization by showing how the

Eskimo have varied their art forms to meet changed economic conditions. Today's Eskimo artist has developed an individualistic rather than collective style mainly in response to the demands of an "outside" market. The existence of this market and concern for it have further linked the Eskimo to the broader world environment.

This is not meant to be an exhaustive account of the history, culture, and present position of the Eskimo of Canada. Nor is it meant to be of professional use to the specialist in Eskimology or in one of the sub-disciplines of social science. As with other works in the Carleton Library Series, this one is aimed primarily at students and the general reading public. For those who may wish to deepen and broaden their knowledge of the Canadian Eskimo, we have included a select bibliography of recent works.

For reasons of economy, we have reduced editorial comment to a minimum and have omitted most of the footnotes in the original texts, except for explanatory notes and references connected with direct quotations. As an example of how drastic some of this cutting has been, the first article in the book, by William E. Taylor, contained 36 noted references; we reduced the number to 6. Charles Martijn's article on Eskimo carving covers 50 pages in the original. We have excerpted only 7. Considerable condensation of the works of David Damas, Diamond Jenness and John and Irma Honigmann should also be noted. All omissions in the text are indicated by ellipses. In some cases, we have supplied titles for articles excerpted from various sections of a monograph.

VICTOR F. VALENTINE
FRANK G. VALLEE
Carleton University
April, 1968

PART ONE:

TRADITIONAL ASPECTS OF ESKIMO CULTURE

An Archaeological Overview of Eskimo Economy

WILLIAM E. TAYLOR, jr.

This paper attempts to highlight certain qualities of the Eskimo economy seen in overview. If it repeats some anthropological clichés, the repetition serves a purpose, for clichés often become such by innate worth, and some reviewed in this paper seem to have been largely forgotten in recent literature on Eskimo prehistory. A rare exception, and a point of departure for this paper, was recently offered by Collins, who notes:

> *In America, however, there is sometimes a tendency to see an overly close relationship between specific cultural manifestations and particular kinds of environment, and to overemphasize the role of environment in the dissemination of culture. In the Eskimo field this point of view is reflected in the related concept of a rather sharp dichotomy between inland and coast, with the former the center of origin – a kind of* fata morgana *that has beset Eskimo archaeology for decades and which still exerts its residual influence, even though the concept in its original elaborated form no longer finds acceptance.*[1]

The three parts of this paper are: first, a brief recalling of prominent hypotheses on Eskimo origins, because they are so embedded in ideas about the nature of Eskimo economy; second,

SOURCE: This is a revised version of a paper delivered by Dr. Taylor as the Boyd Memorial Lecture, Department of Anthropology, University of Toronto, October, 1963. Only the second half of the paper has been published previously, the part from page 11, which is here reprinted from "An Archaeological Perspective on Eskimo Economy," *Antiquity*, Vol. XL (1966), pp. 114-120. Reprinted by permission of the author and publisher.

[1] Henry B. Collins, "Bering Strait to Greenland," in John M. Campbell (ed.), *Prehistoric Cultural Relations between the Arctic and Temperate Zones of North America* (Montreal: Arctic Institute of North America, 1962, Technical Paper 11), p. 134.

a review of the economics of major prehistoric and historic Eskimo groups; and last, from these data, observations on the fundamental nature of the Eskimo economic adaptation.

Hypotheses on Eskimo Origins

In 1767, Cranz suggested that the Eskimo were originally an Asiatic people who, because of population pressures, migrated to northeastern Siberia and across Bering Strait to Alaska, and then continued east reaching Greenland in the fourteenth century A.D. In 1887, Rink pioneered a different approach to the question, presenting a theory based on a consideration of specific elements of Eskimo culture and the environmental conditions necessary for their origin. He saw the Eskimo as an originally inland group, inhabiting the interior of Alaska and perhaps of Canada as well. Their transition from an inland to a coastal life was seen to have occurred as they gradually descended the rivers to the sea adapting to new conditions *en route*. Subsequently they spread across the Arctic, to Greenland and to Siberia.

Murdoch, in 1888, opposed the Rink theory on the grounds that the progressive development of Eskimo culture from south Alaska to Greenland was ethnologically less regular than Rink had proposed. Murdoch thought rather the opposite, that the south Alaskan variant was the highly specialized form and that the truly primitive form occurred in the Central Arctic, the variant construed most specialized by Rink. Murdoch also proposed an inland origin south of Hudson Bay, with migratory movements west and then north to Greenland, east of the bay to Labrador, and inland across northern Canada to the Yukon, Alaska, and Siberia. Boas saw an inland origin indicated in the folklore, but placed the homestead west – not south – of Hudson Bay.

The Jesup North Pacific expedition ushered in the present century with a fine flourish of field research involving Boas, Swanton, Bogoras, Jochelson, Teit, Laufer, and Harlan I. Smith. Their work demonstrated many affinities, especially in folklore, between the cultures of northeastern Siberia and the northern Pacific coast of North America. This lead to the "Eskimo wedge" theory – the idea that the two regions had maintained intimate and extensive contact exclusive of the Eskimo, and that the Eskimo had only rather recently entered Alaska from the east, forming a wedge which severed contact between northwestern America and northeastern Asia.

In 1904 a linguist, William Thalbitzer, suggested that the region about Bering Strait was likely the original home of the Eskimo. Ten years later he proposed that the "Eskimo mother-group" came from the coasts of Siberia. Sapir agreed that the linguistic evidence suggested a western source, and noted that this challenged the idea of an eastern interior origin.

Theories of western origin were rejected by Steensby in 1916 in his important article, "An Anthropo Geographical Study of the Origin of the Eskimo Culture." Steensby applied the concept of culture strata so popular in its day, and still popular in traditional guise; he also introduced the terms "Paleoeskimo" and "Neoeskimo."* The hypotheses on Eskimo origins became increasingly complex. Steensby proposed an original northern inland Indian beginning, a culture whose winter-hunting techniques had become specifically and strongly developed by adaptation to the winter ice of the central Arctic to produce the Palae-Eskimo stratum with sea-ice hunting, dog sled, and snow house. He suggested that the shift from the northern inland Indian to the Palae-Eskimo probably occurred around Coronation Gulf. Having come down the rivers and out to the sea in this area, the Palae-Eskimo then spread to Alaska and Greenland. In Alaska, under influence from Pacific Asiatics, especially the Japanese, there occurred the subsequent transition to Neo-Eskimo with the addition of such features as the umiak (a large, open family boat), open-sea kayak hunting, and the bird dart.

Gudmund Hatt published his views in 1916 and, using the culture strata concept, came to a rather different conclusion than Steensby. Hatt considered that the north coast of America was first occupied by an old coast-adapted culture brought from northeastern Asia; the Palae-Eskimo stage was coastal and Asian. The later culture stratum was the inland, American Indian form, based on the snowshoe and snowshoe-hunting of

---

*Henceforth in this paper the author's own rendition of these terms as Palae-Eskimo and Neo-Eskimo is used. (Editors)

reindeer and moose, the birch canoe, and the conical lodge. Its influence ranged from Lapland to Labrador and, by migration and diffusion, was carried downstream from the northern Canadian interior to the older coast culture, giving it the kayak and absorbing and partly transforming the coastal culture. The Neo-Eskimo form that resulted was extended to Alaska and Greenland.

In a brief and lucid statement made in 1923, Kroeber suggested that Eskimo culture began in Siberia, with some influence from Asian and European centres of higher civilization, and that only the finishing touches were added to the culture after it had spread across arctic America. In 1925 Bogoras expressed a view essentially in accord with Thalbitzer, Sapir, Hatt, and Kroeber.

In 1927 a new phase began, with the publication of Mathiassen's archaeological studies from the Canadian eastern Arctic. This was the first systematic archaeological work in arctic America, introducing in a new way the dimension of time to the problem of Eskimo origins and, for that question, it marks the beginning of a trend away from careful ethnological speculation toward more empirical archaeological deduction. Mathiassen discovered the prehistoric Thule culture which he considered the oldest stage in the eastern Arctic and derived it from Alaska. In general Mathiassen said that Eskimo culture began in the west as a sea-coast culture.

In 1925, with a preliminary report on Thule culture at hand, Jenness studied a collection of artifacts sent by Eskimos living at Cape Dorset. Jenness defined Dorset culture, placed it earlier than Thule, and postulated the existence in the eastern Arctic of a pre-Dorset culture.

In 1926 Jenness initiated systematic archaeological work in Alaska by excavating at Cape Prince of Wales and on the Diomede Islands. He identified the Old Bering Sea Culture which he recognized as pre-Thule and northeastern Asian in origin. Soon after, he strengthened his views on an Asian origin and wrote in terms of culture-drifts from Asia in the second or preceding millennia B.C. Jenness, then, pictured the original homeland of the Eskimo not in America but in northeast Siberia, and he suggested that Dorset culture had spread to the

Canadian Arctic from Alaska no later than the first millennium B.C. His seemingly daring age-estimates were widely ignored until their recent vindication by radiocarbon dating.

Birket-Smith disagreed strongly with Mathiassen, his colleague on the Fifth Thule Expedition. In his monumental study of Caribou Eskimo culture published in 1929, Birket-Smith presented his hypotheses on Eskimo origins – a view similar to, but more elaborate than, that of Steensby. Based in part on an exhaustive ethnographic trait distribution study, Birket-Smith proposed four culture strata. The original "Proto-Eskimo" stratum centred perhaps around Great Bear and Great Slave Lakes. Some of its descendants lingered there to become the Caribou Eskimo of the Barrens; others followed the northward-flowing rivers and the seasonally migratory caribou herds to the arctic coast between Coronation Gulf and Boothia Peninsula. The latter adapted their basic inland techniques of spearing and harpooning fish in frozen lakes and rivers to a sea-coast setting. This second stage is the Palae-Eskimo stratum, which later spread west to Alaska where it developed to the Neo-Eskimo level by local revisions and influences from the Northwest Coast and from Asia. Superior to the previous stage, it readily spread from Alaska, across Canada, to Greenland. In the latter case, the movement was like that of Thule culture. In the Canadian Arctic, with the subsequent decline of whaling, Thule lost a major economic resource, went into eclipse, and was displaced by the fourth stratum, Eschato-Eskimo, another stage of inland Eskimo moved out to the sea from the region west and north of Hudson Bay.

In 1937, Collins published a classic work, *The Archaeology of St. Lawrence Island, Alaska*. In it, he proposed that Eskimo culture began on the northern coast of Eurasia when inland peoples followed the great rivers northward to the Arctic coast where the environmental conditions necessary for the development of a maritime culture based on sea-mammal hunting existed. Once that development occurred, the culture was carried eastward to Bering Strait and across arctic America. If Mathiassen and Jenness jointly fathered the trend away from ethnological towards archaeological interpretations of the Eskimo origins question, Collins' monograph nourished it to

youthful maturity. Like Mathiassen and Jenness, Collins provided heavy opposition to the long-popular inland origin
hypotheses.

Archaeology provided the next major step in the parade of
hypotheses, but this time in the direction of inland origin.
Larsen's and Rainey's report of 1948, on the prehistoric Ipiutak
culture of Alaska hunting, postulates a Proto-Eskimo stage in
the Siberian interior, an inland stage primarily of caribou-
hunting and secondarily of sealing, which was carried by migration to Alaska in the first millennium B.C. The Palae-Eskimo
stage and its Ipiutak expression of about 200 A.D. are members
of the Alaskan stratum which was soon spread across the coast
of arctic Canada, mainly as a caribou culture but adaptive to local
resources. Some remained inland to become the Caribou Eskimo
– and in Alaska, to become the Nunatarmiut, derived from Ipiutak. Other Palae-Eskimo Ipiutak people remained on the Alaska
coast permanently. They evolved into the Neo-Eskimo stage
through indigenous changes, diffusion, and migration of newer
peoples from Siberia. Larsen and Rainey call their Neo-Eskimo
stage the Arctic Whale Hunting culture because of the main
economic distinction between it and the Palae-Eskimo. Better
adapted to the arctic coast, Neo-Eskimo spread across northern
America, generally replacing the earlier variants. Although
formidable doubts beset the Ipiutak theory and although it has
been buffeted somewhat in the storm of post-war work, the
theory carries special value as a recent, largely archaeologically
derived view in a series of genetically related theories descended
from that of Rink in 1887.

It may be that the Ipiutak theory, and Birkett-Smith's
recent refinement of his Caribou Eskimo theory (published in
1959), stand as the last in that series. Gidding's discovery of the
Denbigh Flint Complex in 1948 and his subsequent work;
MacNeish's work in the sub-arctic; Harp's finds in the Barrens;
the recognition of, and rapid development of work on, Pre-
Dorset; the millrace of research in northern Alaska's Brooks
Range; recent developments in the Aleutian area; and the newer
aids to chronology are among the bewildering host of factors
that have added to the complexity of the question of Eskimo
origins. With such as these, and with what Hans-Georg Bandi

brightly and rightly terms the Arctic small paper tradition, it would be rash if not redundant to attempt to explain the origin of Eskimo culture or to summarize views on that question. Gratefully, I may add, it would also go beyond the defined scope of this paper. Let it suffice to note here that no two views are identical, although the majority seem to agree that the origins of Eskimo culture lie in Asia prior to 3500 B.C.

The large question is, then, What is the nature of Eskimo culture? But the business of this paper is to provide a part-answer to a vital fragment of this large question – that is, What is the nature of the Eskimo economy? In the traditional hypotheses just reviewed, there are three persisting themes: first, that the Eskimo economy is fundamentally distinguished as an arctic coastal economy specialized in sea-mammal hunting; second, that the basic quality of Eskimo economy is dichotomy of inland caribou-hunting and fishing versus coastal sea-mammal hunting; and last, that Eskimo culture evolved from an inland caribou pattern or economic polarity to a coastal sea-mammal pattern. There is a frequent assumption of simple to complex development.

In the following section, a review of Eskimo economies past and recent is set against the historical background of the first section to suggest that the inland-coastal dichotomy is inaccurate and inadequate, that the evolutionary sequence may be invalidated by archaeological data, and that the sea-mammal aspect may have been overstressed.

Some Eskimo Economies Summarized

Ethnological examples of the inland ecology are the Caribou Eskimo and the Nunatarmiut. The former were indeed caribou-fish-inland oriented but one may note that in 1925, according to Birket-Smith, about one-quarter of their number summered on the coast hunting seal and walrus, and that two or three families wintered there as well. Further, the slender evidence of archaeology suggests that the former are descended from a Thule culture group that moved inland. Their language would also be compatible with the suggestion of a Neo-Eskimo Thule origin rather than indicating that Caribou Eskimos are survivors of an old Proto-Eskimo stratum.

As for the Nunatarmiut of Alaska, although a few may never see the coast, most spend about two months of summer on the coast, travelling there by kayak and umiak to hunt seal, walrus, and white whale and to trade for coastal products. They intermarry with coastal families and speak a closely related dialect. Birket-Smith considered them a coastal people recently moved inland, and his view finds support in the archaeology of the Brooks Range, reported by Campbell in 1962.

Ethnological examples of the coastal orientation must include the St. Lawrence Islanders, the Aleuts, and the Ammassalik Eskimo. These have purely maritime economies and it could not be otherwise, for their environments scarcely contain a significant resource of land mammals. Another coastal group, the Tikerarmiut of Port Hope, hunted caribou with lances from kayaks in the lagoon there and traded with inlanders for caribou furs; Larsen and Rainey note that caribou-fur clothing was "essential" in the bitter conditions of Tikerarmiut winter-coast hunting. The coast Eskimo at Barrow also traded and hunted for caribou fur. Spencer has termed North Alaska its own specialized area and notes:

> Its economic development arises in far greater dependence than was true of any other Eskimo group on the great baleen whales. This made for a group of specialists, hunters who, in obtaining vast amounts of surplus food, made possible the inland economy of caribou hunting. Maritime life and whaling, with the associated hunting of other sea mammals, seems crucial, for without the stability afforded by the trading of the products of the sea to the inland, the quasi-nomadic inland bands with their exclusive caribou-hunting could not have flourished.[2]

Since he also notes, "That the result was to create a balance and an economic interdependence between the two,"[3] perhaps no more need be said on this facet of the review. The Labrador Eskimo and the bands on the central arctic coasts all hunted caribou, musk-ox (where available), wolf, hare, and fox. They did so, often diligently, using bows, lances, drives, traps, and snares. Generally, maritime Eskimo groups harvest caribou if they are available. One might add that since caribou herds often migrate near the coasts and across frozen bodies of water, and since, within the Eskimo area, they sometimes forage near the coast in winter or summer, it is rather difficult to construe the caribou as strictly inland game.

Turning to archaeology, the usual examples offered for an inland adaptation have been Ipiutak, the Denbigh Flint Complex, Pre-Dorset, Dorset, and the prehistoric Kobuk River, and Brooks Range sites. The last-named may be part of a dual economy whose old coastal sites now lie drowned victims of marine submergence. The Kobuk River sites are indeed inland and date back to 1250 A.D. Most of them contain evidence of skin boats and harpoons, and indications of summer travel to the coast for sea-mammal hunting from sites at least 75 miles upstream (Ahteut, 1250 A.D.) and for trade from locations over 100 miles upstream (Ambler Island, 1730 A.D.). Further, Collins has argued that the greater part of the Kobuk culture had a coastal—not an inland—origin. In Alaska, Denbigh-like sites occur both on the coast and in the interior, and sealing as well as inland hunting seem part of the Denbigh economy. In the central and eastern Arctic, the Pre-Dorset stage has produced both inland and coastal sites, harpoons and sea-mammal bones as well as caribou remains. The few score animal bones recovered from a Pre-Dorset midden on the Ekalluk River (very near the southeast coast of Victoria Island) were overwhelmingly of caribou and only rarely of seal and fish. For Dorset (often accused of a forest aroma), its only inland occurrence yielded an abundance of caribou bones, but also a harpoon head and walrus ivory. Other Dorset sites are coastal and usually reflect a sea-mammal economy. Indeed the large T-1 site included less than one per cent caribou bone in its animal-bone count. Other Dorset sites have much caribou bone.

Ipiutak, however, elegant, is a more complicated matter: Birket-Smith and Larsen and Rainey place it in the Palae-Eskimo stage of coast-adapted people with an inland heritage — as a vast summer site of people who wintered in the interior.

Such Ipiutak-like inland sites are scarcely common. Perhaps the type site-houses were winter dwellings with summer tent camps scattered elsewhere. The Ipiutak people may even have practised the classic winter-sealing technique of breathing-hole hunting, since some of their harpoon foreshafts seem to be of that type, and since no harpoon float gear was found. One authority suggests that shore-lead hunting was likely more common at Port Hope than breathing-hole hunting because local ice conditions rarely favour the latter. The very pertinent Ipiutak animal-bone count showed 88 per cent sea mammals, 10 per cent caribou, and 2 per cent all other.

Archaeological examples of the coastal subsistence system are often called Neo-Eskimo or—in the Larsen-Rainey terminology—the Arctic Whale Hunting culture. They include Old Bering Sea, Punuk, Birnirk, Thule, and recent prehistoric phases across the Arctic. Except on St. Lawrence Island and similar locales where they occurred, caribou, musk-ox, wolf, fox, hare, ground squirrel, and, in addition, fish and birds were taken. Sea mammals were usually the prominent part of the diet, notably the great baleen whales which so permeated the cultures as found by prehistorians. In Thule sites in the Canadian high Arctic, for example, house ruins fairly bristle with whale bones and baleen. In balance, however, some Thule sites, as on Mansel Island, Victoria Island and the Labrador and Ungava coasts yield only moderate or scant remains of whales. Two winter houses in small Thule villages near Cape Parry, tested in 1963 for the National Museum of Canada, showed the presence of baleen and whale-bone objects and fragments, but not the abundance of whale-bone structural material in house-building which occurs in the area of Bathurst, Somerset, Cornwallis Islands, and Boothia Peninsula for example. At Cape Parry, an abundance of driftwood had provided a building material superior to whale bones as in sites farther to the west.

In a Thule winter village I excavated in 1963, at Lady Franklin Point in southwestern Victoria Island, the animal bones reflect a near-denial of the whaling heritage of Thule culture. Of some 5,900 identified bones, 82 per cent were of caribou, 17 per cent were of seal, and only 1 per cent was of all others — including bearded seal, bear, walrus, bird, fish, and whale. Whale bones totalled .15 per cent of the sample. A similar situation existed in small Thule sites tested at Cambridge Bay and on the Ekalluk River flowing into Wellington Bay in southeastern Victoria Island. I cannot say anything about Cambridge and Wellington Bays, but Lady Franklin Point was a coastal gathering place for the migrating caribou, and also for Eskimo hunting them. These Neo-Eskimo Thule examples of a stress on caribou provide a marked contrast to the Ipiutak results showing 88 per cent sea-mammal bones. Other observations noted above suggest marked regional variations in Thule whale-harvesting elsewhere than in the Coronation Gulf-Queen Maud Gulf region where, it seems, the seas were too shallow for baleen whales.

Highly germane to a review of Thule culture's economic variation are the inland winter residences and other Thule remains of the Lake Hazen area in Ellesmere Island. Although referring to a limited number of sites in his 1960 publication, Maxwell's data and his careful discussion of subsistence and seasonal movements of the prehistoric Lake Hazen Eskimo provide, in an excellent statement, another example of the exploitive permutations within this single culture.

Giddings' recent barrage of work in the Kotzebue Sound area pertains directly to this paper. In a partial summary of the economies of five culture stages in a single area he reports a remarkable variety, as follows:

Old Whaling complex (1800 B.C.) much whaling, no caribou;

Battle Rock complex (1500 B.C.) no whales, much caribou;

Choris complex (1200 B.C.) no whale, much caribou, scant seal;

Ipiutak complex (200 B.C.) equally sea and land game, but no whaling;

Thule complex (800 A.D.) much whale.

As Giddings notes, these observations "indicate periodicity in the availability of food animals."[4] Thus – if it need be said – there can be marked subsistence variation through time in a

[4] James L. Giddings, "Cultural Continuities of Eskimos," *American Antiquity*, vol. 27, (October, 1961), p. 171.

single arctic locale, just as in a single widespread culture such as Thule, Dorset, Pre-Dorset, or recent Central Eskimo. All these recently gained data lead one to recall Collins' bold line of a decade ago when, referring to northern North America, he observed that "The earliest Arctic cultures were thus adapted to both a coastal and inland environment."[5]

Observations on the Nature of Eskimo Economy

This scanty review from archaeology and ethnology, spread across arctic America and back some six millennia, also reveals that unilineal evolution cannot be substantiated in accord with the traditional inland hypotheses: the record does not reveal a progressive development from inland caribou hunters to a maritime people. A greater knowledge, however, of the prehistory of dog-traction, whaling, breathing hole hunting, and so on, might reflect refinements – Kroeber's "finishing touches" – that comprised a greater efficiency in the basic Eskimo adaptation to the environment. The record also refutes any wide applicability of the inland-coastal dichotomy in the study of Eskimo origins: archaeological chronology denies its proposed sequence of forms; its two categories are neither all-inclusive nor adequately exclusive. For example, Battle Rock and Choris of Kotzebue Sound seem to have had primarily caribou-oriented economies but they lie on the coast; Thule has produced examples of coastal caribou-oriented economies but also its more common coast-located sea-mammal stressing economy so that it belongs perhaps to both categories; Dorset sites include examples of an inland caribou-based economy, coastal sea-mammal stressing economies, and coastal caribou-oriented and perhaps fish-centred economies; the Pre-Dorset sites provide similar examples. In short, the basic inland-coastal dichotomy is inadequate in the light of archaeological data. As Collins has noted in a discussion of the importance of Ipiutak, "My basic objection is to placing all known forms of Eskimo culture in two rigid, sharply defined, and mutually exclusive categories."[6] Since inland Eskimos come to the coast for marine hunting, and since marine hunters elsewhere camp on the coast to hunt caribou, one may, risking a *reductio ad absurdum*, question not only the dichotomy of economies but also the means of dividing the two environments to which those economies are adapted. The preceding review of archaeological and ethnological evidence of Eskimo economies does suggest, however, a mixed caribou–sea-mammal economy with wide local variation in each major prehistoric and historic group, with few exceptions. These exceptions, pure inland and pure sea-mammal economies, are sufficiently rare that they might better be considered as ecological anomalies, explainable as special cases rather than as polarities from which to derive syntheses regarding the nature or origins of Eskimo economy and culture.

Seen everywhere in the Eskimo world is an economy that is omnivorous, or tending to be so, by which the band exploits a wide range of faunal resources – even man – if starving. Fundamentally, Eskimo economies are neither inland nor coastal-adapted but rather arctic-adapted (and to some degree, occasionally sub-arctic adapted), and the degree to which different species are exploited reflects primarily the environment and the faunal resources, and only secondarily reflects an economic heritage. Referring again to Aleutian Islands prehistory, the findings of Laughlin and his associates constitute eloquent testimony of the omnivorous nature of adaptation in the Arctic. Exceptions such as St. Lawrence Island, Aleuts, and some Caribou and Nunamiut Eskimo exemplify this basic quality, since they exist in unusual environments fostering specialization of one or more of the economic supports, and reducing others to vestiges or to nothing. However, stressing omnivorousness as a basic and general quality of Eskimo subsistence-patterns is not claiming omnivorousness to be universal in the Eskimo world. Perhaps the Polar Eskimo of about 1850 A.D. offer the most blatant exception. Kane, who in 1856 gave the first detailed description of them, reported that they neither hunted the caribou gathered on the nearby coastal hills nor fished the available salmon. The example is in no way weakened by Steenby's account in 1910 of the migration to the Polar Eskimo of Pond Inlet people who re-introduced the techniques and equipment for caribou-hunting and salmon-fishing.

---

[5]Henry B. Collins, "The Position of Ipiutuk in Eskimo Culture–Reply," *American Antiquity*, vol. 20 (July, 1954), p. 61.
[6]*Ibid.*, p. 80.

If omnivorousness is a fundamental of Eskimo economies, there is at least one other flexibility. The economies adjust to regional variations in the environment while being generally omnivorous. It is not enough to be able to hunt whales or seals or walrus or caribou. One must be able to harvest seals – or whatever – over a long part of the year, to get fish at different seasons, to build up a surplus, and to have means of storing that surplus. One or two species may sustain the band for nine months of the year, and so we call them caribou hunters or seal hunters or whalers; fish or birds or ground squirrels may, however, carry them through the other three months and, thereby, in a narrow sense, be as necessary as the major resource for the band's existence. In the omnivorous and flexible harvesting of a wide range of game from whales to shellfish and from caribou to lemmings, the Eskimo reveal an opportunistic quality which may also pervade other aspects of the culture including social organization and religion.

The Eskimo hunter was rarely a neat specialist hemmed into a murderously narrow ecological niche; rather he lived by a versatile exploiting of all available niches. It could hardly be otherwise, for he has persisted perhaps some six thousand years and spread from Siberia to Newfoundland in an environment that is rarely bountiful or benign, subject to gross seasonal variation, and regionally quite varied.

In rejecting the inland-coastal dichotomy as the basic concept for arctic archaeology, I must note (since they are sometimes confused) that this does not deny the merit of the taiga-tundra dichotomy. Even if that becomes a blurred and wavy line for the anthropologist, it remains valuable to studies of northern Indians and Eskimos. The taiga-tundra dichotomy seems fundamental indeed to northern archaeology, but the variable stress on land game or sea mammals within the arctic-adapted economy, although obviously germane to some questions, has been grossly over-exercised in attempts to reconstruct arctic prehistory.

Almost all writers of the past sixty years consider the marine adaptation the distinguishing quality of Eskimo culture. Despite preceding paragraphs I agree and would add, in echo to many, that it was a necessary precondition to the initial spread of Eskimos across arctic America. Conversely the marine adaptation was not alone sufficient to fuel the movement from Bering Strait to Greenland and Newfoundland, however essential to that event. Rather it was the omnivorous flexible economy, the versatile arctic-adapted economy, that permitted and fostered the expansion and persistence of the Eskimo. We could be overly bewitched by the chilly pinnipeds, for as some Nunamiut and Caribou Eskimo indicate, sea mammals are not absolutely essential to aboriginal survival in the Arctic. The marine adaptation was a necessary precondition and a distinguishing attribute of Eskimo economy, but not the basic quality. At root lie those ingenious heterogenous opportunistic qualities. Thus it is difficult to accept the frequent suggestion that by tracing origins of the maritime adaptation we will find Eskimo origins. Such would surely give a major part, but not the whole, of the answer to the old questions of the origins of Eskimo economy and culture.

An Eclectic Review of the
Physical Anthropology of the Eskimo

DAVID R. HUGHES

Physical anthropology today is interested in the description and analysis of human variability, in the evolution of man and other primates, and in the reconstruction of the human biology of past populations. It is this last interest, perhaps, that most readily gains the attention of the archaeologist. In connection with the Eskimo, then, one of the main preoccupations of the physical anthropologist is the problem of the origin, affinities, and antiquity of this very distinctive human population. There is much that he can contribute to the pool of knowledge derived from the combined efforts of archaeologists, linguists, sociologists, and ethnologists.

Man's interest in the variability of his kind is an ancient one, and is manifested in some of the earliest written records. The interest of Europeans in the Eskimos may be presumed to go back to the original contact between the two peoples. It is claimed that this took place on the American continent, and that it is referred to in the saga of Erik the Red. The voyage to Vinland of Thorfinn Karlsefni (1003-1006 A.D.) is mentioned, with a reference to meeting "Skraelings" in Markland; but there is no description of the physical appearance of the indigenes. In subsequent sagas, and other historical accounts of the period, there are occasional and cursory references to contact between the Norsemen and the Eskimos; and artifactual evidence of such contacts is now preserved, of course. in archaeological collections.

The first anthropological description of an Eskimo cranium appeared in 1722, when J. Winsløw, a Dane living in Paris, published some measurements and observations characterizing the distinctive cranial morphology of this people. It is of interest, too, that this is often claimed as being the first published

SOURCE: Specially prepared for this volume.

craniometrical description of a skull. The first evidence of Eskimo facial morphology and general physical appearance, apart from indirect literary evidence, comes from portraits painted towards the end of the sixteenth century. The earliest, painted in Bergen in 1654, shows a group of four West Greenland Eskimos.

It is very apparent, from a survey of the published literature, that there has been great scientific curiosity concerning the origins and affinities of the Eskimo, particularly over the past three hundred years.

The earliest scientific contribution specifically devoted to the physical characters of the Eskimos of Canada appears to be a short paper published by Richard King in 1848. The first systematic field work in the Canadian Arctic was reported by Boas (1888-1901) who personally studied the Central Eskimo and the Eskimo of Baffin Land and Hudson Bay. The growing interest in problems of Eskimo affinities, based on work in Greenland and Alaska, led to the Fifth Thule Expedition (1921-24) under Rasmussen, one outcome of which was a report on the skeletal remains of the Central Eskimos by Fischer-Moller in 1937. Further observations on the Central Eskimo and the Smith Sound Eskimo, incorporating studies of living subjects, were made by Hødlička in 1910 and on the Copper Eskimo by Jenness in 1923.

The Eskimos of Greenland and Alaska were studied more extensively during the same period. A notable contributor was Hansen who published a number of studies of Greenland Eskimo between 1886 and 1914. Expeditions under Wegener went to Greenland twice between 1929 and 1931. Le Gros Clark in 1920 and Cameron in 1928 contributed further cranial studies on Greenland Eskimo material. Meticulous analyses of Greenland Eskimo dentition and skeletal characters have been published more recently by Pedersen and Jørgensen respectively, although the statistical treatment of the data remains somewhat simple. Micro-evolutionary studies on the Greenland Eskimo based upon non-metrical cranial features, considered as genetically determined discrete traits, have been made by Laughlin and Jørgensen. This paper represents a contemporary and promising approach to micro-evolutionary studies of population isolates.

Contemporary studies of past Canadian Eskimo population samples include the work of Stewart and, more recently, Laughlin and colleagues on the Sadlermiut Eskimos, and of Laughlin and Oschinsky on remains, often very fragmentary, of Dorset Eskimo individuals. The numerous Eskimo remains preserved in the National Museum of Canada are currently being comprehensively re-examined.

A great deal of our knowledge of Alaskan Eskimo and Aleut osteological variability comes from the indefatigable labours of Hødlička who published some twenty or so articles and monographs on Alaskan indigenes, including a long catalogue of Alaskan remains preserved in the U.S. National Museum. Another even more elaborate catalogue, relating to Greenland Eskimo material, is the *Crania Groenlandica* of Furst and Hansen.

More recently, Debetz has studied past population samples from the Ipiutak and Tigara sites, Laughlin has studied remains from the Chagula site, and Levin has contributed to our knowledge of Asian Eskimos.

So far, mention has only been made of some of the many studies of cranial, post-cranial, and dental characters of Eskimos and of some of the anthropometric and anthroposcopic observations made on living subjects. The physical anthropologist today is interested in many more aspects of human variability than these, so mention will next be made of some relevant studies. The contemporary approach, however, whenever practicable, is very much that of a synthesis of different techniques as is examplified in a recent paper on the Eskimo by Laughlin.[1]

The earliest reported serological investigations of Eskimo population samples appear to be those of Heinbecker and Pauli, published in 1927, and relating to Eskimos of the Cape York and Godhaven Pröven regions of Greenland. In the following year, the same workers reported on a Canadian Eskimo sample from Baffin Island. Numerous similar inquiries followed in subsequent decades. The resulting ABO blood group system gene frequencies have been listed in Table 1, together with phenotypic frequencies for those samples too small for gene frequency computations. The complete references to the original published papers may be readily obtained from the indispensable compilations of Dr. A. E. Mourant.[2] It will be noted that there are disparities in the listed frequencies, suggestive of some degree of heterogeneity amongst the samples studied for this particular blood group system. Thus the frequency of the gene for blood group A (conventionally indicated by p) will be seen to range from 8.77 per cent (Cape York) to 42.26 per cent (Angmagssalik) within Greenland, and up to 43 per cent in Alaska (Barrow); that of B (indicated by q) ranges from .34 per cent (Labrador and Baffin Island) to 18.56 per cent (Alaska). Some of this apparently wide variability is undoubtedly caused by sample bias introduced by one or more of such factors as degree of consanguinity, genetical isolation, sample size, and hybridization. Disparities of this kind must be viewed from the perspective of what is known about other genetical markers, however, for too much is often read into them when they are considered in isolation.

There are two points of comparative interest regarding these ABO gene frequencies that deserve special mention. The first is that, whilst Eskimos, in general, may be said to possess antigens of group B, American Indians, on the other hand, apparently do not. This is often quoted, incidentally, to support the temporal dichotomy that is supposed to separate Indian and Eskimo arrival in the Americas. The second point is that, in general, Eskimo ABO gene frequencies overlap and resemble those of many European population samples. This is coincidence and not indicative of affinity, of course, but it makes analysis of the degree of hybridization affecting some Eskimo samples difficult to follow through.

---

[1] W. S. Laughlin, "Blood Groups, Morphology and Population Size of the Eskimos," in *Origin and Evolution of Man* (Cold Water Springs, N.Y.: Cold Water Springs Harbour Symposia on Qualitative Biology, vol. 15, 1950), pp. 165-173.

[2] A. E. Mourant, *The Distribution of Human Blood Groups* (Oxford: Blackwell Scientific Publications, 1954). See review of Eskimo blood group frequency data on pp. 142-143.

TABLE 1: *ABO Blood Group System Gene Frequencies for Various Eskimo Population Samples*

LOCALITY	SAMPLE	NUMBER TESTED	GENE FREQUENCIES (%)		
			p(A)	q(B)	r(o)
1. CANADA					
Baffin Island	Eskimo	166	25.12	0.61	74.27
Labrador and Baffin Island	.. Eskimo, "pure"	146	25.47	0.34	74.19
N.W.T.	Eskimo "pure" and "mixed"	272	30.88	2.61	66.51
Hudson Bay	Eskimo	67	25.62	1.50	72.88
Ungava	Eskimo	64	35.33	1.20	63.47
Victoria Island	Copper Eskimo	320	29.14	3.16	67.70
2. ALASKA					
Alaska	Eskimo	341	30.15	9.52	60.33
Alaska	Eskimo	655	29.89	12.54	57.57
West Alaska	Eskimo	2954	28.54	9.38	62.08
West Alaska	Eskimo, White hybrids	258	25.85	9.16	64.99
Nome	Eskimo, "pure"	254	25.90	7.40	66.70
Nome	Eskimo, "mixed"	68			
Point Barrow	Eskimo, "pure"	329	29.10	6.31	64.59
Point Barrow	Eskimo, "mixed"	172	38.94	7.14	53.92
Anaktuvuk	Eskimo	43	38.55	18.56	42.74
Aleutian Islands	Aleut	144	26.84	3.18	69.98
Wainwright	Eskimo	111	36.00	9.00	55.00
Barrow	Eskimo	64	43.00	3.00	54.00
Anaktuvak Pass	Eskimo	65	39.00	17.00	44.00
Beaver	Eskimo	65			
Kodiak Island (Old Harbor)	Konyag	161	24.36	3.00	72.64
Kodiak Island (Kaguyak)	Konyag	51	21.89	5.39	72.72
Kodiak Island (Karluk)	Konyag	95	34.16	8.10	57.74

3. GREENLAND

Greenland	Eskimo	607	23.14	3.68	73.18
Greenland	Eskimo, White hybrids	101	16.31	13.95	69.74
S.W. Greenland	Eskimo	186	30.85	4.68	64.47
Angmagssalik	Eskimo	644			
Angmagssalik	Eskimo, "pure"	569	40.69	10.48	48.83
Angmagssalik	Eskimo	21			
Angmagssalik	Eskimo	180	42.26	7.80	49.94
Cape Farewell	Eskimo	484	33.07	2.51	64.42
Cape York	"nearly all pure"	124	8.77	3.25	87.98

The evidence of other blood-group systems that are possibly less subject to modification indicates clearly the common Mongoliform affinities of Eskimos and Indians, although there are occasional local variations in gene frequencies. This evidence comes from the MNS and Rhesus systems. Data existing for these systems are far less numerous, however, than those accumulated for the ABO system. An abbreviated list of gene frequencies relating to the MNS blood-group system appears in Table 2. There are numerous other blood-group systems that may be used as genetic markers, and which are of assistance to the physical anthropologist, but it will suffice to direct the reader to a recent concise summary by Chown and Lewis.[3] The example of the Diego blood antigen might be quoted here: American Indian population samples generally possess it in various frequencies, whilst it appears to be entirely absent in Eskimos. Evidence of this kind appears to confirm the linguistic and cultural dichotomy between the two peoples.

Many substances in the blood, other than the now well-known blood-group antigens, are of interest to the physical anthropologist. Some of these are transferrins, haptoglobins, and haemoglobins. There are numerous studies containing comparative data for Eskimos and American Indians.

---

[3] *Op. cit.*

TABLE 2: *MN Blood Group System Gene Frequencies for Various Eskimo Population Samples*

LOCALITY	SAMPLE	NUMBER TESTED	GENE FREQUENCIES (%) M*	N
1. CANADA				
Ungava	Eskimo	64	64.84	35.16
Victoria Island	Copper Eskimo	320	84.22	15.78
	Eskimo	67	80.60	19.40
2. ALASKA				
Wainwright	Eskimo	111	82.00	18.00
Barrow	Eskimo	65	80.00	20.00
Anaktuvuk Pass	Eskimo	55	89.00	11.00
Aleutian Islands	Eskimo	142	84.51	15.49
Alaska	Eskimo	341	68.62	31.38
Alaska	Eskimo	604	79.14	20.86
Kodiak Island (Old Harbor)	Konyag	161	71.12	28.88
Kodiak Island (Kaguyak)	Konyag	51	70.59	29.41
Kodiak Island (Karluk)	Konyag	95	62.23	37.77
3. GREENLAND				
East	Eskimo	569	91.30	8.70
West	Eskimo	733	81.65	18.35
South-West	Eskimo	187	81.55	18.45

*M and N are alleles – that is, two different mutant forms of a basic MN blood-group gene. For easy comparison, an M gene is like the gene that gives you blue eyes rather than brown eyes.

An example of the relevance of the study of these substances to the eludication of Eskimo origins and affinities may be seen in Table 3 which is extracted from a recent review article by Parker and Bearn,[4] and modified so that gene frequencies are shown as rounded-off percentages. The figures relate to the frequency of the gene responsible for one particular haptoglobin type, called Hp^1.

TABLE 3: *Haptoglobin Gene Frequencies for certain Mongoliform Population Samples*

SAMPLE	NUMBER TESTED	PERCENTAGE WITH Hp^1 GENE
Chinese	115	34.0
Japanese	488	27.0
Alaska Eskimo	418	30.0
Baffin Island Eskimo	67	23.0
Alaska Indian	82	44.0
Navajo Indian	263	45.0
Maya Indian	414	59.0

It will be observed from these gene frequencies that the Eskimo samples are closer to the Asiatic samples than to the American samples. This could be interpreted again as indicating that Eskimos are "more recently evolved" Mongoliforms (as are Japanese and Chinese) than the American Indians, who are often considered to have evolved from an earlier and more archaic Mongoliform population. However, one must express caution about drawing conclusions from one set of gene frequencies, since little is yet understood about the possible selective value of haematological characters like the haptoglobins. The evidence of the haptoglobins cannot be said to contradict the customary hypothesis that seeks to explain the entry of Indians and Eskimos into the New World.

Another marker gene that is of great interest to the physical anthropologist is the one responsible for the ability to taste the chemical phenylthiocarbamide (P.T.C.) or related substances. In samples of Navajo Indians and Cree and Beaver Indians from Alberta 98 per cent could taste this bitter chemical. Brazilian Indians tested also showed 98.8 per cent to be tasters. Of the Labrador Eskimos, only 59 per cent could taste it, and of the North Alaskan Eskimos 74.2 per cent were tasters.

Studies have now demonstrated that the differential excretion of B-amino-*iso*butyric acid is under genetic control. As more samples are tested, it has become apparent that different human populations vary considerably in their frequency of high

---

[1]W. C. Parker and A. G. Bearn, "Haptoglobins and Transferring," *Annales Humana Genetica*, vol. 25 (1961), pp. 227-240.

and low excretors of this substance. The following percentages of high excretors have been reported for Indians and Eskimos: Alaskan Athabascan Indians, 56 per cent; Apache Indians, 59.2 per cent; and Alaskan Eskimos, 23.3 per cent. Europiforms appear to be different from Mongoliforms: a sample tested in New York yielded 10.2 per cent of high excretors.

Dermatoglyphics have an attraction for some physical anthropologists as finger, palm, toe, and sole prints are largely genetically determined and are unaffected by the normal post-uterine environment. Fingerprint patterns have been investigated for a number of Eskimo population samples and the results are listed in Table 4. It will be noted that sample size is given as the number of prints studied. Faulty prints or missing fingers account for discrepancies between totals of individuals (n) and totals of prints ($10n$), as does the use by some writers of numbers of individuals studied irrespective of any missing fingers. Many frequencies and indices have been computed for this table by the writer from the published data. Arches, loops, and whorls are abbreviated to A, L, and W, respectively. Male and female are abbreviated as m and f.

An impression of dermatoglyphic heterogeneity is gained from an examination of the frequencies and indices. Samples from Greenland do show higher intensities of patterns than those from the Canadian Arctic and Alaska, however. The three Alaskan samples appear to form a more homogeneous cluster than do the others. Meier attributes the high incidence of arches, particularly noticeable for his males, to the fortuitous inclusion in the sample of a consanguineous sub-sample possessing a far higher number of arch patterns than usual in Mongoliform peoples.

Through the years of scientific interest in the Eskimos many claims of biological differences between them and the immigrant Europeans (and their descendants) have been put forward. The tenuousness of some of these claims has been demonstrated recently by Pett and others[5] who made detailed observations on nearly six hundred Canadian Eskimos over a period of five years. Amongst their findings were the observations that the amounts of serum proteins, plasma chloresterol, and plasma lipids detected in Eskimos lay within the observed normal ranges for other non-Eskimo populations in Canada. Although male and female Eskimos were, on the average, two inches shorter in stature than the averages for non-Eskimo Canadians, their body-weights corresponded to the national averages for their stature and age. Skinfold thicknesses proved

TABLE 4: *Dermatoglyphic Data for Various Eskimo Population Samples*

SEX AND LOCATION OF SAMPLE	NUMBER OF PRINTS	% A	% L	% W	$100_A/w^1$	$100w/L^2$	P.I.I.[3]
1. CANADA							
Southampton Island – *m*	280	2.1	57.8	40.0	5.3	69.2	13.8
Baffin Land – *m*	2340	4.1	66.8	29.0	14.1	43.4	12.5
Southampton Island – *f*	340	6.4	48.0	45.4	14.1	94.6	13.9
Baffin Land – *f*	2180	1.8	58.5	39.6	4.5	67.7	13.8
Southampton Island – *mf*	614	4.6	52.5	43.0	10.7	81.9	13.8
Baffin Land – *mf*	4609	3.8	41.4	54.8	6.9	132.4	15.1
Coronation Gulf – *mf*	239	2.9	62.7	34.4	8.6	54.9	13.2
2. ALASKA							
Kodiak Island – *m*	555	8.3	49.1	42.3	19.6	85.7	13.4
Kodiak Island – *f*	400	4.0	55.6	40.5	9.9	73.0	13.7
Kodiak Island – *mf*	955	6.5	51.9	41.6	15.6	80.0	13.5
Point Barrow – *mf*	300	2.3	51.3	46.3	5.0	90.3	14.4
St. Lawrence Island – *mf*	590	4.4	48.8	46.8	9.4	95.9	14.2
3. GREENLAND							
Angmagssalik – *m*	350	0.0	35.1	64.8	—	184.6	16.5
Angmagssalik – *f*	280	3.2	46.7	50.0	6.4	107.1	14.7
Angmagssalik – *mf*	630	1.6	39.7	58.7	2.7	147.9	15.7
East Greenland – *mf*	680	0.8	26.9	72.2	1.1	268.4	17.3
West Greenland – *mf*	1400	3.5	54.1	42.5	8.2	78.6	14.0

[1]Dankmeijer's index.
[2]Funihata's index.
[3]Cummins and Midlo's Pattern Intensity Index.

[5]L. B. Pett, P. Verdier, and J. E. Monagle, "A Review of Biological Data on the Canadian Eskimo," *Federal Proceedings*, vol. 20, Part I (n.d.), 96 pp.

to be smaller in Eskimos than the average for other Canadians – throwing some doubt on the theory that unusually thick adipose tissue offers the Eskimo protection against climatic extremes of cold. There was no evidence of vitamin deficiency in the subjects studied, and the presence of both hypertension and arteriosclerosis in the sample, together with the small proportion of individuals in the sample exceeding forty years of age, appeared to disprove earlier arguments that these conditions did not occur in Eskimo populations. The somewhat stocky build of the Eskimo seemed to be reflected in a heart-chest size ratio less than that observed for other Canadian populations. The transverse diameter of the heart was observed to be within the normal range however, when the factors of body-weight and stature were taken into account.

It does appear confirmed, on the other hand, by a number of studies that thermoregulation in the Eskimo is associated with basal metabolism higher than normally observed clinical standards and higher than is normal in individuals of lean body mass. The carefully designed clothing of the Eskimo furnishes him with what is virtually a portable tropical microclimate within which excess metabolic heat is dissipated through sweating. The suggestion has been made that Eskimos have more sweat glands than other human populations, but this has yet to be demonstrated convincingly by the latest counting techniques.

Adaptation to cold in the Eskimo appears, therefore, well-documented, although certain physiologists have reservations concerning the number and influence of variables that may affect the repeatability of observations. Experimental evidence derived from laboratory tests shows that Eskimos have a greater tolerance to cold in the hands than non-Eskimos. The usual tests are based upon finger- or arm-temperatures following immersion in near-freezing water. Milan has also reported, under field conditions, that Eskimos retain their body heat even whilst lying on the winter ice, hunting seal.[6]

This eclectic review has attempted to show the development of the physical anthropology of the Eskimos and to cover certain contemporary aspects of the study of these populations. There has been no mention of the innumerable theories concerning the origin of this distinctive people, but a full historical treatment, covering some sixty past opinions, claiming Asian, American and even European origins for the Eskimo, was published almost thirty years ago by Hødlička. A lucid exposition of contemporary thinking about the problem (including a review of linguistic evidence) has been published by Laughlin,[7] who has also recently demonstrated, with Reeder and other colleagues, the feasibility and value of studies combining archaeology, ecology and various aspects of anthropology and human biology in an effort to define more clearly the eco-system in which arctic Mongoloids have and are evolving.

One of the most promising current developments in Eskimo physical anthropology is the organization, under the auspices of the International Biological Programme, of a combined Canadian–United States–Danish Human Adaptability Project intended to study intensively, from as many scientific aspects as possible, Eskimo populations from Alaska, the Canadian Arctic, and Greenland. This will be a long-term interdisciplinary project, financed by the three governments concerned, with the aim of producing in due course the fullest description and analysis of the Eskimo peoples hitherto attempted. It will, in fact, be one of the most intensive studies ever carried out within the fields of human biology, physical anthropology, and associated sciences.

---

[6]F. Milan, Unpublished Thesis, University of Wisconsin, cited by W. S. Laughlin, in *Science*, vol. 142 (November 8, 1963), p. 644.
[7]W. S. Laughlin, "Generic Problems and New Evidence in the Anthropology of Eskimo-Aleut Stock," in J. M. Campbell (ed.), *Prehistoric Cultural Relations Between the Arctic and Temperate Zones of North America* (Montreal: Arctic Institute of North America, Technical Paper 11, 1962).

Spatial Concepts in the Eskimo Language

RAYMOND C. GAGNÉ

In this paper we touch on some of the idiosyncrasies of the Eskimo language when compared to Indo-European languages, and relate some of these idiosyncrasies to the peculiar cultural and ecological settings of traditional Eskimo life. After a brief introduction dealing with some general features of Eskimo language, we look in some depth at some of the spatial concepts in the language, specifically at what we call "localizers." This in-depth approach is taken in order to transmit to the reader a feel for the nuances and flexibilities in the Eskimo language, something difficult to do in an account of only general features or vocabulary.

Eskimo Culture and Language

The Eskimo language is a distinctive one, a kind of "stock" of its own. It is spoken over a vast northern expanse ranging from Greenland, across Canada and through Alaska, to Siberia. It is comprised of several dialects, some of which are virtually unintelligible to other dialect groups. In Canada, the largest dialect gulf is between those dialects of the Mackenzie Delta region and those of the regions to the east of them, although minor gulfs occur within each of these broad groupings.

In the popular mind, the notion of dialect is rather vague, and rests most often on differences in lexical items coupled with minor phonetic and intonational variations. To the linguist, a language represents a continuum with a common grammatical core within which there are varying degrees of mutual intelligibility, and in which the phonological, grammatical, and lexical differences can be resolved by the speakers without involving the learning of an entirely new set of structures or a new

Source: Pages 30-33 were written especially for this volume; pages 33-38 are excerpts from Mr. Gagné's Eskimo language course, Department of Indian Affairs and Northern Development, unpublished MS, 1966. Reprinted by permission of the author.

linguistic code. In some parts of Africa, for example, the speech patterns in a certain area are referred to as a three-day dialect, or a three-week dialect and so on, indicating the time it takes to achieve an easy mutual intelligibility. Geographical distance is not necessarily a guide to the degree of mutual intelligibility: the Eskimo spoken in Labrador, for example, is closer to that of northwestern Alaska than it is to east Greenlandic or the latter to west Greenlandic. Before we are able to divide the Eskimo language as spoken from Siberia to east Greenland into a set of distinct formal dialects, on sound scientific principles, detailed studies of the various structural levels would have to be made and accurate mutual intelligibility tests devised. In the meantime, it might be more significant to highlight the remarkable fact that the Eskimo language continuum does range over such a wide expanse of the Arctic, in spite of a long history of migration coupled with geographical isolation of small numbers of people.

Many theories have been offered by linguists and anthropologists about the geographical and cultural origins of the Eskimo language, but contemporary authorities discount most of them. Perhaps the only point upon which the experts are in agreement is that, according to linguistic evidence, the Eskimos originated somewhere on the Asian continent and migrated to North America via the Bering Straits.

Despite the fact that Eskimo is spoken by a relatively small number of people, it has received more scholarly attention than dozens of languages that are spoken by much larger populations. Nevertheless, there are still relatively few good scientific studies of the language. The Eskimo spoken in Greenland has had the advantage of a literary tradition of more than two hundred years. The sizeable body of Greenlandic literature has made the Eskimo language more accessible abroad for research and other purposes than in Canada. Although they number only 1,200 or so, the Siberian Eskimos know how to read and write their language with the use of the cyrillic alphabet. As for the Alaskans, there is no standard system of writing which has official government sanction. About a decade ago, the Canadian government launched a scientific study of the Canadian dialects with a view to designing a standard Roman orthography. This new system of writing is about to be implemented in the Canadian Arctic in a vast literacy program in the Eskimo tongue.

Like all human languages, Eskimo is a tightly-knit set of structures within structures, serving as the principal vehicle to express the culture of its native speakers. Sapir once observed that there are no high or low cultures in any absolute sense. It follows, because of the intimate relationship between language and culture, that there are no high or low languages. An important implication of this relationship is that the Eskimo language, like English or French, must be studied as an independent and autonomous system whose *raison d'être* is to contain and reveal the particular view of reality and the particular set of emotive responses to this reality of the Eskimo speakers.

A few examples will suffice to show, in a general way, how the Eskimo language expresses Eskimo cultural orientations which are quite different from those of people whose native tongue is an Indo-European language. There is no Eskimo concept for *time* or for its myriad sub-divisions, as indicated by such expressions as *to save time*, *to kill time*, *to gain time*, and so on – sets of concepts and expressions which form an intricate micro-structure in most Indo-European languages. Words for time are lacking in Eskimo for the simple reason that time, as we know it, does not have the same relevance in traditional Eskimo culture as it does have in our culture. Further evidence of this is found in a careful analysis of the tense-system where the present, immediate past, and immediate future are by far the most frequently used. The distant future, on the other hand, is used relatively infrequently, since the Eskimo culture, unlike our own, is not future-oriented. Planning beyond the immediate future is not common among the Eskimos.

A more familiar example – often quoted in the literature – of the elaboration in Eskimo language of concepts which are not elaborated in most other languages, concerns the phenomenon of snow. The Eskimos have one word (*aput*) which is translated into English as "snow in general," but there are dozens of specific words for different types of snow: snow in different stages of hardness and softness; snow suitable to accept sled runners, or to build blocks for houses; and so on. The reasons for such elaboration are plain to see, given the crucial significance of snow in the Eskimo habitat and economy. As a final example, we might point out that the colour spectrum is divided differently from ours by the Eskimos; and the fact that, traditionally, the Eskimos did not distinguish between green and blue does not mean that they suffered from poor eyesight or from some peculiar eye defect.

Such considerations bring to mind the famous Sapir-Whorf hypothesis, which suggests that the particular view of reality, the particular way of perceiving the world, is conditioned by and confined within the limits of the grammatical categories and structures of the mother tongue. To illustrate from a previous example: if there are not two separate words for green and blue in the Eskimo language, the child who learns and internalizes his linguistic patterns is, without his being aware of it, conditioned to overlook that colour distinction. We now proceed to show how language structures the perception of "reality" among the Eskimos by examining how spatial relations and patterns of localization are handled in their language.

Spatial Relations and Patterns of Localization

Localizers are sets of words, found in every language, which enable the speaker to locate or identify a thing or a place within his range of vision. He may do so by pointing to it, or by indicating it in some other way, within an area immediately surrounding him (his hereness); within an area beyond his hereness but roughly on the same level as himself (his thereness); within an area above him (his upness); within an area below him or below his pointing level (his downness); within an area immediately circumscribing the place he is in, for example, an igloo or tent (his outsideness); or finally, within an area inside an enclosed space, such as a house or a box, of which he is outside (his insideness). Note that outsideness and insideness are meaningful only in opposition to each other. This means that the speaker must be inside a house or some other structure before he can use an "outsideness" localizer and so on. We now examine the particular ways in which localizers are used by the Eskimos.

From my studies of Eskimo language and culture, I have been led to believe that all visible phenomena which can be localized by the speaker – whether things, beings, places, areas, or surfaces – are viewed two-dimensionally. Moreover, all of them fall into two basic categories: first, those whose visible limits are in fact, or appear to the speaker to be, of roughly equal dimensions, such as a ball, an igloo, a box, a patch of grass, or an ice surface; and second, those that are or appear to be of unequal dimensions (that is, things that are distinctly longer than they are wide), such as a harpoon, a gun, a rope, a road, or a river. Any area without easily definable limits, such as a wide expanse of land or sea, is automatically classified as of unequal dimensions. However, within a broad expanse of land, the speaker may choose to cast his eye and locate areas, places, or surfaces that have definable limits; and these two-dimensional surfaces will fall in either one category or the other, that is, of equal or unequal dimensions. For example, he may cast his eye on a river (unequal dimensions) or on a roughly round or square patch of grass (equal dimensions) or on a rock path crossing the patch of grass (unequal dimensions), and so on. In the case of objects, it may prove more convenient to refer to them as slender and non-slender rather than as of equal or unequal dimensions.

The spatial world of the Eskimo is divided into three basic pairs of opposites, which we have chosen, in the terms used above, to call: first, hereness/thereness; second, upness/downness; and third, insideness/outsideness. The actual measurable and delimitable range of space of each of these areas is subjective, impressionistic, and entirely dependent on the concrete situation or spatial context surrounding the observer or speaker. Within the context of a small habitation, the physical range of a speaker's hereness in relation to his thereness will be proportionately much smaller than it would be if he were on the tundra on on a large body of water. By the same token, the presence, and distance from the speaker, of mountains or icebergs will significantly alter the physical proportions of his spatial relations. Some of these have been consecrated by time and experience. For example, even though the level of water may appear to a non-Eskimo hardly lower than the land on shore immediately surrounding it, the Eskimo speaker standing on the shore will automatically identify observable phenomena on the water as being "down there" rather than as being "over there."

Because the speaker is always at the center of all spatial categories, it is proper to speak of *his* hereness, *his* thereness, and so on. All unambiguously delimitable phenomena in his hereness, his upness, and so on, will be located with the use of the localizers. In the case of ambiguity, instead of using a localizer, such as *panna*, "that slender thing up there," the speaker will give more details, such as "that slender object up there on the canvas near the kayak."

So long as the objects localized by a given speaker are in direct relation to him, the localizers in their root form will be used – thus, *kanna*, "this non-slender object (in the speaker's downness)." However, if the object or person or place mentioned is in the hereness of the person spoken to or about, or of another thing or place referred to, the prefix *ta* will be added to the root – thus, *takanna*, "that non-slender object (in the hereness of the person spoken to or about) down there (in the speaker's downness)."

In the present discussion the following symbols are used for the sake of brevity: (x), which stands for all delimited phenomena real or imagined of roughly equal dimensions; and (//), which stands for all delimited phenomena of distinctly unequal dimensions, as well as all non-delimited or not easily delimitable phenomena (for example, tundra or sea). These phenomena may either be actually visible to the speaker or only partially visible. In the latter case, he can classify them as being of a certain shape or dimension according to his personal experience, imagination, and memory – if you will, in his mind's eye.

All living things are automatically classified as (x), except when in motion (walking, running, flying, and so on) when they are classified as (//). However, interestingly enough, babies, small animals, and close friends – even if dead – are still (x). It should be added that a caribou, when grazing lazily, even though moving, does not create the linear illusion (//) required to group it among the slender objects. The same holds true for a dog chasing its tail. However, a dog running around an igloo would be categorized as (//). Any object normally classified as (x), such as a ball, also changes its classification when in motion. The important thing to remember is that the motion of the animate being or the inanimate thing must cover a real or imagined distance great enough to create the optical illusion of a line for the observer who is the speaker. Compare the following examples:

1. *takkuuk kanna tuttu!* Look at the caribou (motionless) down there!

2. *takkuuk unna tuttu!* Look at the caribou (in motion) down there!

3. *arsaq inna aiguk!* Go and get the ball (motionless) over there!

4. *arsaq anna aiguk!* Go and get the ball (in motion) over there!

As pointed out earlier, the choice of localizer depends to a large extent on the impressions and arbitrary decisions of the speaker in a given situation. Physical conditions, such as distance, light, visibility, and powers of perception all play a significant role. Furthermore, the size and shape of an object and the area of delimited space, real or imagined, that it may in fact or potentially occupy are interrelated. For example, "Please put this thing over there!" can be translated in four ways in Eskimo, namely:

1. *ililauruk una* (x) *ikunga* (x)!
   Please put this non-slender thing over there (i.e., on that surface of roughly equal dimensions)!

2. *ililauruk manna* (//) *ikunga* (x)!
   Please put this slender thing over there (i.e., on that surface of roughly equal dimensions)!

3. *ililauruk una* (x) *avunga* (//)!
   Please put this non-slender thing over there (i.e., on that surface of distinctly unequal dimensions)!

4. *ililauruk manna* (//) *avunga* (//)!
   Please put this slender thing over there (i.e., on that surface of distinctly unequal dimensions)!

Suppose *una* (x) in the first sentence is a box 2′ wide by 2½′ long and the surface on which it is to be placed (a table, a piece of canvas, etc.) is 8′ x 9′, then the speaker can delimit various 2′ x 2½′ areas on the table in his mind's eye, which he can specify by pointing to any of the four corners of the table or even to its center, and thus refer to this area as *ikunga* (x). So long as the particular 2′ x 2½′ area pointed to can be reasonably distinguished from other potential 2′ x 2½′ areas on the table, the person being addressed can follow the instructions of the speaker with fair accuracy. Also, the speaker might simply have pointed to the table from a certain distance without indicating any particular specific area on the table, hence he would use *avunga* (//), and the person taking the order could then place the box anywhere on the table. However, if the table were 3′ x 4′, only *ikunga* could be used to refer to its surface in relation to a box 2′ x 2½′; *avunga* could not be used because it would be impossible to delimit more than one 2′ x 2½′ area on a 3′ x 4′ table. Broadly speaking, if the surface area of the object to be placed on another one is more than half the area of the latter, there can be no choice between (x) and (//) localizers to refer to the surface on which the first object will sit. In other words, surfaces of roughly equal dimensions will take (x) localizers, whereas surfaces of distinctly unequal dimensions will be referred to with (//) localizers. If the opposite proportions hold true – that is, that one thing is less than half the surface area of another – both (x) and (//) localizers can be used with reference to the latter area, so long as pointing clearly delimits the (x) areas.

It is important to note that the contrast between a (x) and (//) localizer can carry meanings that we would normally spell out with additional instructions in English. This is illustrated by the following example, in which the localizers refer to objects measuring 10′ x 2″ x 4″):

1. *ililauruk manna* (//) *avunga* (//)!
   Please put this (slender thing) over there (lengthwise on that slender thing)!
2. *ililauruk manna* (//) *ikunga* (x)!
   Please put this (slender thing) over there (crosswise on that end of that slender thing to which I am pointing)!

In the second sentence, *ikunga* automatically means that the one ten-foot 2″ x 4″ will have to be placed crosswise on the end of the other ten-foot 2″ x 4″, which is indicated with the finger, for if placed lengthwise, the localizer would have to be *avunga*.

*   *   *

To the uninitiated, the foregoing discussion will appear complex, but the reader may be assured that we have only scratched the surface on this topic of spatial relationships in the Eskimo language. However, we trust we have provided enough material to give him a feeling for the nuances in the handling of spatial relationships, and to evoke some notion of the complexity and flexibility of the spatial categories in the Eskimo language.

Through the study of Eskimo language, we gain insights into the way the very categories of thought and perception are structured and how these categories are congruent with traditional Eskimo culture and habitat. This congruence has become familiar to social scientists through the widely quoted examples in the literature of the rich elaboration of words for snow and the lack of elaboration of time concepts. In this article a further example of congruence among language, culture, and habitat has been given by spelling out some of the ways in which Eskimos transmit messages about spatial location. It could be argued that Eskimos are able to specify, with more precision than is found in most languages, where things and places are located, how to reach them, their attributes in relation to their settings, and so on. It is obviously vital to Eskimos whose very lives depend on success in locating game and on travel over vast, uninhabited, and untracked reaches to develop cognitive maps adequate for these purpose. Their language is the underpinning for these cognitive maps.

The Timeless Present in the Mythology of the Aivilik Eskimos

EDMUND S. CARPENTER

> Time present and time past
> Are both perhaps present in time future
> And time future contained in time past.
>
> **T. S. ELIOT**

The beginning of the Aivilik world is, strictly, at a point out of time. Aivilik cosmogony contains no doctrine of creation *ex nihilo*, no philosophical conception of creation from nothingness. No supreme power ever acted as creator, maker, or artificer. Nothing came first and of itself. For there had already been forms of existence which looked upon the transformer in admiration and amaze. Nor is mention made of a mythological age when all animals lived a human life. With the exception of stories of metamorphosis, which involve neither "change" nor "origin" in our sense of these words, no attempt is made to account for the beginning of anything.

Aivilik mythology simply ignores the question of creation. The world never came into existence; it has always been, exactly as now. Before the coming of Christianity, when the goddess still lived beneath the sea in the person of a woman with tangled hair and mutilated hands, spirit beings were perhaps more active than now. But they are the same ones who inhabit the world of today, and it is inconceivable that they will ever change or disappear.

It follows that the Aivilik experience no desire to set a beginning to the chain of events to which they belong. Indeed, they see no chain! If we, as outsiders, regard this attitude as editorial indifference or outright error, we miss the whole point, for Aivilik mythmakers reject the question of creation and

SOURCE: *Anthropologica*, vol. 3 (1956), pp. 1-4. Reprinted by permission of the author and publisher.

beginning. They regard the "past" as merely an attribute of the present, as something immanent in all Aivilik being. Instead of describing attributes, they give an account of mythical and historical past by presenting essence.

History and mythical reality, then, are not the "past" to the Aivilik. They are forever present, participating in all current being, giving meaning to all their activities and to all existence. The Aivilik will speak of a whale which their fathers hunted, or the one which the mythical *Oomanetook* killed, in exactly the same terms with which they will refer to a whale which they themselves are hunting now; and it will give them satisfaction to do so.

In all their undertakings this "past" is present, giving these undertakings validity and value. Wherever they go, their surroundings have meaning for them; every ruin, rock, and cleft is imbued with mythical significance. For example, there lie scattered along the southern shore a number of tiny tent rings which the Aivilik declare to be the work of the Tunik, strangers from the past whose spirits still linger somewhere in the ruins. Of the stories that are told of these mythical folk, perhaps none is quite so fascinating as that which accounts for their swiftness in the chase and the smallness of their homes. For it is related that they slept with their legs propped against the tent walls and their feet overhead so that the blood flowed from their legs and thereby promoted their speed as hunters. Other stories tell how these people, a physically superior race, were driven from this land by the more dexterous Eskimo. Yet the Tunik do not in any sense belong to the past, to an earlier age, to the dead-and-bygone world. They remain forever in the present, inhabiting the ruins, giving these stones a special quality, bestowing on them an aura of spiritual timelessness. For in these myths it *is*, always *is*, however much they say *it was*. The tales bestride the tenses and make the *has-been* and the *to-be* present in the popular sense. In them life and death meet, for they conjure up timelessness and invoke the past that it may be relived in the present.

This is true even of legends surrounding the Sadlermiut Eskimos, a remarkable group wiped out by epidemic in 1902-3. Some of the older Aivilik visited this community before it was destroyed and even adopted two Sadlermiut children, one of whom lived until recently. Added to this direct knowledge is a vast store of legend concerning these people and their ancient homes. There is, for example, a tale which accounts for the presence of a great boulder on the top of a steep hill at Native Point. Tradition has it that it was deposited there by Avalak, famed Sadlermiut hunter. I have no idea whether or not Avalak actually did transport this great rock – a feat which would require extraordinary strength – but the Aivilik assert that he did (pointing to the rock as proof), and this belief somehow changes the quality of the stone.

Material objects are not alone in possessing the "past" as an attribute. Certain old songs and secret prayers, for example, are thought to have once belonged to spirit beings and to have been passed down through a number of generations until finally inherited by their present owners. The personal history of each is often known, and its owner gets satisfaction out of recounting incidents in the past where it was successfully employed to combat sickness or thwart disaster. Chronology and historical sequence are quite irrelevant here; the history of each song or prayer is important not as development but as an ingredient of being.

Indeed, the Aivilik have no word for history. When they want to distinguish between different kinds of occasions, they will say, for example, *eetchuk*, that is, "time before known time," not a previous phase of *this* time, but a different kind of time. More frequently they will use the term "in the time of my grandfather's father," which does not refer to an earlier phase of this time, and definitely not to the actual generation of their great-grandfathers. Rather it is comparable to the phrase *tamnagok*, "once upon a time," with its double sense of past and future and its true meaning of everlasting now.

History, for the Aivilik, is not a confused repository of anecdote; they are merely uninterested in chronological sequence. For example, I recorded Ohnainewk's autobiography which was given with complete disregard to chronology. He was apparently uninterested in narrating his story from the ground upward, for he began with the crisis, so to speak, and worked backward and forward, with many omissions and repetitions, on the tacit assumption that my mind moved in the same groove as his, and that explanations were needless. It produced the most extraordinary effect, one reminiscent of that achieved by Joyce and other sophisticated writers who deliberately reject sequential time. I was later forced to rearrange clusters of statements so that they represented an historical sequence – only then did they become coherent to me.

Chronological sequence is of no importance to the Aivilik. They are interested in the event itself, not in its place within a related series of events. Neither antecedents nor consequences are sought, for they are largely unconcerned with the causal or telic relationship between events or acts. In their mythology, concepts of spirit beings are particularistic, not organized into groups or hierarchies. They have a capacity for recounting brief, minutely-detailed legends, but they show little interest in organizing such accounts into wholes with a significant meaning. The details are of interest for their own sake, rather than as part of some larger pattern. When we inspect this mythology we find no emphasis upon past, present, or future, but a unity embracing complexity. *Everything* is in mythology, and everything in mythology *is*, and is together.

Religious Rituals and Beliefs

RT. REV. ARSÈNE TURQUETIL, O.M.I.

. . . At the time of childbirth the mother has to have her own separate hut. If the infant is born in an igloo or tent inhabited by the family – a thing which does not happen, except unexpectedly –it becomes necessary to abandon the habitation. After birth, the mother is isolated for a month if the infant is a boy and for two months if it is a girl. The eighth day after birth there takes place the ceremony, conducted by the medicine man, of consecrating the infant to a protective spirit and then giving the child a name.

The name! For the Eskimo this means everything. If the infant dies before it is given a name, there is no mourning. If it is a girl of which they wish to rid themselves, they smother it before the eighth day, but to smother it after it has received its name would be looked upon as a real murder which would call for vengeance.

The name given an infant is that of a deceased relative. If a small boy receives the name of his grandmother, his father will address him as mother, his mother will address him as mother-in-law, his brothers and sisters will call him grandmother, and he himself so soon as he begins to talk well at four or five years of age will address them as my son, my daughter, and so forth. The Eskimo does not, however, believe in metempsychosis, in a real reincarnation of the soul. But, he says, the dead person lives again through his name (*le mort revit par son nom*). He is glad to see his name preserved among his own people, and these in turn are glad to perpetuate the name of their ancestor whom they loved. It is only the names of the wicked that are blotted out forever. Such a mentality is certainly a very human one.

After the giving of the name comes betrothal, a commercial contract. Part of the price agreed upon is paid at once; the

SOURCE: "The Religion of the Central Eskimo," *Primitive Man*, vol. 2 (July/October 1929), pp. 57-64. Title supplied by the editors. Reprinted by permission of the publisher.

balance will be paid when the two who are betrothed reach maturity.

It should be further noted that female infanticide is practised only among the very small isolated groups, where no one can learn of the birth of the infant or ask for the female infant in marriage. Consequently the smaller the population, the greater the danger of extinction. On the other hand, one will find the grown-up men buying and paying in advance for an expected infant, under the condition that it will be a girl, with the intention of making her his wife later. For, in many places, female infanticide has led to a scarcity of women. Among the Netchiliks, there were recently one hundred and thirty-eight boys and only sixty-six girls, and even today at Cape Eskimo the missionaries are in touch with forty families among whom there are twenty grown-up young men who are not able to find wives anywhere. Thus there come polyandry, fighting, and also, unfortunately, murder followed by blood revenge.

The education of the infant is very simple. He does whatever he pleases. Nobody commands him and nobody scolds him. But the native folklore and traditions are taught him under the form of wonder stories that become encrusted, as it were, on his soul, and make of him a true Eskimo.

I do not know of any special puberty rites. The young girl merely puts on the clothing of a mature woman, with the long hood at the back, and then is joined in union with the man whom she has been accustomed from infancy to consider as her husband. She is so attached to him that in case her future husband is absent the young girl resists, often to blows, any violence which libertines might attempt. There is certainly here a touch of modesty, of natural probity that is interesting to note.

Polygyny and polyandry are permitted, but cases of them are rather rare. Monogamy prevails. Divorce is permitted. I have seen cases of forced divorce, commanded by the medicine man. Sometimes an individual covets his neighbour's wife and is not willing to share her in a polyandrous union. Then there takes place a wrestling match for the possession of the woman. The woman belongs to the victor. In case of divorce, a child too young to hunt remains with its mother. Marriage does not occur between blood kin, cousins, uncle and niece, aunt and nephew.

I have come across a case of an Eskimo who had at the same time two sisters as his wives. Ordinarily, however, affinity is in itself an impediment to marriage.

The treatment of illness is exclusively the task of the medicine man. Medicinal herbs are unknown as vegetation is lacking. Surgery, however, is very much in honour. Cutting, opening, lancing abscesses and tumours of all kinds, even the most deep seated, without sterilization of instruments and without anesthetics, antiseptics, dressings or bandages, are all matters of common usage. It is the medicine man's job to discover what fault has aroused the anger of such or such a spirit and so caused the sickness. Having discovered this, he prescribes nothing but proscribes much. The life of the Eskimo is honeycombed with these prohibitions or taboos, a great number of which take their rise in the treatment of disease.

At death we see the reappearance of the idea which prevails at birth. The sick man must not breathe his last in the tent or igloo that he inhabits. If this happens, in spite of what everybody can do to prevent it, it becomes necessary to abandon the hut. There is a taboo against touching the corpse. The whole family and, in fact, the whole tribe, must fast for twenty-four hours after first receiving news of the death of one of its members.

Folklore is a powerful influence making for unity of view and observance as well as for conservatism. It reveals to us also the soul of a people. Eskimo folklore gives us such an insight into the Eskimo solution of the problem of life.

The thing that stands out first and foremost in their folklore is their anxiety to be successful hunters.

Once upon a time, the story will run, there was a hunter who never came back empty-handed. They then describe in minute detail his hut filled with meat, and all the members of his family as big, fat, dressed in beautiful new skins, happy in an igloo where the lamp never went out and where the song of the *Yayaya* ever witnessed to everyone's happiness. This is the zenith of contentment.

And here is the antithesis. Once upon a time there was a hunter who never had any luck in the chase. His igloo was dark and chilly. There was no oil or fat for his lamp. Hunger tormented his ragged children, for there was nothing to eat. One heard nothing but the cry, "I am hungry, I am hungry." This is the nadir of misery.

Such themes speak eloquently to the child. The ambition and desire to become a good hunter is born within him and grows apace as each evening he falls asleep, his imagination filled with these marvellous stories that his grandmother tells to the family before the family gets ready for bed. The next morning on awakening he will ask his grandmother: "Grandmother, what happened to that hunter of whom you were talking last night?" "My child, that hunter observed faithfully all the ordinances, usages and customs established by the spirits of the sea, and so he lacked nothing, and nothing could hurt him." And then the good old woman will explain in detail the observances that have to do with birth, with the hunt, with death, and so forth. The child drinks in these instructions from the first awakening of his imagination. He determines to be a real Eskimo.

The same theme is brought home just as eloquently to the girl, who dreams of a husband who will be a good hunter. She sees his tent and igloo full of comforts and of happiness. How pleasant it will be for her to hear the happy cries of her children enjoying life. And on the other hand, how she will shrink from the thought of being united to a hunter who is unskillful, unlucky, sick, powerless, or too old.

In the second place, the Eskimo folklore gives us an insight into the native's concern for the interests of his soul. Religion may appear as if relegated to the second place and as if bound to the service of material interests. But we must not conclude that it is for the Eskimo a luxury, a matter of phantasy or of simple opportunism. It is an integral part of that ensemble of impressions, ideas and points of view which make up Eskimo mentality.

The pagan Eskimo believes firmly in the immortality of the soul and in a moral sanction in the other life. No doubt, absorbed as he is entirely by his preoccupations as a hunter and deprived of supernatural light, the Eskimo thinks of his future life as a material paradise abounding in the choicest game, and one where success in hunting is assured without work. This dream of the future life is explained by the environment in which the Eskimo lives. His hell, too, is a material one, a land of desolation and of famine, without food or raiment or lamp, where he is forever engaged in the Tantalus-like pursuit of game which he can never take or overtake. In this there is a real idea of a sanction, but the question remains: Have we to do here with *moral* good and evil?

It should be said at once that starting out, as the Eskimo does, from a material point of view, he develops this point of view with a rigorous logic and concludes that those will go to the paradise of abundant game whose life has been lived in conformity with the pleasures of the two goddesses of land game and of sea game.

Now he who here below is a good hunter evidently is in the good graces of these divinities. Success in the hunt is therefore the sign of a good life, just as lack of success is the proof of a moral disorder, and this even from the religious point of view. For religion is nothing but the totality of man's relations with the deity, and the object of the acts of religion is to please the deity and to conduct oneself in accordance with the deity's pleasure. Thus, though starting out from a false principle, the Eskimo follows his reasoning to guide his hunting in accordance with the will of his god.

Success in the chase does not always come even to the best hunter. He then concludes that he has committed some fault which has displeased the deity or else that evil spirits have interefered, for the Eskimo admits the double principle of good and evil. Thus the purpose of the act of religion is to propitiate good spirits, to obtain their protection, and to keep at bay these evil spirits. Thus the deity is not inaccessible – the sorcerer is famous for his voyages to the moon and to the bottom of the sea. The deity is even coercible – he can be forced to act by formulas, by sacred rites, by fetiches and by amulets. Fetiches and amulets act homeopathically, Carrying a rabbit paw gives rapidity of movement, possession of a fox nose assures good smelling ability and guides one surely towards game, and so forth.

The evil spirit is also accessible but only through the aid of the protecting spirit, and instead of being propitiated or conciliated, he is fought with, he is forced to beat a retreat, he is even killed. I have said "through the aid of the protecting spirit."

The good principle is therefore superior to the evil one.

The functions of the sorcerers are: to see that the usages and customs established by the deity are faithfully observed; to prevent or to discover faults, that is, breaches of these regulations and to assure expiation of these breaches through confession and penance; to interpret omens, auguries, and extraordinary natural happenings, such as thunder; to discover sacred spots, and so forth; to prevent evil spirits from approaching the camp, or, if they have already done so in spite of everybody, to force them to go away.

I may add that among the magicians there are men who stab themselves with knives, shoot themselves with guns, die and come to life again in an instant without any signs of wounds. Among the more primitive inland Eskimo, the sorcerer is chosen to act in the name of the tribe and enjoys very great authority. Even if he is a child he takes precedence over the oldest men at the feasts and at the semi-religious dances he wears tonsure and girdle; his word is law. He can, however, resign whenever he wishes. The sorcerer sometimes makes evil use of his art and then we have black magic. He makes a sort of monster with the head of a bear, with the body of a wolf, with the wings of birds, with the tails of fish, and so forth, gives life to this formidable being, and launches it in pursuit of his enemy, who will then infallibly succumb.

Add to sorcery certain phallic rites, ritual promiscuity and you have the broad lines of Eskimo religion.

Some Preliminaries on the Soul Complex in Eskimo Shamanistic Belief

SVEND FREDERIKSEN

It has not been known before that the Eskimo universal deity was metamorphic and clearly anchored in the myth about the Sun and the Moon, who are respectively associated with sister and brother. It has been known that *silap inua* (literally: of air, its person) was some sort of an Eskimo supreme deity, without, however, a knowledge and understanding of what this deity actually was, its role and its function. The descriptions have been rather confused and distorted, not alone because of many observers' lack of understanding of the Eskimo language (which to be sure has often proved a serious impediment) but also because its counterpart and metamorphic character were not at all sensed. The many recordings I have in Eskimo from my field research in Canada, Alaska, and Greenland, leave no doubt about this question. However, descriptions which we have as early as the sixteenth and seventeenth centuries strongly indicate that the Eskimos felt themselves allied with the cosmic elements.

The Sun and the Moon are regarded as a hole, or window, in the universe. At this hole, in day appears the sister, who at the time of sunset becomes the brother and at dawn becomes again the sister. We could so far also call the universal deity the universal soul, as it is the identical counterpart to each and everyone of the life souls. The life soul is the corporeal soul which is physically present within, and bound to, the body. Every person's life soul is the counterpart of the metamorphic deity or the metamorphic universal soul.

The night side of the deity, the "moon"- brother in the sky, is an embryo creature, which at the turning point from night to

SOURCE: *Journal of the Washington Academy of Sciences*, vol. 54 (April, 1964), pp. 109-112. Reprinted by permission of the author and publisher.

day takes its seat in the adult woman, who becomes pregnant. All child-bearing women are thus the mothers of the metamorphic deity, but of its night side only. We have here something in the nature of a parallel to Jung's Animus-Anima statement. The day side, the sister, has the form of a bird, which is in itself the symbol of resurrection, and to the Eskimos a religious reality.

A metamorphic event takes place at the initiation of the male Shaman novice when he receives his Shaman name and has his night side life soul turned into a day side life soul of a bird shape. This is exactly what we see in the world-famous Lascaux caves in France, which have been determined by radiocarbon dating to be about 16,000 years old. There we have a prostrate man, shown with the face and beak of a bird, and next to him a bird sitting on a pole, the *axis mundi* – sitting on the top of the world. The concepts of the bird-soul and of the *axis mundi* – the world tree or tree of life – are found in many religions in different parts of the world.

The Eskimo soul complex is, however, dualistic beyond the relationship of the corporeally bound (life) soul, with its counterpart in the deity. The individual soul, which also could be termed the free soul, the image soul, or the name soul, is a non-physical counterpart soul, which like the universal, physical, life soul, splits off in an amoeba-like manner.

This has not been recognized in the scholastic literature, although it has been known that individual soul and name are identical. It is on the basis of the individual soul that misconceived and confused ideas of so-called Eskimo multiple souls have been described. The name represents the image of the person. The mirroring image as seen in the water would represent the individual soul of the person there reflected. Thus any picture taken of the person represents his individual soul. Naturally Eskimos, as other aboriginals, were frightened, years ago, when pictures were taken of them. I have myself experienced such an incident, which however is now an extreme rarity.

The Eskimo name system – and we cannot describe the individual soul without relevance to it and without realizing the purpose of the personal name in Eskimo belief – has not been recognized in all its essential facets in the scholastic literature, nor has its far-reaching significance in Eskimo culture, language, and religion been sensed. This is not only because of unfamiliarity with the Eskimos' language and thought processes, but also because concepts from our modern world have been projected as extraneous elements into the old Eskimo culture. This is one of the reasons why the concept of counterpart souls, their structure and function, has not been understood.

Each given name is related to successive cycles of human life as: (1) embryo, (2) birth, (3) puberty(and its opposite, the menopause in women), and, in addition, (4) illness (temporary name). At each of these stages a new name is given, each being a soul name. When a person dies, his name soul splits into two parts, one of which remains in the realm of the dead while the other is transferred to another person, for example a newborn baby, a boy or girl at puberty, or a Shaman at his initiation or during illness. In the case of an infant, the name given must be that of a person who has died recently. When the novice Shaman receives his new name, it must be that of a long-dead ancestor. Nicknames also occur, but they are not regarded as real names; they are not soul names.

It follows logically that when a soul name is discontinued, is in the process of being shifted, the Eskimo conceives of himself as "dead" for a period. Often the expression: "In some way I died," is used. The most crucial impact of the name shift on a person's consciousness would be where he is first able to visualize the consequences of the name shift; this usually happens at puberty, where the person must undergo the Shamanistic novitiate. All the horrors of death and the great novelty of resurrection are here experienced.

It may also be realized as a logical consequence that the entire Eskimo community is educated and geared for Shamandom. In the name system, the name given at birth is the name which leads to Shamandom. The fact that Eskimos often may travel long distances and live far apart in small groups also underlines the necessity of this Shamanistic extension. However, not every adult may be regarded as a full and actual Shaman. To be called a Shaman, it is necessary that the person be able to perform in public. A Shaman is one who can face the realm of death and easily enter into and out of it. We must note that to die means for the Eskimo only a transition. Death is not conceived as extinction. The realm of death is just another transcendence. All the dead ones are alive, and their individual souls have their namesake among the actual living.

It must be emphasized that the counterpart souls are coexisting souls. The old soul continues to exist in the realm of living "dead ones." This is not the same as incarnation or reincarnation, phenomena of some of the so-called higher religions. What happens is that two soul units, both of them formed in amoeba-like fashion, are brought together and that both are subject to constant mutation.

When a person dies, his name must not be mentioned until he has been renamed. This is quite understandable because of the great mobility of the individual soul (which even in dreams is supposed to leave the body). If the counterpart of the name soul of the dead is not properly transferred to the living, danger and disorder will result. If the deceased is called by his own name, it would mean that the person mentioning that name would be possessed by the name soul of the dead one, and that he himself would die. The entire soul system must have a chance to regroup and to be brought in order again. Nothing is so dangerous as a disordered soul system. The Shaman has this order-bringing task.

But we realize then that the fact of a name which cannot be used for a certain period gives rise to the necessity for a parallel language, the Shaman language. A name that cannot be mentioned could be one that was very useful or essential in daily life. Thus, it would be inconvenient not to have another name or metaphor for Polar Bear than *nanoq*, if a person by that name had died. After renaming, the word *nanoq* could be used again.

Let me use here a concrete example from a late Eskimo friend of mine, a Shaman from Chesterfield Inlet. His name leading to Shamandom, the name he received at birth, was *nanoq*, meaning Polar Bear. We will see how at his Shaman novice initiation he literally experiences the coming to life of the Shaman language.

A relative of his was a female namesake, *nanoq*, who lived very far away. (Whether it was a female or male namesake would make no difference; sex has no role in connection with counterpart name souls). According to this Shaman's autobiography, which I recorded in Eskimo, he postulated that he was telepathically informed that his relative had died. As her namesake identity he had to die too, and he felt that he did. His individual (name) soul left his body entirely as it was. But it did not go out of existence. It mutated, it went over to another transcendence during his initiation as Shaman novice. It transmuted, and as a polar bear it became a member of his faculty of helping spirits, even becoming the leader of them. But since he could not conceive of himself any longer as *nanoq* until his dead relative had been renamed, he could only think of the concept of Polar Bear under the metamorphical expression *pisuktse*, "the land animal," "the one you have as walker." After his dead namesake had been renamed, it was safe to use the word *nanoq* again in conversation, but it would never again be his name.

One may here sense that Shamanism is a dive into the unconscious, which happens at every trance and seance as a regression of mind, where the Shaman language is used in communication with the helping spirits. In this regression he seeks the origin of the ancestry (in the name soul complex) and of the deity (in the life soul complex).

At my friend's initiation to the Shaman novitiate, the officiating Shaman "dreamt" a visitation to the mythical ancestress of the Eskimos, the woman who lives at the bottom of the sea, who once was married to a dog. From her husband *kanajoq*, Sea Scorpion, the officiating Shaman learned that my friend, who formerly had the name *nanoq* now had to answer to the new name *qimukserâp*.

In his initiation as a Shaman novice, my friend "dreamt" about the male night side embryo metamorphic deity, which up to now had been his counterpart universal (life) soul but which now at his "awakening" was transmuted to the female bird-like day side counterpart soul. He thus experienced unity with the female day side bird-like metamorphic deity. This was his resurrection, and this happened on the fifth day of his initiation, when he received his new name from the officiating name-giving Shaman. He now was a regenerated individual with a new universal counterpart soul and a new individual counterpart soul. But in spite of the new life, the new being he had become, the transmutations preserved a link with his past, with his previous existence, his origin in ancestry, and his origin in deity.

As to the metamorphic Shaman language, the point is that it is used in the unconscious state, when the Shaman is in a trance, etc., as well as in the conscious state, in the entire oral traditional literature of the old Eskimo culture.

Until now very little has been recorded of the Shaman language, and its significance and meaning have not been understood. The Shaman metamorphic words have been translated as ordinary words, when they are something entirely different. They are expressions of his soul, a part of himself, expressions too of the soul of his fellow Eskimos – a part of themselves. The myths, the legends, the entire "literature" of the aboriginal Eskimo are interwoven with Shaman words. This has definitely not been known before. There is much, much more to be recorded. We must study this "literature" in an entirely new light, and it must be done now, while some of the older Eskimos who possess this unique knowledge are still alive. In a few more years it will be too late.

Witch-fear among the Aivilik Eskimos

EDMUND S. CARPENTER

The Aivilik Eskimos, who are a branch of the Iglulik, live in scattered communities along Roes Welcome, north of Hudson Bay. On Southampton Island they total about 120 individuals, or roughly half the native population. The remainder belong to the Okomiut, Akianimiut, and Kidlinikmiut groups.

Although the Aivilik are gradually being drawn into the world economy, life on Southampton Island is still ruled by the old ecological cycle. Subsistence is by the chase – hunters prey upon all nonhuman animals around them. In recent years trapping incomes have been supplemented by stevedore work and employment on scientific expeditions. But at heart the Aivilik remain hunters; the only labour in which they delight is the chase. They not only depend on game for most of life's necessities, but they have the hunter's outlook on the world. Although acculturation processes have by no means left their culture "purely" aboriginal, changes are often more apparent than real. The Aivilik of today, in spite of their dependence upon civilization, represent in thought and act individuals foreign to the Western mind.

Earlier writers on Aivilik life have stressed the importance of magic, recording literally thousands of formulas for controlling game, disease, weather. In these activities the magician did not *cause* things to be done; he *did* them. Just as the hunter with his material implements harpooned the seal, built the igloo, or paddled the kayak, so the magicion with his various formulas "drove out the evil spirit," "stopped the wind," or "took the bear's spirit." This was not influence, nor the force of magic; rather it was "to magic." Magical action was understood as action, not cause. The validity of the magical spell lay not in results, nor in proof, but in its very being. It lay in its inheritance

SOURCE: *American Journal of Psychiatry*, vol. 110 (September, 1953), pp. 194-199. Reprinted by permission of the author and publisher.

and its being performed by the appropriate person within a patterned activity. To seek validity through proof was foreign to Aivilik thinking.

Today most of this is gone. By 1950 magic was almost completely a thing of the past, a memory. Yet witch-fear was everywhere. Bewitching was a constant threat. Every man's hand suspected of being against every nonrelative. Tension, jealousy, and suspicion were always present. Even marriage did not necessarily guarantee suspension of hostility, for a wife came from outside the trusted circle. Indeed, she above all others was not to be trusted. Only within the extended family, the nuclear economic unit – and even here only with close relatives – could one find a haven. Witchcraft has replaced magic.

Records of over 100 cases of Aivilik magic and witch-fear indicate the witch-hunting dated back no further than about 1930 when the Aivilik found their survival imperilled by tuberculosis and a declining food supply. Its life was brief but colourful. It developed gradually during the 'thirties and 'forties until by 1950 it reached a point where it dominated the thinking and behaviour of every native. Then suddenly many of the forces that brought it into existence lessened, and today witch-fear is definitely on the wane.

Witch-fear, then, was neither an aboriginal nor a "normal" phenomenon in Aivilik society. Fundamentally, it was a socially disintegrating philosophy based on a belief in the potential malevolence of other people and reflecting great insecurity in interpersonal relations. This insecurity appeared to derive not from traumatic situations of early childhood, retained throughout life, but from contemporary situations that frustrated the Aiviliks' feeling of safety in their environment.

The Aivilik had sound reasons for feeling insecure. Deadly diseases had increased tremendously following white contact. Game herds had been decimated. Hostile Eskimo groups lived in close proximity on Southampton Island where they competed for women and an ever-decreasing food supply. The economy was based in part on the uncertain fox trade. There was a general loss of traditional values, of methods of meeting crisis situations, and of fear-reducing mechanisms. As the aboriginal religion changed, it became increasingly difficult to blame misfortunes or antisocial behaviour on either angry deities or malevolent ghosts; instead most were blamed on human agents. Where once misfortune was a community problem, now it became a personal one. Instead of community cooperation to appease a deity or drive out a ghost, now there was interpersonal strife. This was no joking matter in a society where large families spent the long arctic winter face-to-face in small igloos and where some women literally did not leave these igloos for months on end. And finally, a general loss of faith in the effectiveness of the magician's tools led to their discard. Yet belief in psychic powers persisted and took the form of witchcraft.

For Aivilik witchcraft was a psychic art. Practitioners performed no rites, uttered no spells, possessed no medicines. They could injure others in virtue of some inherent quality that had no external symptoms. Aivilik did not profess to understand the mechanics of witchcraft. At times a witch was actually unknowing. A malicious thought, by no means rare among these people, apparently sufficed. That it could kill and injure was obvious. Beyond this they did not inquire.

Belief in witchcraft did not in any way contradict empirical knowledge of cause and effect. On the contrary, natural and mystical causation supplemented one another, the former explaining *how*, the latter *why*. Most misfortunes had their natural cause; to witchcraft was attributed the role usually assigned to fate, coincidence, or accident in our society, *i.e.*, selecting the sufferer, the occasion, and the means. In short, witchcraft explained the particular conditions in a chain of causation that related an individual to a natural happening in such a way that he sustained injury.

Thus all Aivilik willingly conceded that the cause of disease was bacteria, insofar as they understood such modern concepts. What concerned them, however, was why a particular person should be singled out for illness. If someone were not bewitching him, how else could one account for this selection? Bacteria caused the disease, true. But every Aivilik was exposed to the same bacteria, and yet not everyone became ill. Why? Because no witch brought them into relation with germs in such a way that they suffered.

Let me give another illustration. On two occasions Towtoongi was shot while hunting. There was nothing remarkable in this. Most Aivilik owned rusty rifles and faulty ammunition, neither of which was used with caution. On hunts, boats were generally overcrowded. Yet little care was exercised, and it sometimes happened that a hunter was standing in the line of fire at the time of an accidental discharge or careless shot. That a rifle should go off accidentally was easily intelligible to the Aivilik. They knew that this was caused by a worn sear, and they repaired it. That a careless hunter should stand in front of a muzzle was also understandable. He was probably excited and moved forward to obtain a better shot. But why, the Aivilik asked, should these two events have occurred at precisely the same moment in time and space? Witchcraft, of course.

It was by no means illogical for them to conclude, in this instance, that Ookpuktowk, recognized enemy of Towtoongi's father, was the agent responsible for these two woundings, although in neither case had he actually fired a weapon. (The charge went undenied.) Nor did this exclude a recognition of natural causation. It was merely a logical interpretation of the whole problem in terms of Aivilik culture.

To our mind the only relationship between these two independently caused facts was their coincidence in time and space. We offer no explanation of why two chains of causation intersect at a certain time and a certain place, for, unless we accept witchcraft or hold that the cosmos is controlled by an omnipotent power, we recognize no interdependence between them.

Aivilik philosophy supplied the missing link. It explained what we do not. The world known to the senses was as real to them as it is to us. They were well aware of the immediate, natural causes of Towtoongi's wounds. But they recognized plurality of causes, and they selected for emphasis that cause that to them was the socially relevant one. Thus it was not simply that the flesh had been torn, but that a hunter – a food-provider – had been disabled. It was also the attempted murder of a member of a family and a community. Of the two causes of injury, natural and mystical, the latter alone had social significance.

Proof of witchcraft was twofold: the occurrence of misfortune, particularly disease and death, and confessions. Since witchcraft caused death, therefore death was evidence of witchcraft. A confession confirmed the fact; counterwitchcraft avenged it.

This doctrine of witchcraft was not used to explain every failure or tragedy. It often happened that the social situation demanded a common-sense, and not a mystical, judgment of cause. Thus if a man lied, or stole from another man's traps, he could not elude punishment by saying he was bewitched. Here witchcraft was quite irrelevant; for it was not necessary to seek a witch when a man stole – the culprit was already known and had to be stopped.

But generally all sickness, particularly the fatal case, was explained in terms of human agents. For death from disease, heart attack, or stroke was much more difficult to understand than somebody's dying because he was mauled by a bear or murdered by someone who hated him. Natural death was far less understandable than unnatural death. The following example is a case in point:

Kainuk and Mikkoshark remained married for years, although the union proved singularly unpleasant. In the end he bewitched her, causing her death in 1951. But before she died, Mikkoshark realized what Kainuk had done and publicly stated that, though she could not kill him in her lifetime, her ghost would take him after her death.

Following his wife's death, Kainuk's behaviour became so unbalanced that there was talk of doing away with him. He became convinced that the goddess Sumna was irrevocably determined to betray him at every turn in his life and to torture him eternally in the next. He was visited by apocalyptic visions; mind-freezing apparitions of his wife shrieked in his ears. On several occasions, mistaking a daughter for his wife's ghost, he attacked her with rocks and edged weapons. Everyone expected his wife's spirit to take him quickly, but then he seemed to recover and for the better part of one day was calm and restful. The next morning he did not awaken from his sleep, and all knew that his wife at last had won.

In cases like this, where no natural cause of misfortune was known or suspected, mystical causation stood alone. This was particularly true in fields like mental illness where the natives were, by our standards, quite ignorant. It would appear that, before the Aivilik assimilated many European explanations of natural crises such as sickness, they had but a single interpretation for a given phenomenon. But as they learned the white man's knowledge and made it complementary to the older belief. Natural and mystical causation thus came to exist side by side, offering a dual, though not conflicting, interpretation. Whether this duality existed in aboriginal belief or not is difficult to say, but all evidence points to the contrary, and it is probably safe to regard this as an acculturation phenomenon. Today in those fields where the whites do not, or cannot, offer the Aivilik a natural explanation, only one interpretation is made. We might call it a mystical interpretation, but to the Aivilik it is merely *the* interpretation. Let me give a striking example of this:

A young Okomuit woman named Shenarkiyark had long suffered at the hands of a cruel father. This was exceptional for generally children were treated with kindness and respect. But among other things he beat her and abandoned her without provisions for over a week at a time. She developed the habit of stealing from neighbours. These thefts were widely known but overlooked. However, on one occasion, in the winter of 1942, fearing her father's anger, she stole a fox from an Aivilik hunter, Ookpuktowk, to replace one destroyed by dogs. This theft was regarded as serious, but at the time Shenarkiyark was not suspected.

That spring she married and the next year gave birth to a daughter. She had always been considered rather simple, but it was only just before the birth of the child that her behaviour occasioned any comments. After the delivery she became quite unstable. She kept rubbing her stomach and complaining that there was something within her. Others felt of her abdomen and agreed. One old woman commented that she must have committed some crime to which she had not as yet confessed.

A few days later Shenarkiyark admitted to the theft of the fox, and the artifact in her abdomen was immediately identified as the stolen animal. Once during the middle of the night she declared that she heard a fox barking outside and asserted that it had gone beneath the igloo and was at that moment approaching her from the direction of the entrance. Her husband searched outside but found nothing.

Shenarkiyark continued to insist that the fox was within her, and once, baring one of her feet, said, "Look! My foot is like a fox's!" And, according to witnesses, it was. She said she had conceived orally and at one point tried to deliver the fox in this manner. She reached down her throat to grab it and, grasping several whiskers, tried to hold the fox by pinning these against her inner cheek. But she succeeded only in tearing a corner of her mouth. Later she screamed that the fox was coming out of her vagina, and on another occasion pointed to a great penis coming up through the igloo platform. One old woman, who had long suspected her of incest and mechanical eroticism, was inclined to associate the penis with these activities.

Finally when her daughter was taken from her, she went completely mad. She was unable to care for herself, constantly hummed tunes, imitated others, barked like a fox until she was hoarse, and had to be forcibly restrained from biting people. A coffin-like box with bars across the top was constructed, and she was imprisoned within it. There she remained for months.

Up to this point she was treated with kindness and concern. But gradually the natives became terrified, and limitations to this kindness were set. Finally, when the natives felt their lives endangered, they prepared to take the matter into their own hands. However, at this point Shenarkiyark was evacuated by the Royal Canadian Mounted Police to Brandon Mental Hospital where her case was diagnosed as schizophrenia, catatonic type.

In 1951 Ookpuktowk, owner of the fox, was asked why all this had happened to Shenarkiyark. His reply was brief. He said "*Akumnit anawakateelaogoma* (paternal uncle mine − clothes-sharer was with me)." What he meant was that his late uncle, a renowned hunter, was his *anawakatee*, that is, had given him at birth an old piece of clothing. This gift established the uncle as Ookpuktowk's guardian and guaranteed that the uncle's spirit would always look after the younger man. In this particular case, even though restitution was made by the girl's father, it was quite impossible for Ookpuktowk to call off the evil powers afflicting her, for the owners were not his, but his uncle's. And even if he had been so inclined, he would not have dared rebuke his guardian. To do so would have offended the spirit-ghost of his uncle, who might then have withdrawn his support or even turned against his ward. All were agreed that an earlier confession by Shenarkiyark might have averted this tragedy.

At times it was held that sins had been inherited, an aboriginal belief given added support by the biblical threat about visiting the iniquity of the fathers upon the children unto the third and fourth generations. Even here, no matter how far removed, there was always the implication that, at some time and place, a wrong was committed. In the past, the inheritance of sins related to immanent justice or offended deities. In 1950 the revengeful agent was an angry witch who achieved satisfaction against enemies by harming their children.

Let me illustrate with two cases of women who were hospitalized as catatonic schizophrenics in 1945 and 1944 respectively. The first, Oomayoarluk, an Akianimiut, had been unstable since birth. This condition became pronounced shortly after she was deserted by two successive husbands, both white. In 1941 she moved from Sugluk to Southampton Island, where she felt herself unwelcome and denied the prestige to which she felt entitled. When she first came ashore, it was observed that she smilingly used one of her hands as a looking glass. She continued in this habit, spending hours each day examining her nonexistent image. (This point may be of more than passing interest, for in both Aivilik and Akianimiut philosophy an individual's *tungnik*, or spirit-name-soul, is regarded as separable from his body and visible as a reflected image or shadow.) From this point on she was withdrawn, incompetent, promiscuous, hostile, at times even violently dangerous. Voices from beyond spoke to her, and she obeyed their irrational commands.

She was never asked to confess and thereby achieve absolution and relief, for it was recognized that since birth she had been possessed not by her own *tungnik*, but by that of an evil guardian. Therefore her affliction was attributed either to sins she had committed in earlier life or, more probably, to sins inherited from her parents. Since they were not available from whom to exhort a confession, her case was regarded as hopeless. She was treated kindly, but with caution, perhaps even fear.

Until evacuated, she was confined for months in a barred chamber off an igloo.

The second case was remarkably similar. The woman had long been regarded as a bit odd. Like Oomayoarluk, she was an "outsider," a Kidlinikmiut who came to the Island in 1939 from Port Burwell. (When selecting natives for transfer to other posts, the fur traders generally choose those individuals whom they regard as the least desirable; it is quite possible that both women were selected on this account.) While in her middle twenties, she experienced a series of personal conflicts of considerable magnitude and in consequence became convinced that she was engaged in several witchcraft duels, the most deadly with her new step-father. It will suffice to state that her life at this time was marked by almost incredible fears and stresses. Her behaviour became increasingly unstable. There were scenes of uncontrolled anger. On several occasions she attacked children. She imitated others, constantly hummed and talked to herself, and refused to cooperate in daily tasks. Things became so bad that she and her mother were turned out of one igloo after another.

In spite of this, the community generally showed only kindly tolerance and concern. But one night, according to a young man's account, she was observed being raped by a great hairy beast, who was none other than the goddess Nuleeiayuk's husband, an incubus who rose from the nether world to rape and bring disaster. The terrified community acted quickly. She was tied up and tortured until she confessed her transgressions. When these proved of little consequence – the worst was masturbation – the community was certain of what it had long suspected: she was being forced to suffer for parental sins. For it was widely known that her mother was responsible for her father's death. Clearly her illness was punishment for her mother's sin. To make his wife suffer, the ghost of the father had actually driven the *tungnik* from his own child. He had achieved revenge against his wife even though it meant striking down his own daughter.

Realizing that her case was helpless, the girl requested that her name, within which her soul resided, be given to a child *in utero*. The community readily assented, for this guaranteed that there would be no malevolent ghost seeking revenge. While she stood by and actually watched, the ancient ceremony of reincarnation was performed and her soul was incarnated in the body of another. In short, she attended her own funeral.

Both of these cases, plus the preceding one, parallel standard Western forms of catatonic schizophrenia. What influence social factors may have had in precipitating latent disorders here, increasing or minimizing their intensity, and aiding or hindering their resolution, is difficult to ascertain. We know that unbridled fear is a powerful and destructive force in life. In individual cases it can disrupt bodily processes and sometimes even kill. Anthropologists have noted that in primitive societies the incidence of mental disorder appears to increase during the periods of acculturation. If this is so, then perhaps it is not coincidental that these three cases, which were the only ones known from memory, all occurred at a time of great anxiety and social unrest.

Moreover, in one case the individual was burdened with a sense of guilt that was deeply rooted in native philosophy and corroborated by her associates. And finally, all three regarded their cases as beyond remedy. They were without spirit-souls, indeed without names, without identity. In fact, in one case, the woman's "soul" had actually been reincarnated in the body of a child.

The will to be cured must have been greatly minimized by such convictions. And the three women probably had little faith in, or understanding of, modern medicine, so that they were left without the benefit of their culturally prescribed techniques of disease-curing and fear-reduction. Even before they were evacuated, they were left alone with their problems and fears, cut off from friendly associates and deprived of what emotional support a sustaining and heartening philosophy might possibly have offered them. Caught thus with anxieties unresolved by institutionalized and socially sanctioned facilities, these women were forced to face their problems alone.

Now I am not for a moment suggesting that social factors here were a *sufficient* cause, but I do believe that they were contributing factors, and in several cases perhaps even necessary ones. Each of the women had been unstable for years. That there was a constitutional basis or component for their disorders, possibly of genetic origin, can hardly be questioned. The postpartum factor in Shenarkiyark's case is clear. But that there are maladies here that, as Dostoievsky said, "arise from the abnormal conditions of society," also cannot be denied. It is my opinion, perhaps because of my anthropological bias, that these conditions, when projected into a philosophy of witch-fear, not only determined the content of the psychoses but increased their intensity, hindered their resolution, and, in the two latter cases, perhaps even acted as a "trigger mechanism," changing latent or mild mental disorders into severe ones.

We know, for example, that violent, destructive fears, culturally inspired and prescribed, when let loose on unfortunate victims "in the interests of society," can be disastrous. This is especially true when such fears have validity within the philosophy and value systems of that society.

The case of Santainna, a mature, athletic Aivilik hunter, is relevant here. I had come to know Santainna quite well. So when, in the winter of 1952, I learned that he was in distress, I immediately went to see him. I found no fever, no obvious symptoms or signs of disease. He complained of pain, but said it was not localized. First it was here, then there. It was obvious, however, that he was not only seriously ill and extremely weak, but partially paralyzed. Then I learned that he was convinced that his wife's ghost had bewitched him and that consequently he must die. Several years earlier she had been evacuated to a tuberculosis sanatorium where she remained until her death late in 1951. Before she died she became convinced that her husband was the cause of her sickness and that he was killing her so that he might take a younger wife. Indeed, Santainna's behaviour did much to encourage her in this belief. While she lived he evidenced little fear of retaliation for, obviously, his was the greater power. But in Aivilik belief it is held that after death an individual's spirit acquires powers often greater than those it knew in life. When Santainna learned of his wife's death, he was literally paralyzed with fear.

Since no medical facilities were available, I decided upon a harmless experiment: I gave him two aspirin tablets, which I assured him were counter-charms designed to offset bewitching. The relief was almost instantaneous: within a few hours he was back on his feet, apparently happy again and without complaint. The next day he left for his traps.

The question naturally arises as to how trustworthy were my critical judgments in this particular case. Was there a physical cause for the ailment that I failed to observe? How fearful, sensitive, and suggestive was Santainna as a particular individual? And finally, what other life stresses may he have been undergoing at that moment? These questions must all remain unanswered. But while conceding their cogency, it is still my impression that Santainna was, perhaps in the true sense of that word, bewitched. I believe his fears were of sufficient magnitude to actually disrupt bodily processes. They might conceivably have proved fatal. Aivilik witch-fear, then, was not only a socially, but at times a biologically, disruptive philosophy.

As a final comment it is interesting to note that within the last two years the intensity and destructiveness of witch-fear in Aivilik life have greatly diminished as a direct result of improved economic and social conditions. Tuberculosis has been brought under partial control, at least temporarily. Government assistance has helped to stabilize the economy. Eskimo ingenuity has resulted in improved housing conditions. And intentionally or otherwise, Catholic mission activities have given the natives new rites for fear-reduction and have reaffirmed the validity of the confessional. Fear of witches is lessening. And gradually the Aivilik and their neighbours are embracing a less colourful, but a more co-operative and perhaps more practical, philosophy that emphasizes natural rather than mystical causation.

Canadian Eskimo Carving
in Historical Perspective

CHARLES A. MARTIJN

So-called "primitive" communities tend to achieve a close integration of art with everyday life. The extensive material culture of the traditional Eskimo, and to some extent that of the historical Eskimo, bears this out quite clearly. Four primary categories of function may be attributed to Eskimo carvings of yore:

1. Decorative – Objects for daily use were often ornamented or carved in the form of animals or humans. In order to lend emphasis to this important aspect, a number of things externally transformed in such a manner are listed below. They illustrate clearly how utilitarian objects have served the Eskimo as a stimulus for artistic expression. The examples cited cover the whole range of arctic geography and history: arrow shaft straighteners; bodkins; boot-sole creasers; box and bucket handles; cord attachers; drag handles; drum handles; earrings; fish decoys; harpoon boxes; harpoon heads; harpoon socket pieces; helmet decorations; kettle-hooks; knife sharpeners; knife handles; line clasps; needle cases; needle case attachments; netting weights; nose-plugs; personal ornaments; pipes; powder horns; root picks; snuff and tobacco boxes; spear rests; swivels; thimble-holders; and toggles.

2. Magico-Religious – Carvings often served as charms to bring good luck in hunting or to ward off malign influences such as illnesses etc. Among various tribes it was also customary to deposit with the dead small models of useful objects such as lamps, harpoons, knives, etc., whose "spirits" could then be utilized in the afterworld by the deceased.

3. Toys and Games – Eskimo children were given toys to play with in the form of miniature lamps, animals, cooking pots,

SOURCE: *Anthropos*, vol. 59 (Fascicule 3-4, 1964), pp. 557-561 and 571-574. Reprinted by permission of the author and publisher.

kayaks, dolls, and sleds. Animal figurines were also used for certain games. Boas reported on one similar to dice, called *Tingmiujang* or "images of birds." "The players sit around a board or a piece of leather and the figures are shaken in the hand and thrown upward. On falling, some stand upright, others lie flat on the back or on the side. Those standing upright belong to that player whom they face; sometimes they are so thrown that they all belong to the one who tossed them. The players throw by turns until the last figure is taken up. The one getting the greatest number of the figures being the winner."[1] In another game, *Ajegaung*, an ivory polar bear or some other animal form perforated with holes is sometimes used. The object is thrown up and for a specific number of times must be caught upon a stick in one of the holes or successively in a whole row of them.

4. Self-Entertainment – Although most likely no longer true today, Eskimos in former times often carved for their own amusement in order to while away idle moments. Boas recounts that "all the Eskimo tribes, east and west, are very fond of carving . . . and produce many small animal figures that serve no practical purpose but which are made for the pleasure of artistic creation."[2]. . . [However, we should be] cautioned against interpreting such activities as a manifestation among "primitives" of that peculiar intellectual abstraction which we term "art for art's sake."

Once contact had been established between Eskimo and Whites, a fifth function for carving developed which eventually displaced all others. Economic incentive led to the making of figurines for sale to outsiders. As a result, carving ceased to play an integral traditional role in Canadian Eskimo life, and a change-over to a culturally peripheral activity took place.

Certain writers have placed much emphasis on the "geographical remoteness" of the Canadian Eskimo, which supposedly preserved his art from outside influences. Upon closer examination this argument turns out to be fallacious. Eskimo-White contact, though not necessarily continuous, did take place regularly in the Far North throughout the nineteenth century. Provision ships of the Hudson's Bay Company plied steady routes. Each year whaling vessels, mainly Scottish and American, went to Baffin Land and Hudson Bay in pursuit of their cetacean prey. Apart from bartering with the Eskimos, some of these sailing crews wintered up there, and frequently hired on natives as extra help in their operations. Exploration parties moreover kept on returning in search of the North-West passage, while traders, travellers, government officials, and missionaries followed in their wake. By the end of the second decade of the twentieth century, these people "had completely shattered the ancient Eskimo culture over most of the Eastern and Western Arctic, and were launching an assault on the still primitive central region."[3]

Odd though it may sound at first, carving was one of the aspects of Eskimo culture which turned out to be most sensitive and receptive to White influence. The reason for this is simple. Carvings came to be in demand as souvenirs, and this brought with it a gradual transformation in their form and function. Canadian Eskimos began to look on them primarily as commodities for the "tourist trade."

. . . [Some writers] venture the opinion that arctic carving as first encountered in early historical times never possessed a predominantly magico-religious orientation, as is the case in certain other "primitive" communities. Hence it was a simple matter for the Eskimo artist to effect a shift from creating pieces for himself or his own group, to making them for foreigners. MacPherson has contributed the astute observation that "from the first years of the nineteenth century increasing contacts with European whalers, traders, and missionaries exerted pressures under which a change began to take place in the character of Eskimo handicrafts. Around the posts, objects conforming to the ideas of what outsiders believed to be typical of Eskimo life were most saleable and so were most often made."[4] For example, apart from being fashioned to stand upright, and carved fully

---

[1]Franz Boas, "The Central Eskimo," *Sixth Annual Report of the Bureau of Ethnology* (Washington: Smithsonian Institute, 1888), p. 566.

[2]Franz Boas, *Primitive Art* (New York: Dover Publishers Inc., 1927), p. 124.

[3]Diamond Jenness, *Eskimo Administration: Canada* (Montreal: The Arctic Institute of North America, Technical Paper 14, 1964), p. 25.

[4]Dorothy Macpherson, "Eskimo Handicrafts," *Encyclopaedia Canadiana*, vol. IV, p. 44.

dressed (which may be partially due to missionary influence) so as to give them a typical Eskimo appearance, these statuettes of the contact period assumed increasingly less stiff poses. Incisions representing facial features or decorative patterns had formerly been rubbed with dirt to bring out the figures in black on a white background of ivory. In historical times additional means came into vogue, such as home-made ink, and later even battery-carbon or crayon pencils of different hues.

[Reports of early travellers suggest that] throughout the whole nineteenth century there was a steady demand for Eskimo souvenir carvings in the Eastern Arctic. . . .

During the 1920's Speck decribed in detail a number of remarkable walrus tusks from Labrador and Northeast Hudson Bay. These were unusual in that they had been carved as complete units, with up to a dozen animal and human figurines extended in a group along their length. He affirms that "no other specimens quite like them seem to exist in the Eskimo collections of other museums. Coming from the northern Labrador coast they seem to stand out either as a local development in the historical growth of Eskimo art or as the exclusive property of a division of the race which has long had the style among its property though unobserved by students of the Eskimo." There does not seem to be any stylistic connection between those carved tusks and Dorset "multiple mask" finds. Other negative evidence from both archaeological and ethnological work would appear therefore to favour the first of Speck's two hypotheses. We now know that around this very time a strikingly similar development was taking place in Alaska as a result of European stimulus. In view of this there can be little doubt as to the inspirational source behind the above-mentioned Labrador art form. More recently, the making of such tusk-carvings as a means to illustrate Eskimo myths has been encouraged by Father Steinmann at Povungnetuk.

By the 1930's, supplying carvings to outsiders whenever the opportunity arose had become a commonplace occupation for Canada's Innuit. The Hudson's Bay Company handled a considerable quantity, and even shipped out a number of commissioned orders. An Eskimo art exhibition held at the

McCord Museum in Montreal provided the general public with an additional opportunity for acquainting itself with the forms of creative expression practised up north. Apparently the Eskimos even numbered Nascapi and Algonquin Indians among their clientele!

In 1938, Twomey observed with interest how Belcher Island natives busied themselves "feverishly" at their task of turning out ivory carvings for sale to the crew of a visiting schooner. Apparently the commercial function of carving had not yet overridden all other considerations, for he hazarded the opinion that during the long winter months ahead the unsold items would become toys for the Eskimo children. In contrast to what is produced today, such carvings then were reckoned much less valuable and lacked a year-round market. Many months might pass between ship visits, and no one was too concerned about what happened to their surplus carvings in between those dates. There would always be plenty of time to make some more for the next arrivals. Under different circumstances, the same kind of casual approach was witnessed by Carpenter among the Aivilik who might indifferently drop the finished object into a tool-box, or simply lose it.

A decade later this easy-going attitude was destined to change drastically at the less isolated communities. Not only had contacts become more frequent but carvings now could be sold directly to the trading-post at any time. With such a favourable set-up, Eskimos became noticeably less negligent about the disposal of their output. The impact of these new developments may be gauged from Leeghman's disclosure that "before World War II, when the R.M.S. *Nascopie* took tourists into the Eastern Arctic each summer, there was some sporadic trade in carvings, model kayaks, and dolls, but this was never an important source of revenue. Now that there is an immediate and guaranteed market for such work, production has increased and nearly everybody, it seems, is busy carving, more than 75 per cent of the people according to one estimate."[5]

From all the evidence cited above, it becomes quite clear

---

[5] J. D. Leechman, "Eskimo Sculpture in Stone," *Canadian Geographical Journal,* vol. 49 (September, 1954), p. 95.

that historical Canadian Eskimo carving was never the "hitherto undiscovered" and "free from any outside influence" art which certain present-day writers have mistakenly believed it to be.

*　　　　　*　　　　　*

A twofold problem confronts every "outside" observer who strives to attain an intelligent appreciation of the art produced by any "primitive" group. The initial requisite of insight into aesthetic values must be supplemented by at least some understanding of the world-vision and way of life which play a primary role in the molding of each artistic creation. By ignoring Eskimo categories of thought and experience, people have all too often misinterpreted what the aboriginal artist was attempting to express.

Certain members of our society have subjected contemporary Canadian Eskimo carving to a critical evaluation using the same criteria that they ordinarily apply to creative modes of their own cultural milieu. . . .

Some of these critical appraisals can of course be justified on the grounds that the contemporary carving phase is in reality a hybrid art form with only limited traditional content, and that as such it falls properly within a sphere of creative activity where Western values prevail. There still remains a lingering impression that no one has had either the courage or the insight to spell out what critical standards would actually be applicable to authentic traditional Eskimo art.

This was precisely why Carpenter launched forth on a campaign to make the public realize that "the study of Eskimo art must be a study of the Eskimo world-view. It demands the utmost concentration on what the Eskimo is saying to fellow Eskimo. Not what this art means to us, but what this art means to the people for whom it was intended." The first step would be to distinguish clearly between the more traditional ivory carvings made to satisfy a need for self-expression through the release of half-hidden forms, or for religious and ornamental purposes, and the soapstone carvings created to please the non-Eskimo world. . . . Carpenter has attempted to show that the aboriginal Eskimo fused time and space into a four dimensional concept of reality in which nothing is stable and no fixed boundaries exist. According to him this concept of reality has been shaped by the peculiar physical nature of the arctic world where often nothing in particular stands out or is separable from the general background. For long periods during the winter months everything is turned into a meaningless whirl of cold and white. In such an environment all forms are temporary and transient and do not possess a definite invariable shape. Through carving and song, by recognizing and releasing emergent forms which held some meaning for him, the traditional Eskimo assisted in this perpetual process of transformation. He represented the force that revealed form and cancelled nothingness. When engaged in the act of carving, no attempt was made to force the medium of ivory into uncharacteristic effects. The artist simply responded to the material itself. The carvings as such were only of secondary importance. Art was "an act, not an object; a ritual, not a possession."[6]

Another theory expounded by Carpenter is that the truly aboriginal Eskimo relied more on auditory than on ocular powers in apprehending reality. This was carried over into their art, which in this sense might be called an "acoustic art." The traditional carver did not preoccupy himself with the task of placing a carving in a deliberate setting, or associating it with an explicit mood. For this reason, "each carving lives in spatial independence. Size and shape, proportions and selection, these are set by the object itself, not forced from without. Like sound, each carving creates its own space, its own identity; it imposes its own assumptions."[7]

Interpreted in this light, most traditional carvings reflect such an Eskimo concept of space-time by the very fact that they do not represent specific episodes or static "moments in time." Small and easily handled, they lack a single, favoured side for viewing, and can readily be turned this way and that way for multiple perspectives. This is in sharp contrast to so many contemporary soapstone carvings which portray a "moment in time" from domestic or outdoor life: (man-spearing-seal etc.), are best viewed from a specific angle, and have been made stationary by being mounted on a pedestal and by increased size

---

[6]E. S. Carpenter, R. Flaherty, and F. Varley, *Eskimo* (Toronto: University of Toronto Press, 1959), p. 38.
[7]*Ibid.*, pp. 27-28.

and weight. This contemporary carving style fits in harmoniously with our classic occidental approach to art, but is foreign to the old traditions of the north. The ancient Eskimos lacked such artistic "refinements" because these did not fulfill any need in their way of life. Only later on were they taught to think regularly in terms of separating time from space where carving was concerned.

A unique instance of this took place during the early 1920's. An Igloolik Eskimo named Au described to Rasmussen how on one occasion four large walruses on an ice-floe had drifted past his dwelling. The Danish explorer handed him paper and pencil and asked for a sketch of this scene. Unsuccessful in his attempt at drawing, Au offered to carve it in ivory. Six months later he produced a carving of "a male walrus and three females drifting on an ice-floe, while Au watches them from land through a telescope; with his wife and daughters seated beside him."[8] Here then we have an "outsider" stimulating the native carver to produce an "episode" carving.

A similar influence helped bring into being the contemporary phase of Canadian Eskimo carving, with Houston and others suggesting to the Eskimos that they depict scenes from their hunting and domestic life. Once these natives had been taught to visualize in this manner, they went ahead and created a spectacular new Eskimo art form frequently centred around "moments in time."

Such developments have also taken place in Alaska, and among the Siberian Eskimo and the Chukchi where guidance was provided by industrial art co-operatives and the Siberian Arts and Crafts Board.

The organization of carving projects in the Canadian Arctic brought with it insistent demands for technical perfection, which led in turn to greater self-consciousness about minute detail and complex form. Under pressure to produce work of a certain standard, a new type of artist has come to the fore, in some respects less free to express himself without inhibitions, in other respects able to explore new avenues.

Man used to be depicted as quite independent of his surroundings, freed from association with a single location or a specific temporal event. The very opposite is often true today.

Canadian Eskimo carvings have become kinesthetic, preoccupied with settings, and time-conscious, while deriving new scope for artistic composition from the form of bulky, rounded shapes and smooth surfaces typical of arctic clothing In contrast to the partial or complete nudity of early Eskimo art, modern human figurines are invariably fully dressed. At one community there has recently developed a trend back to nude figurines. This represents perhaps a different concept of nudity, more closely allied to Western eroticism, and something that has already taken hold in Alaska.

Not unexpectedly, a study of the sculptures that have come out of the Canadian north every year since 1949, shows contemporary carving to be a melting-pot of aboriginal concepts and new Western ideas. The ratio of inspiration drawn from these two founts varies not only in time, but also from settlement to settlement, and from individual to individual. To state about this modern phase, as Carpenter does, that its roots are "western" is therefore not altogether correct. Its roots are both Euro-Canadian and aboriginal. As has been demonstrated in Alaska, the latter influence cannot be so readily eradicated from the Eskimo mind. In Canada, the older generation of carvers has certainly retained it to a minor degree. This is particularly noticeable where animal figures are concerned, but much less so with human effigies. Stylized, symmetrical animal carvings which lack a "favoured point of view" are not yet rare, and will probably never disappear, although in deference to Kabloona tastes they may be naturalistically decorated and provided with a base.

---

[8]T. Mathiassen, "Material Culture of the Iglulik Eskimos," *Report of the Fifth Thule Expedition*, vol. VI, part A (Copenhagen: Glyndalske Boghaindeln, 1928), p. 104.

Caribou Eskimo Legal Concepts

GEERT VAN DEN STEENHOVEN

Law: needs formal criterium

Law – if we consider it not from the lawyer's limited standpoint but as a social phenomenon – can be said to be those rules of secular conduct to which we have to adhere not only for moral or "social" motives, but *because these norms are administered by an authority which has the power to apply physical coercion*. And "legal concepts" can be taken to refer to those common notions about conduct which are generally felt to be embodied in law. Most of us agree that formal codes, courts and constables are not necessary for the determination of law; for the present purpose, I [take] as basic criteria of law: authority and (threat of) physical compulsion. The chief criteria of law will therefore be *formal*, and not functional.

Malinowski: functional criterium

The latter, functional view of law was held by Malinowski, who regarded law as a system of rights and duties, governed by the principle of reciprocity: "as the specific result of the configuration of obligations, which make it impossible for the native to shirk his responsibilities without suffering for it in the future"; and as "effective custom." I believe, however, that some of his critics have rightly pointed out that this functional criterium leaves law and custom undistinguished; and although Malinowski turned himself against the view that all custom was law (among primitive peoples), his definition seemed to have the opposite effect.

"Customary Law": a confusing term

Other scholars – feeling that some customs, though they were not law, were not mere customs either – have adopted the

SOURCE: *Proceedings of the 32nd International Congress of Americanists* (Copenhagen, 1956), pp. 531–538. Reprinted by permission of the author and publisher.

existing term of "customary law" for this category of rules. But I think that De Josselin De Jong was right when he held "that the essential problem of the relation between phenomena of law and phenomena of custom has been obscured again and again by gathering all dubious cases into a separate category which is neither law nor custom but a certain 'tertium quid' which does not require a sharp definition."[1] And, as a muddled terminology may be an impediment to clear thinking he proposes that we should begin by abolishing the term of "customary law." I feel that it is useful to adopt this suggestion in cultural anthropology in general, and particularly in studies of the law of societies whose legal system is so utterly different from our own.

Hoebel's working-definition

Adamson Hoebel, who has done so much to further the study of the law of primitive peoples, refined and elaborated the concept into the following definition: "Hence we may say that privileged force, official authority, and regularity are the elements that modern jurisprudence teaches us we must seek when we wish to identify law. On this basis, for working purposes, law may be defined in these terms: *A social norm is legal if its neglect or infraction is regularly met, in treat or in fact, by the application of physical force by an individual or group possessing the socially recognized privilege of so acting.*"[2] And many are the examples which he gives of the existence and process of law among peoples which have no codes, no government, no state, no constables, no jails. Three points in Hoebel's definition need perhaps special mentioning: First, for a norm to be called legal, there must have been a number of consistent "cases" ("regularity"); second, "authority" can just as well reside in the community as such or in a private individual (e.g., the complaining party himself) or group, acting with a kind of "ad hoc" status, with approval – implicit or explicit – of the other

---

[1] J. P. B. De Josselin de Jong, "Customary Law – A Confusing Fiction" (Amsterdam: Koninglijke Vereeniging Indisch Instituut), *Mededeeling 80, Afdeeling Volkenkunde*, vol. 29, 1948.

[2] E. A. Hoebel, *The Law of Primitive Man* (Cambridge, Mass.: Harvard University Press, 1954), p. 28.

members of the society; and third, all supernatural sanctions (on the violations of taboos) are excluded.

Thus guided by Hoebel's formulation, I undertook my field-research among the Caribou Eskimos. During and after this research, however, I felt that the following three observations might be made with respect to the definition. First, I felt that the authority of the pater familias, or his equivalent, inside his family sphere, should be considered as excluded from the definition. Second, I have some doubts whether "physical coercion," or the threat thereof, is really the first essential for a definition of law; I am not yet prepared to argue this point and maintain the requirement – in accordance with prevailing legal theory – only with the reservation that I feel "administering authority" to be definitely more characteristic of "law" than "physical coercion." Third, during a recent discussion of this subject, some remarks by Professor De Josselin de Jong brought to light quite another aspect of "law" and the "legal" which does not run contrary to Hoebel's, yet seems to throw a different and meaningful light on the problem.

De Josselin De Jong's observations

As De Josselin De Jong pointed out at that occasion: if there exists law, *it must be felt by the members of the society concerned* to exist as such: some segment of their norms must be regarded as separated from the other norms in that their infraction calls for a tendency towards special procedure; violation of these norms will be met not in the spontaneous manner which is characteristic of the infraction of mere customs. If the norm is legal, the reaction is *non-spontaneous*, there is a tendency to "find the law" which should here be applied, to involve the help of specialists. A norm is legal, if infraction is known by the community to be met with something else than mere social disapproval; and this distinction should be recognized in *formal* characteristics. Of course, there may be border cases and – no society being entirely stable – there may also be transition cases from custom to law or even vice versa; but this does not affect the principle, that it seems a true guide for the determination of law to *ascertain how the society concerned regards the norms and the nature of the reactions in question*. I feel that this additional criterium can be used as a useful tool to make the proof whether or not a norm meeting Hoebel's rational definition, in reality may be said to have the level of law.

Summary

My already most summary introduction can therefore be summarized as follows: I consider law to need a formal, not a functional criterium; I shall not use the confusing term "customary law," thus restricting myself to "custom" on the one hand and "law" (codified or non-codified) on the other; and Hoebel's working-definition of legal norms (laws), viewed in the additional light of De Josselin de Jong's observation, seems an acceptable manner of dealing with the social phenomenon of law, both primitive and modern.

With the foregoing in mind, I might now be allowed to consider from a bird's eye view the conclusions from the available Caribou Eskimo field-data.

Caribou Eskimo reactions to norm-infractions

If one listens to the opinions given by the informants in reply to questions as to what is done in case of violation of a rule, these replies suggest a preference for withdrawal from situations of conflict, general nuisance, or trouble. Akpa – one of the most respected Padlermiut hunters, and one whose physical courage and moral responsibility cannot be questioned – once said to me: "In case of conflict or dispute, I would rather run away than fight." Again and again, the replies indicate that one who steals, or who lies, or who is lazy and neglects his wife and children, or who violates other strongly favoured rules, especially one who *persistently* trespasses the norms, is regarded as "one for whom we do not care," an unpleasant man, one who lacks brains, pitiful, and a nuisance. In a very serious case, the camp might move elsewhere without warning him, in an attempt to rid itself of the undesirable one; but he will not be actively expelled, nor will he be refused some food if he would be starving. Not one opinion revealed any consciously felt or regularly practised legal sanctions for the violation of a rule, but instead a largely unpredictable choice from possible customary communal reactions against the one who upsets social balance by his violations, ranging from just social disapproval to leaving the troublemaker behind by moving elsewhere. And if the issue is between two parties without involving the community as such, predictability of what action – if any – the wronged party will take, and how he will proceed, is similarly lacking, since there are no fixed procedures and all depends upon the "then and there" of the situation and on the moral or psychological superiority of the one over the other.

However, more positive reactions to wrong sometimes do occur, though without regularity or apparent community involvement. A choleric mother-in-law was killed, a few years ago; another case shows that the relative of a wife came to take her back from her husband who neglected her and who had gambled away his possessions; sometimes, with respect to goods that can be expressed in trade-values, the creditor will try to even it out via the trader, rather than directly approaching the debtor or thief. These incidental occurrences clearly have nothing to do with law.

The case "Alickewa vs. Ollie"

I shall enter with some detail into one of the very few more pronounced cases of dispute or trouble which I encountered. A wife was taken away by her brother from her husband, who had failed to pay the bride price. The woman, by the name of Ootnooyuk, had been married several years to her husband Ollie, when her brother Alickewa – in Ollie's absence – travelled to his sister and took her, as well as some or all of her children, far inland to give her in marriage to the shaman Pongalak, whose wife she is to this day and near whom Alickewa was living at the time. It is believed that Pongalak – who is a notorious "schemer" – conceived of the project which, of course, had to be carried out by Ootnooyuk's brother, Alickewa. Although the deserted husband Ollie – who is still looking around for another wife – is not known as a good hunter or trapper, it seems unlikely that she was badly neglected by him. The case is interesting in so far as physical action (effecting a kind of annulment of the marriage) was taken by the nearest relative; Ollie seems to have resigned to the incident, and other Padlermiut Eskimos at Eskimo Point, where he was staying last summer, expressed as their opinion that Ollie had felt Alickewa's action as difficult – if not impossible – to resist against. He had lost his case by not paying the promised bride price, which is definitely regarded by these Eskimos to be wrong. But can we now conclude that "this infraction is regularly met, in threat or in fact, by the application of physical force (by her brother) possessing the socially recognized privilege of so acting"? Or that here is shown the presence of "privileged force, official authority and regularity"? Perhaps we are close to finding here a case meeting the requirements to be called "legal"; here we have socially recognized action, implying the application of physical force. It is true that the action taken was not felt to be automatically the only one possible under the circumstances (and – perhaps significantly – it was performed during the absence of the husband), nor does the social recognition suggest more than an utter minimum of passive "official authority" – if any; and regularity, though to some extent suggested by the occurrence of similar reactions in somewhat analogous cases, is by no means established. But it cannot be denied that the case shows a certain conformance with the respective requirements of Hoebel's working definition of law, which I had adopted for the present study; although the case stands alone so that it cannot carry conclusive weight, it might nevertheless be felt to present something of the "legal" in its barest bones. On the other hand, a feeling of uncertainty and dissatisfaction with the vagueness of such a conclusion cannot be avoided. It is here that the above suggested "test" of De Josselin De Jong should be applied: examine if these people *themselves* regard this rule to be a norm different from the others, in that its infraction calls for specific non-spontaneous reaction and procedure. The test will clearly show a negative answer and the case "Alickewa vs. Ollie" is therefore not a legal case.

Habitual troublemakers

So far, then, we have seen that it is up to the wronged party to take or not to take any customary action. The other families in the community who are not involved in the issue, will not consider it proper to interfere – though they will certainly have their own opinion. The situation becomes different if someone is repeatedly causing trouble so that he becomes a menace to regular and peaceful camp life. In those rather rare cases, the *camp as such* may gradually come into action, but it is a "passive" action: not visiting the undesirable any more, not sharing their plans with him, perhaps even moving camp altogether, without warning him. In short: withdrawal from the nuisance. Habitual liars, thieves of foxes or meat caches, and lazy people are – in practice – perhaps the worst social nuisances, in the eyes of these Eskimos: these characters make life uncertain and their unpredictable attitude works disruptively in the daily routine. It is my feeling that an Eskimo from these regions might easily "get away" with conduct that is very wrong in the eyes of everyone else around, as long as these others feel that he is not going to make a habit of so acting. That may well explain why Idjuadjuk, after he killed in one stroke the entire family which opposed his marriage, was not only tolerated, but even very popular: for once he had got his wife, it was felt by the others that he was satisfied, and his known cleverness and advice were in high regard.

Conclusion

It is my opinion, then, that the pertinent research data are negative as regards the privileged force, the official authority, and the regularity of application, which are the basis of Hoebel's working definition of law. The lack of cases reported is not entirely due to the imperfections of my research: the replies to many questions implied the unlikelihood of any positive "cases" to occur in the fields concerned. To the contrary, external anarchy prevails here as in other important aspects of Caribou Eskimo life, which knows only a minimum of private property, no land-ownership in any form, no state, no tribes, no chiefs; neither do they know the institutionalized song duel as in Greenland, or formal expulsion, or executions of intolerable wrong-doers with positive community consent, which are sometimes reported from other Eskimo regions. My search for the social phenomenon of law among these Eskimos, then, has had a negative result. If there be question of law among other Eskimo groups, I did not encounter it among the Caribou Eskimos which I visited, or in the relevant research literature; neither have I reason to feel that they ever had legal norms or law in the past. The negative nature of my conclusions and the non-legal character of their norms and practices are, however, none the less interesting, for that matter; though on the other hand it seems by no means a shocking discovery for anyone who does not dogmatically presuppose "law" in the above defined sense to exist as a universal social phenomenon.

It seems superfluous to stress for an audience of ethnologists that, even if we cannot speak of "law" among these Eskimos, it would be quite wrong to call them "lawless" in the sense which some people like to give to this term when they think of societies quite different from their own. These Eskimos do have definite opinions on right and wrong, and their small societies do manage generally to carry on their social life cheerfully by the force of mere custom, governed by common sense and a strong *"sympathie sociale."* Their traditionally small numbers, scattered and nomadic existence, and hazardous natural conditions of life might well have prohibited the development of an indigenous system of laws as most other peoples have developed in the course of their history.

Maintenance of the peace

If there is only custom and no law, when does the community as such come into action? Dr. Birket-Smith has given us the answer when, after emphasizing that there is never question of *judicial action* among these Eskimos, he wrote with reference to the entire Eskimo area: "in essence it is not the mission of the community to execute law and justice, but exclusively to restore peace, using this word in the medieval sense of the ordinary, regular course of life. On this basis the settlement may, for instance, combine in killing a man or a woman suspected of witchcraft, for such persons are a menace to the peace of the community. The killing is not, however, a *punishment* for the practising of witchcraft, for the community may in the same manner get rid of a man with a wild and brutal temperament, or of old or sick people who are a burden upon the settlement."[3] I feel that Birket-Smith's observation gives us the answer to the question of what motivation the community needs to take or

---

[3] K. Birket-Smith, *The Eskimos* (London: Methuen & Co., 1936), p. 156.

approve any action against one of its members, and that the infraction of a norm *per se* is no prerequisite for any such action. This explains why these communities can on the one hand cause the death of a man merely because he is sick or invalid, and on the other hand remain entirely passive as such if one of its members is murdered by another. The community seems to act only when safety, security, quiet, and order are felt to be in imminent danger: and even then its action is essentially passive, at any rate among the groups which I visited.

Final remarks

As a rule, these Caribou Eskimos seem to maintain a fine and peaceful social existence. Though justice does not seem to be regarded by them as something that should be maintained, if necessary, with the help of physical coercion; or rather: though justice as an independent concept is unknown among them, there is a common and strong feeling for fair and reasonable practices in routine daily interactions. Self-criticism, realism, common sense, and a happy absence of "righteousness" govern their secular activities.

But, *to us*, structure seems to be lacking to *administer* this fairness in case of repeated, habitual and troublesome violations, except by various degrees of social disapproval and avoidance, and in extreme cases by more or less impulsive killings either as a private or as a direct (or indirect) communal action; I must admit that no cases of killing as a communal action have ever been reported in the region, but on the other hand I feel that such action is nevertheless *conceivable* among these Caribou Eskimos. There is no social control on the legal level; and this absence does not seem to harm their present social life, except in the rare case when they have to deal with a habitually troublesome camp member or neighbour who has enough character to face the disapproval and contempt of the others.

But, fortunately, trouble is no favoured pass-time among these people. A young hunter at Eskimo Point, whom I asked what he would do if they had to put up with an undesirable camp member, answered: "We won't care for him, but we won't let him starve." Then, as if to correct himself, he added: "An Eskimo, however, would *always* be likable."

Igluligmiut Kinship Terminology and Behaviour: Consanguines[1]

DAVID DAMAS

One way of classifying kinship behaviour between categories of relatives is by means of a respect-to-rough-joking series or a most formal-to-most-intimate arrangement of categories. These approaches are not particularly apt in the case of the Igluligmiut behavioural system, however, because joking and a sort of familiarity abound throughout most of the system, and this behaviour does not seem to be arranged in any hierarchical order. There seems to be no "joking-cousin" relationship as reported by Heinrich from Alaska. The only institutionalized joking relationship that I was able to discover was that pertaining between pairs of non-related or remotely related individuals called *mangariik*. The joking in this relationship seemed to take a rough form, and when the partners were separated by long distances, jokes were sent by mail (these are written in the Eskimo syllabary), carried by dog team. Avoidance and respect relationships are, on the other hand, sometimes carefully prescribed between classes of relatives. There is a deepened respect relationship between brother and sister after about the age of puberty, which is also in effect between opposite-sexed cousins, though to an attenuated extent. Brother and sister, when adults, seldom address one another and generally will not appear alone in a house together. Avoidance and respect reach their greatest development between *ai* or opposite-sexed in-laws. Formerly, those in that category were *illirjuariik* or those relatives who could not mention the name of each other; these

SOURCE: *Igluligmiut Kinship and Local Groupings: A Structural Approach* (Ottawa: National Museum of Canada, Bulletin 196, Anthropological Series 64, 1963), pp. 47-57 and 203-212. Reprinted by permission of the author and publisher. Title supplied by the editors.

[1]The Igluligmiut terminology for consanguines will be found in figures 1 and 2.

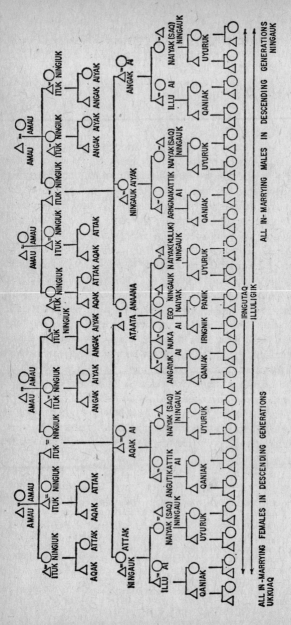

FIGURE 1. Igluligmiut consanguines, male ego.

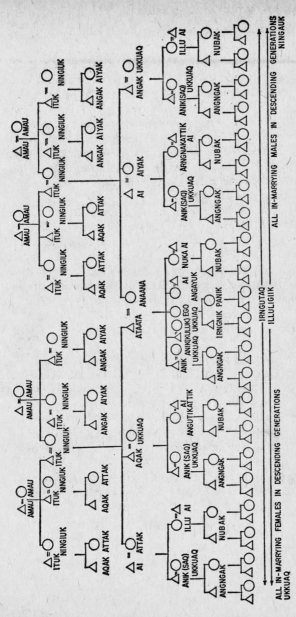

FIGURE 2. Igluligmiut consanguines, female ego.

had to be addressed through a third person. This pattern seems to have largely broken down, but the respect relationship is still marked. There seems to exist an asymmetrical respect relationship between father-in-law and son-in-law and between mother-in-law and daughter-in-law; that is, the parent-in-law need not reciprocate the respect given him by those affines named. Between the fathers-in-law, however, the respect relationship is symmetrical. Thus, among the relatives where we would expect a great deal of contact in the household situation, certain respect regulations can be seen to operate in regulating daily contact situations and in militating against the conflicts inherent to such circumstances.

Appraisal of the system as a conceptually consistent arrangement of behavioural norms was not forthcoming until the investigator realized the frequency of the use of the terms *ungayuk* or "affection" and *nalartuk* or "obedience" in the natives' description of the status relationships. Conceived in terms of these two concepts, much of the system becomes understandable; for within the realm of *nalartuk*, the dominance-subordination relationships are arranged, and within the confines of *ungayuk* the degrees of closeness in their co-operative bonds are shown.

Ungayuk is especially important in understanding the cousin system of the Igluligmiut. From the above, it is evident that there is a terminological identification of opposite-sexed cousins with opposite-sexed siblings. Behaviourally, there is an extension of the avoidance relationship shown to exist between brother and sister to opposite-sexed cousins. This is in actual practice somewhat attenuated in the case of collaterals, and some informants indicate that there is a greater electiveness involved in the behavioural realm among opposite-sexed cousins than among opposite-sexed siblings. Even though relations between *anik* and *naiyak* are marked by avoidance, there is a close bond between them, and *ungayuk* characterizes the reserve that is evident. Between cousins of the same sex, the more complex "three cousin" system has a logic in terms of *ungayuk*. The male Ego males in his generation have brother or brother-like relationships. A complementary situation occurs for female Ego with her sister and sister-like relationship to females in her generation. The three sorts of cousins of the same sex are ranked hierarchically with regard to affectional closeness according to the principle of the solidarity of the sexes. For male Ego, paternal parallel cousins as the sons of two brothers form the closest sort of brother-like bond outside the actual sibling group. Most distant of the three cousins for male Ego is the maternal parallel cousin. The logic of that arrangement is that the maternal parallel cousins are related to one another through parents who are both opposite in sex to either of the cousins. Intermediate in affectional closeness are the cross cousins. This is still consistent with the principle of the solidarity of the sexes, for in that case one of the connecting relatives is of the same sex as the cousins in question and one is of opposite sex. A complementary picture obtains for female Ego. Since the maternal parallel cousins are related through two females, this is the strongest sort of cousin bond, the most sister-like outside the actual sibling group. The paternal parallel cousin is the "weak" cousin with regard to closeness on the same principle, and the *illu* or cross cousins are intermediate.

The terminologies of the first ascending and descending generations have been explained in terms of each other and just so can the behavioural correlates be understood. Here again the principle of the solidarity of the sexes operates through the connecting relatives. The children of brothers and of male cousins are more son-and-daughter-like to male Ego than those of sisters and female cousins. The opposite is true of female Ego because the children of sisters and female cousins are closer with regard to affection than the children of brothers and male cousins. As outlined above, avuncular-nepotic relationships are conceived of in terms of dualities, as for instance *aqakqaniaq*. Collaterals in the first ascending generation can be conceived as being surrogate mothers and surrogate fathers. Following the principle of the solidarity of sexes again for male Ego, *aqak* is closer to Ego than *angak*, because he is related through father (i.e., the complement of the Ego-*qaniak* situation), whereas *angak* is related through mother. The situation is reversed for female Ego, for whom *angak* is more father-like than *aqak*. Among the aunts, *attak* is a closer mother-surrogate for male Ego than is *aiyak*, for again the latter is related through father or same sex (with Ego) relative. For female Ego, *aiyak* is closer than *attak* according to the same principle.

In terms of *ungayuk* and the principle of the solidarity of the sexes, then, three generations of the Igluligmiut' consanguineal system can be plotted in hierarchical order. Using the values "1" to "4" as close-to-distant with regard to affection, Table 1 indicates the organization of cousin-sibling and avuncular-nepotic dyads.

It should be noted that only same-sexed relatives in Ego's generation are listed here. As I have indicated in the descriptive section, female cousins and sisters for male Ego and male cousins and brothers for female Ego are merged in the terminology. The siblings are seen as closer, despite the terminological equivalence with cousins, but there is no indication that the hierarchy of close-to-distant applies with regard to the parentage of the cross-sexed (for Ego) cousins as it does with same-sexed cousins.

In the remaining ascending and descending generations, the principle of sex solidarity does not operate. It should be noted, however, that *ituk* or *ningiuk-irngnutaq* are closer sorts of relationships than *amau-illuligiik*. The grandchild-grandparent tie shows a pattern common among primitive peoples, one of indulgence and affection mingled with informality and joking not found on the parental level. The relationship between Ego and father (and the father-like figures *aqak* and *angak*) is tinged with respect, though informality often prevails. The father-son and mother-daughter bonds are the most solid of actual bonds in the actual social life of the people. The same-sexed offspring is gradually and carefully introduced to the pursuits of his adult role and encouraged to gradually assume full status in adult male or female life. A fuller exposition of this relationship is, however, connected to the discussion of *nalartuk* or obedience, the other key concept in the Igluligmiut system.

TABLE 1: *Hierarchies of affectional closeness*

In Ego's Generation:

MALE EGO	FEMALE EGO
1. *angayuk* or *nuka* (brother)	1. *angayuk* or *nuka* (sister)
2. *angutikattik*	2. *arngnakattik*
3. *illu*	3. *illu*
4. *arngakattik*	4. *angutikattik*
All females *naiyak*	All males *anik*

In Adjacent Generations:

MALE EGO	FEMALE EGO
1. *ataata-irngnik* (father-son)	1. *ataata-panik* (father-daughter)
2. *aqak-qaniak*	2. *angak-uyuruk*
3. *angak-uyuruk*	3. *aqak-qaniak*
1. *anaana-irngnik* (mother-son)	1. *anaana-panik* (mother daughter)
2. *attak-angngak*	2. *aiyak-nubak*
3. *aiyak-nubak*	3. *attak-angngak*

In the sibling group, age and sex both figure in determining the dominance-subordinance hierarchy. Thus for male Ego, the older brother is terminologically distinguished from the younger, and obedience is along the lines of age, as is the case with females who show a complementary terminology. Between males and females, however, the female should obey the male sibling regardless of age differences. In actuality, this operates only when both brother and sister are mature. Girls often play a surrogate-mother role for younger brothers, such as carrying them about in hoods, as they do for younger sisters as well. The age and sex principles thus outlined seem also to operate, though in attenuated form, for cousins, paralleling terminological lumping of cross-sexed cousins with cross-sexed siblings. The parent-child relationship can also be partly understood in terms of obedience, though as noted above, deep affectionate factors soften these ties, making them bonds of great closeness and co-operation, as well as being strongly oriented toward leadership and followership. It should be noted, however, that there is at times a tendency for old and ailing men to relinquish much of the practical leadership function to sons, especially in matters of decision concerning the hunt, though unusually deep respect relationships pertain, which are at times in marked contrast to the scorn shown by an Eskimo to the old and feeble, who are not related to himself.

The quintessence of *nalartuk* is found in the relationships among some classes of affinally linked persons. Concerning those marrying into Ego's kin group, the terminology bears out the dominance and solidarity of the consanguineal group. Thus *ningauk* for male Ego and *ukkuaq* for female Ego are definitely subordinate regardless of relative age differences and regardless of generational differences with Ego. The correspondence of this relationship can be seen in Ego's relationship with wife's or husband's consanguines. In the ascending generation, the *sakkik* or parent-in-law is to be obeyed and, as mentioned earlier, certain respect relationships are involved. Involved also for the male is the practice of a year's bride service, which is given *sakkik* or, in his absence, *sakkiaq*. As the common root indicates, the latter seems to be a sort of surrogate *sakkik*. *Sakkiaq* extends downward as well as collaterally among Ego's spouses' consanguines, complementing the picture of the *ningauk* among Ego's consanguines' spouses. The spouses of Ego's spouse's consanguines (co-affines) form with Ego a "quasi-sibling" group. As indicated in the descriptive section above, one's status is determined in terms of the age and generational differences of spouse's consanguines. A co-operative association pertains between those in these positions, and the subordinance-dominance pattern revolves around the apparent age distinctions as among siblings. There is, curiously, no actual age distinction here, however. In general, this group of relatives seems to conform closely to a sibling-like arrangement in which the authority is evident but is more subtly expressed than between directly affinally related persons such as *ningauk-sakkiaq* and *ukkuaq-sakkiaq*.

Iglulingmiut terminological categories thus display the property of being understood in terms of several principles. Some categories carry with them respect and even avoidance directives for Ego; whereas, in general, joking pervades the relationships among those at other places in the system. It does not seem profitable to consider degrees of familiarity and respect as the key to the understanding of a large number of categories. Rather, as we have indicated, many of the relationships can be considered in terms of relative affectional closeness coupled with the principle of the extension of surrogate roles from lineal to collateral relatives. In other words, collateral relatives in the parental generation show relatively greater and lesser mother-like and father-like roles for Ego, those collaterals in Ego's generation assume sister-like and brother-like roles, and in the descending generation son- and daughter-like roles. The principle involved in determining the relative closeness to Ego (or stated another way, the degree of identification with lineal relatives) has been shown to be the solidarity of the sexes. These statements concern chiefly consanguines for both male and female Ego.

Another class of feelings pertaining among relatives is that characterized by obedience and command. Among consanguines this system is determined by age-hierarchy and generational differences. Between Ego and affines it is determined by the locus of authority falling within the blood group. Thus Ego has a large measure of authority over those same-sexed affines marrying into his consanguineal group. At the same time he is largely subordinate to spouse's consanguines.

The terminological and behavioural data that have been discussed give a picture of the several kinds of kin groups with which Ego is associated. First, there are Ego's consanguines, which, as noted above, comprise a largely symmetrical bilateral group with Ego at the centre. The scope of consanguineal relations has fuzzy limits but, in general, seems to extend to the second cousins, in our sense of the term; that is, father's cousins and their offspring seem to fall within the generally recognized circle of consanguineal kin.

*   *   *

The regulation of marriage among the Igluligmiut is closely interwoven with the limits of the terminological system. Ego should not marry anyone for whom he (or she) has a kin term. There are, to be sure, borderline cases. For instance, there is some contradiction regarding marriage eligibility between foster siblings. I have inquired about cases of marriage in such cases and have found that some relatives condone such unions, but others do not. In general my older informants, who were not related to anyone who had practised such a union, were adamant that it should not be allowed and that those who violated the regulation were *issumakittuk* or "simple-minded."

Regarding marriage of the offspring of the spouse-exchange relationship, there is also some contradiction, but mostly uncertainty. These reactions, coupled with those of general resistance toward any questioning in the area of spouse exchange, leave us frustrated in interpreting the situation. On the succeeding two generations, however, there is more certainty, and marriage is definitely not allowed among these persons.

Violations of the directives against marriage of relatives occur within the Catholic segment of the population. Papal dispensation has been extended for cousin marriage for Catholic Igluligmiut. There is, however, evidence to show that another factor besides the desired religious endogamy is important in accounting for this practice. This I shall discuss presently.

With regard to actual incest regulations, or the control of sexual relations among kin, information is lacking, but there is evidently a looser regulation in that area than is found in actual marriage control.

*   *   *

Justification for undertaking a detailed presentation of terminology, especially behavioural ideals, would be lacking if one failed to find some general correspondence between ideal and actual behaviour. Indeed, at times the testimony of the Igluligmiut themselves would seem to conspire against the hope that much correlation could be found between the two universes. The word *"illani"* or "sometimes" entered heavily into the discussion of kinship behaviour with these Eskimo. They are indeed aware of the difference between ideal and actual in kinship behaviour. The electiveness of behavioural directives applied to the various categories is noted in discussions of this sort. For instance, in checking information taken down regarding behaviour of a man toward a female cousin, the informant indicated that "sometimes, if both agreed" an avoidance relationship would prevail. This electiveness parallels to some extent Heinrich's[2] conceptualization of the *natqua* system in Alaska. The circle of "nonoptative" statuses which Heinrich speaks of does not seem to be set off at Iglulik, and there is no term to define such a group. There is present a rather fluid system of allegiance or non-allegiance to norms of behaviour. The writer, however, believes that there is perhaps a greater conformity to norms of kinship behaviour than the Eskimos are themselves willing to admit. An example of this could be seen in the village where I spent the longest stays during my field programme. There, one of my informants, after indicating the prescribed behavioural directives between him and his close male relatives in the village and, as well, the patterns that should prevail among them, laughingly remarked that of course he and his close relatives did not follow such a system closely. He expressed the often-repeated sentiment of the Igluligmiut that the general feelings of good-naturedness should be maintained in contacts between relatives, and that no matter what dominance-subordinance hierarchy should be called for, the latter should be secondary to the joking and warmth that should prevail in co-operative enterprise. Actual observations in the course of hunts, boat launchings, and journeys convinced the writer, however, that the *ningauk-sakkiaq* and *angayungruk-nukaungruk* roles were followed rather closely in the execution of co-operative activity and were constantly reinforced through verbal reference, kin terms being more frequently used than names.

*   *   *

There is not a great deal of data published which show units that can readily be compared to those that I have used in my analysis in this . . . [paper]. Furthermore, there is insufficient space here to deal adequately with the wider functional problems of the Eskimo area in a study which is primarily structural in emphasis. Nevertheless, it may be useful here to examine some of the available comparative material in order to rough out the direction that future studies of depth and pertinent orientation should take in attempting to solve wider problems of function in the Eskimo area.

It has been indicated that the Igluligmiut economy has

---

[2]Albert Heinrich, "Structural Features of Northwestern Alaska Kinship," *Southwestern Journal of Anthropology*, vol. 16 (Spring, 1960), p. 111.

undergone a change toward an adaptation resembling the Neo-Eskimo or Thule culture phase, with an increased permanency of villages that is probably related to the increased accumulation of stores for the winter, based on the boat-and-walrus complex. It has been noted that the aboriginally significant and present-day prominent occurrence of surpluses has allowed in the Iglulik area a higher level of subsistence than that found in most central or eastern Eskimo societies. Stefansson, for instance, observed that the usual number of dogs per (nuclear) family among the Copper Eskimo was two, and the highest number seen was four. Hall, on the other hand, reports teams of from twelve to twenty animals in the Iglulik region. The number of dogs is an important gauge of local prosperity, for among the Igluligmiut today the dogs require more food over the year's time than does the total human population. Mathiassen reports the lack of population-control measures such as infanticide around Iglulik; Rasmussen and Jenness report that practice, especially with regard to female infants, among the Copper and Netsilik Eskimo. One might conjecture, in the absence of concrete demographic-genealogical data, that the effect of infanticide would be the increased fragmentation of groups since the number of members of any given group of brothers and sisters would tend to be small. In addition, the likely early death of adults that marginal subsistence situations could bring about might conspire against the common occurrence of the father-and-adult-son link. Thus the two main building blocks of the extended family as seen at Iglulik, the sibling tie and the father-son tie, might be considerably weakened in the less well-endowed Eskimo regions, bringing about an increased nucleation of the local group. Indeed Rasmussen's census from the Netsilik area indicates that the "household" (which apparently is the residential unit) is most commonly a nuclear family, or a nuclear family with single adults (especially men) attached. There is no information regarding the character of the kinship connections between such peripheral members and the core couple in such situations. Jenness makes a strong case for the nuclear family as being the typical residential unit among the Copper Eskimo. Although he noted that joint houses were occupied by two or more families, he says, regarding such alliances of families:

Sometimes two would decide to build together before they started out, sometimes not until they chose their sites. It was rare for two families that lived together in one settlement to stay together in the next apparently because they had tired of each other's company and were anxious for a change.[3]

If one seeks comparisons in the area of group structure outside the nuclear family, one must be concerned with the patterns of residence after the marriage of young couples. There are little concrete data regarding this in the Eskimo area, only general references. . . . The degree of compositeness or of bilaterality in the larger groupings here or most anywhere in the Eskimo area is not known. This writer was able to gather some information regarding residence from Eskimo patients in several hospitals in Western Canada. On the basis of this preliminary information, one can probably hypothesize a rather widespread occurrence of virilocality. Data from Baker Lake, the Netsilik area, and Pond Inlet indicate that that form of residence was at least the ideal at those places. My informant from Baker Lake, a man of about fifty-five or sixty years of age, indicated that, in winter, fathers and sons and their families shared a common snowhouse or a collection of domes joined together. Band organization above the level of this kind of arrangement was said by this man to have been variable and bilateral. Graburn indicates that in the Sugluk region as well, virilocality prevailed.

The question of defining the extended family in the Eskimo area will probably involve criteria other than the simple sharing of one roof, though the economic criteria, which I used to supplement the residential in the discussion of the Iglulik material, may need modification when applied to a larger area. The relative compositeness, lineality, or bilaterality of larger groupings cannot be more than speculated on at this time, for in spite of the occurrence of considerable field-work in the eastern Canadian Arctic, little space has been devoted to the analysis of the kinship composition of bands in the published reports of such

---

[3] Diamond Jenness, "The Life of the Copper Eskimo," *Report of the Canadian Arctic Expedition, 1913-18, Volume XII* (Ottawa: F. A. Acland, 1922), p. 74.

work. One of the best leads available with regard to group composition comes from Van den Steenhoven, based on his studies among the Pelly Bay Eskimo, Netsilik. Although the groups in that region have joined to form a large winter settlement, the local bands have kept their identification in the compound organization of that settlement. The number of father-son alliances is remarkable within the clusters of two and three nuclear families that make up the large village. On paper, at least, the village organization is reminiscent of the Iglulik groups with units that are apparently virilocally slanted extended families connected by a series of bilateral ties. This author (Van den Steenhoven) interestingly explains two uxorilocal situations in terms of their abnormality and found that genealogical isolation, either local because of immigration, or total because of deaths of relatives, was usually behind such arrangements, as indeed did the writer at Iglulik. On the other hand, the web of relationships seems to have been extended to a far greater extent through pseudokinship arrangements than I found in my field study. The elaborate sharing procedures regarding the seal is a case in point. Perhaps the shift in emphasis from the seal to the walrus and the generally higher level of subsistence at Iglulik obviate the need for such carefully regulated division practises. . . .

Further west, Spencer's treatment of the whale-hunting North Alaskans shows the importance of partnerships and voluntary organizations, especially the boat crew, which reached a fuller development with greater formalization and cultural content than at Iglulik. Spencer says of the general configuration of social features, however: "As the North Alaskan data are reviewed, therefore, it seems evident that here is a basic social organization paralleling that of other Eskimo groups to the east. It is borne out further by the kinship terminologies."[4] This author sees a more significant difference in the lineage developments of the Bering Sea area farther to the south.

On turning specifically to a comparison of kinship terminologies,[5] there seem to prevail a general uniformity of terms on the grandparental and grandchild as well as first descending generations throughout the East-Central Arctic, a greater variation in affinal terms, and much more significant differences in Ego's and first ascending generations. Since such divergences

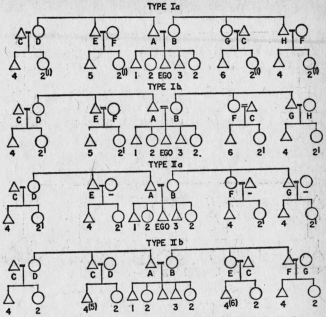

FIGURE 3. Types of East-Central Eskimo kinship terminologies I.
Based on ego's and first ascending generations.

in terminology may be seen to have some significance in broader
Eskimo perspective, I have arranged their distribution in a series
of types (*see* Figures 3, 4, and 5).

It can be noted that Type Ia has a wide distribution,
spanning the area inhabited by groups collectively designated as
"Iglulik Eskimo" by Birket-Smith. It can be seen that the Back

---

[4]Robert N. Spencer, *The North Alaskan Eskimos: A Study in
Ecology and Society* (Washington: Smithsonian Institution, Bureau
of American Ethnology, Bulletin 171, 1959), pp. 448-449.
[5]The conventions to be followed in Figures 3, 4, and 5 are as follows:
the roman numerals and capital letters refer to the parental generation. All like terms are represented by the same letter. Types I, II,
III refer to the classification of members of the first ascending
generation. Arabic numerals and lower case letters are used to
represent members of Ego's generation. Types "*a*" and "*b*" refer
to the classification of cousins. Diacritics indicate *saq* usage. Numbers in parentheses (including diacritics) indicate optional usage.

TYPE III a

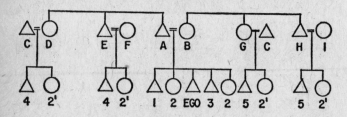

TYPE III b

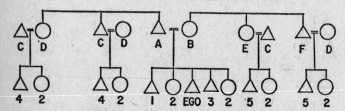

FIGURE 4. Types of East-Central Eskimo kinship terminologies II.
Based on ego's and first ascending generations.

River system contains emergent similarities with the "Iglulik" system on Ego's generation but an overriding of affinal-consanguineal boundaries in the first ascending generation that is not seen in the other system (Type Ia). Type Ib (Baker Lake) shares the cousin system of the Iglulik people, which system is also an alternative one in the Back River region, but in the parental generation differences are noted from both those regions. Type IIIb represents the Chesterfield Inlet and perhaps the Eskimo Point terminologies. Here both generational levels contrast with the systems considered above. The cousin terminology is identical in structure (though the terms are not cognate) with the Lake Harbour system; however, there does not occur an overriding of affinal-consanguineal boundaries in the parental generation of the latter system. Sugluk and Great Whale River show a cousin system that resembles the Back River arrangement (the one that has preference over the alternate – that identical with Iglulik).

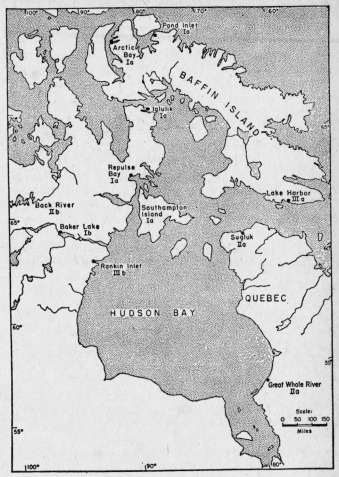

FIGURE 5. Distribution of terminologies in the Eastern Canadian Arctic.

The writer's survey is admittedly sketchy. Terminologies have been taken from a number of sources. Some are, no doubt, highly reliable; others are not. For instance, this writer does not vouch for terminologies taken from single informants from a particular region with the assurance that he can give for the Iglulik terminology which became fairly clear to him only after six months in the region. The lack of opportunity for cross-checking and the ever-present linguistic difficulties that were involved in collecting much of the terminological data weaken attempts at cross-regional interpretation. For whatever my information is worth, then, ecological correlations do not seem to be forthcoming from this examination. For instance, I have noted similarities in cousin terminologies between walrus-hunting Igluligmiut and caribou-hunting Back River people. Conversely, within the barren grounds area of Keewatin one finds three rather distinct systems among people who were all basically adapted to the inland nomadic life of caribou hunting.

The geographical distribution of systems shows somewhat more promise for a cultural-historical or "microdiffusional" approach. For instance, the groups designated as "Iglulik Eskimo" by Birket-Smith (this includes the Pond Inlet, Arctic Bay, Iglulik, Repulse Bay, and Southampton Island terminologies in my survey) show a sharing of terminology as well as of the material cultural traits that led to the setting up of the "Iglulik" cultural sub-area. The two systems from Quebec show conformity. . . . Preliminary investigation shows that the Back River system is probably shared by other "Netsilik" peoples. Chief incongruities with regard to the micro-diffusional explanation can be seen in the distinct systems found at Baker Lake and Rankin Inlet and to the similarities of Lake Harbour and Rankin Inlet which span Hudson Bay.

The expectation that the distribution of terminologies or other features of social structure might display a spread similar to traits of material culture finds varying support from recent workers in social structure. . . .

The expectation that, on the other hand, distributions based on ecological similarities might occur overlooks an important intermediate step in functional analysis. One must first consider the extent of congruence between terminological systems and their behavioural content and other features of the social structure as group composition, marriage customs, and so forth, and then consider the degree of fit that these latter features show with the technological-environmental nexus. One is faced, then, with the problem of the tightness of such fits in other Eskimo areas of the adaptive factors are to be sorted out from the historical in analysing the occurrence of particular terminological features where they appear.

Obviously what is needed to approach these problems systematically is more intensive social structural-functional studies designed for producing integrated descriptions of aspects of kinship other than the mere comparison of terms, and, in addition, a careful study of the relationships of kinship terminological principles with the structural principles of group organization. After such studies are available, one can begin to approach a better understanding of the adaptive, or historical-diffusional factors involved.

On the other hand, on the basis of the material now available it can probably be stated that an overly stringent application of external-adaptive-functional explanations should not be pressed. Although forms of social structure may have jobs to do, it is probable that alternative forms are possible which may perform such jobs with equal or near equal success in a given cultural-environmental nexus.

Perhaps the writer has dealt overly long with the elements of diversity in the terminologies of the area in question at the expense of ignoring the substantial correspondences in terminology. Indeed, it seems possible to outline an "East-Central Eskimo System" on the bases of these uniformities. This system follows, to a large extent, the pattern given by Spier.[6] Accordingly, it can be characterized by one term each for grandmother and grandfather, one term for grandchild, four aunt and uncle terms, and four nephew and niece terms. The age distinctions noted by Spier are also evident throughout the area. Also uniform throughout, but not covered by Spier's system, are the occurrences of one term each for great grandparent and great grandchild.

Divergence from Spier's system occurs in the classification of cousins, the features which he has used as his chief criterion of his "types" of North American kinship systems. Indeed, the classic arrangement of cousin terms which has widely been

---

[6]Leslie Spier, *The Distribution of Kinship Systems in North America* (Washington: University of Washington Publications in Anthropology, vol. I, 1925), pp. 69-88.

posited as the chief diagnostic of "Eskimo type" kinship systems is not found in the terminologies that I have considered. When these data are added to those already available from the western area, it begins to look as if the classic pattern of *one term for cousins separate from sibling terms* will not be found in the Eskimo area.

Regarding the classification of cousins in our sample, it should be noted that in each case there is a separation of siblings from cousins. This is in conformance with "Eskimo type" usage. In future attempts to define Eskimo type kinship, it might be well to dwell on this aspect of classification in Ego's generation rather than focusing on the differences within cousin categories. This characteristic, however, applies only to same-sexed (with Ego) cousins since in the terminologies that have been considered here, a Hawaiian or quasi-Hawaiian system[7] prevails for opposite-sexed cousins.

This brief excursion into the wider functional realm of inter-regional comparison has not been intended as an exhaustive review of material now becoming available in rapidly increasing volume from the Eskimo area, but rather has been designed to show some of the pitfalls and complexities of functional exploration in that area. I have also tried, indirectly, to indicate the desirability of comparative studies of "concomitant variation" or "controlled comparison" sorts which aim toward explanations limited to area or type. The widespread homogeneity in cultural forms and, as it is beginning to be seen, in certain aspects of the social life as well, indicates the historical affinity of the Eskimo area and can be held constant in analysing locally variable phenomena. Ecology can at times be used as another constant and, in other cases, could be hypothesized as the casual factor underlying variable phenomena. My concern has here centred on problems of group composition and cooperative and authority networks. Comparative studies of such controlled type as outlined here would indeed be fruitful in that area of interest, but there are other phases of Eskimo culture and society that could profitably be treated in such a frame. The fascinating congeries of homogeneous and diverse social and cultural elements found in the Eskimo area provide an ideal climate for studies seeking first to establish correlations within one area that later can be tested elsewhere in the world with the hope of eventually arriving at higher level generalizations. In the Eskimo area a great complicating factor in such research is the rapid rate of acculturative change that is going on almost everywhere in the Arctic. In some cases, traditional homogeneity from locality to locality has been obscured by divergent change. In other instances, traditional diversity has been to some extent overlaid by convergent change. There are still available, however, a number of approaches whereby traditional social and cultural elements can be discovered. Records and early censuses by such agents as missionaries and traders and the few early anthropologists have not been fully explored. Our understanding of social and cultural change in the Eskimo region, a concern which is rapidly becoming the chief focus of anthropological studies in the American Arctic, will approach completeness only if the picture of contact society and culture is greatly clarified.

---

[7]Quasi-Hawaiian here refers to the use of the sibling root with the *saq* postbase for opposite-sexed cousins.

PART TWO:

THE ESKIMO IN
THE MODERN WORLD

Differentiation among the Eskimo in Some Canadian Arctic Settlements

FRANK G. VALLEE

This paper is based on the author's fieldwork at Baker Lake, with supplementary and comparative data from seven other Arctic locations in Canada. It is limited to documenting new forms of differentiation and grouping among Eskimos in settlements, and offers some hypotheses concerning the conditions under which these new forms of differentiation and grouping arise.

Traditionally, the main forms of grouping among the Eskimos were according to band, extended family, and household. The literature often refers to tribes, but the Eskimos did not have tribes in the sense used by modern anthropologists. In a given region, a number of camps would share a dialect of the Eskimo language, certain stylistic forms – such as in tattooing, dress, and so on – and a vague sense of identity. We might describe such groupings as regional sub-cultures, but they were not tribes, for they had no encapsulating kinship or political structure. Because of selective interaction with other camps in such a grouping, most marriages would occur within it, but the Eskimo did not objectify this grouping as an endogamous unit of social structure. Examples of such groupings are: the *Aivilikjuarmiut*, the *Padlermiut*, the *Quernermiut*, the *Harvaquormiut*, the *Metsilikmiut*, and the *Kidlinermiut*.

Comprising these gross groupings were social units variously called bands and camps, made up of families which normally camped and moved together most of the year. Such bands or camps varied considerably in size. After the introduction of the rifle and individualized hunting techniques, the size

SOURCE: Frank G. Vallee, *Sociological Research in the Arctic* (Ottawa: Northern Co-ordination and Research Centre, Department of Northern Affairs and National Resources, 1962). Reprinted by permission of the author and publisher with revisions by the author.

of camps devoted to hunting the caribou dwindled appreciably, especially in those areas where trapping assumed a significant part of the economy. In some places the average camp, during the thirties, numbered about three nuclear families, usually related by kinship within the second degree and comprising about twelve to fifteen persons. In other areas, where getting a livelihood required concerted group effort and where important facilities, such as whale boats, were controlled by a headman, the bands numbered between forty and sixty persons on the average. Within such camps or bands authority lines were much clearer and more highly structured than in the smaller, more nomadic bands mentioned earlier. Much systematic research remains to be done on the kinship structure and other features of social organization in groups living in bands of different sizes, and constituted in different manners in the Canadian Arctic. The literature indicates that there were important variations, particularly between people who spent all or most of their time inland, and those who spent all or most of their time in sea-mammal hunting.

In all areas, role and status differentiation were according to sex, age, birth order, domestic or camp leadership, and relations to supernatural beings. Besides, a number of dyadic relationships were institutionalized, such as between song cousins, wife-exchange partners, rivals or duellists. There were, of course, non-structured, personal friendships, animosities and symbiotic relations. But apart from these, the patterned grouping and differentiation just named are virtually an exhaustive list of the forms of traditional social organization among Canadian Eskimo groups.

With the establishment of trading posts, police stations, and missions during the early part of this century, a number of new roles were assumed by small numbers of Eskimos: namely, the trader's helper, the catechist, and the special constable. These people did not realize it, but they were the forerunners of new kinds of groupings, for Eskimo society.

In some places, these outposts of Kabloona[1] society have been established for about fifty years, and in most places for at least twenty-five. This means that the settlement consisting of one or all of the institutions mentioned – the trading post, the police post, the mission – has become by now a vital part of arctic social life.

In recent years, still other roles, familiar to our society but without precedent among the Eskimos, have become commonplace in many arctic localities: day labourer, student, artisan, skilled worker, interpreter and clerk – to mention some from the world of work.

They have become commonplace because of a very significant development in the Canadian arctic since the late forties and early fifties: the proliferation of settlements. New settlements have been created and old settlements transformed in response to pressures of technology, ecology, politics, and defence. To these new settlements are being attracted an ever-growing number of Eskimos from hinterland areas, many of whom take up permanent residence.

In all these communities there is a growing dependence on income derived from wages and from government funds of various kinds. In some, such as Rankin Inlet and Great Whale River, a very large proportion of the total source of livelihood comes from these sources; in others, such as Baker Lake and Port Harrison, the Eskimo population is dependent on these sources for about half of their subsistence; in still others, such as Povungnituk, Sugluk, and Tuktoyaktuk, a substantial proportion of the income is still derived from wildlife which is both trapped and hunted, although in these places too this proportion is decreasing.

Another striking feature of many settlements in the Arctic today is the comparatively large number of whites and the wide variety of the institutions and social types represented by these whites, compared to white representation even ten years ago. As has already been noted, in many Arctic locations the Eskimos have been in contact for generations with limited aspects of outside society, and with a few of its representatives. Now in many locations, they confront substantial numbers of outsiders and are exposed to a much greater variety of stimuli than was formerly the case. Needless to say, the Eskimos have developed patterned ways of dealing with some of these stimuli, and with

---

[1]This is the Eskimo term for "white person."

the outsiders in face-to-face contact, but the sharing of space with substantial numbers of non-Eskimo peoples raises new problems in social arrangements which one can study as though in a large small-group laboratory.

*   *   *

The first kind of sorting-out to note is that between settlement and land people, a division which resembles somewhat the rural-urban one familiar to all of us. In two communities, Port Harrison and Baker Lake, this distinction is already quite marked. For Port Harrison, Willmott remarks,

> The differentiation between camp and settlement results directly from the intrusion of the white establishment into Eskimo society, has nothing to do with functional differentiation with Eskimo society itself. In almost every area of social life differences are apparent between these two groups. We shall refer to those who live in the settlement as settlement Eskimos, those in the camp as camp Eskimos.[2]

He then proceeds to spell out this differentiation in considerable detail.

Writers on the other communities listed are not as explicit about this distinction as Willmott is, although in most of these reports references to settlement people imply that the distinction between them and the non-settlement people is recognized. For Great Whale River, Balikci mentions that settlement dwellers developed from a core of trader's helpers and groups from poor game areas; he notes also that there are tensions between those who continue to hunt and trap and those who work for the whites. For Povungnituk Balikci notes that,

> a small number of Eskimo helpers to the trader settled permanently near the store and act also as middlemen between the trader and the coastal camps. They become increasingly attracted to Euro-Canadian culture as a global way of life and constitute the first step towards the appearance of culturally divergent sections within a larger Eskimo settlement.[3]

At Baker Lake, distinctions between settlement and non-settlement people have crystallized to the extent that some people objectify and label two types of Eskimos, calling one group Nunamiut (people of the land) and Kabloonamiut (people of the White Man). By Nunamiut they mean simply those Eskimos who live outside the Baker Lake settlement and derive the largest proportion of their livelihood from hunting, fishing, and trapping. The denotation of Kabloonamiut is not very clear-cut at present and is applied in a loose fashion. In its most specific sense, Kabloonamiut denotes those Eskimos who are employed by Kabloona and who live in the settlement. In a slightly more general sense, it refers to anyone who lives permanently at the settlement, whether employed by Kabloona or not, and parallels the English usage of "urban" as distinct from "rural." In its most general sense it denotes those Eskimos who are at ease with the Kabloona and who are more conspicuously imitative of Kabloona ways than are the majority of Eskimos.

For purposes of this paper, Nunamiut are classified as those who:

1 reveal a desire to live on the land rather than in the settlement;
2 choose a way of life which requires an acute dependence on the land;
3 choose to follow what traditional conventions still exist in the culture, such as in living arrangements, in the ways they bring up their children – in short, those who appear to be oriented more to the traditional way of life than to the Kabloona way of life.

Kabloonamiut are those who:

1 reveal a desire to live in the settlement;
2 reject a way of life which requires an acute dependence on the land;
3 choose to follow certain Kabloona-like customs where they could just as well follow traditional ones.

---

[2]W. Willmott, *The Eskimo Community at Port Harrison* (Ottawa: Northern Co-ordination and Research Centre, Department of Northern Affairs and National Resources, 1961), p. 4.
[3]A. Balikci, "Some Acculturative Trends Among the Eastern Canadian Eskimos," *Anthropologica*, n.s., vol. 2 (1960), p. 9.

For Baker Lake region we attempted to place all family heads somewhere along a continuum at one end of which is "confirmed Kabloonamiut," at the other end of which is "confirmed Nunamiut." As a basis for judgment we depended primarily on our own observation of behaviour, checking this with the opinions of key informants in both land camps and in the settlement as to where each household head stood with reference to these criteria. It is realized of course, that a household head may have a different "score" from his spouse or his offspring, and that this raises interesting problems; but for present purposes we consider only the rating of household heads and the classification of them on this crude scale, the weakness of which we are the first to acknowledge.

On the basis of the criteria mentioned, we estimate that eleven of the eighty household heads in the Baker Lake region or 14 per cent are clearly Kabloonamiut, and that twenty-six of the eighty household heads or 33 per cent are clearly Nunamiut. In our judgment, twenty-five household heads, or 31 per cent are "marginal Kabloonamiut" in the sense that they are not markedly Kabloonamiut, Nunamiut in outlook, style of living, and so forth. We placed eighteen household heads or 22 per cent as "marginal Nunamiut," regarding them as not markedly Nunamiut, but as closer to the latter than to the Kabloonamiut. Expressed in terms of percentages of household heads in each category, the crude and tentative picture looks like this:

Kabloonamiut	14%
Marginal Kabloonamiut	31%
Marginal Nunamiut	22%
Nunamiut	33%

At the risk of complicating things unduly for purposes of this paper, let us say that not all settlement people are Kabloonamiut according to our classification, for there are some who live in the settlement but remain oriented to the land. Furthermore, not all hinterland or camp people are Nunamiut in our classification, for there are some who would like to live in the settlement but are discouraged from doing so by the authorities or for some other reason.

We give prominent place to the description of the Kabloonamiut because of their special significance in the process of acculturation. Their significance has two obvious features. First, they are Eskimos who are "carrying" the Euro-Canadian culture to the Nunamiut, in the sense that they are becoming stylistic and behavioural models, particularly for the younger generation; second, they are becoming key figures in the networks of interaction between the Kabloona and the Nunamiut.

It should be emphasized that the Kabloonamiut are not simply regarded as the White Man's Eskimo, in the sense that some Americans refer to the White Man's Negro. Attitudes toward the Kabloonamiut vary, but they are regarded as Eskimo first and foremost. Although they have rejected the way of life which requires an acute dependence on the land, they have not given up the skills associated with the land. On the contrary, some of the best travellers, hunters, and fishermen are Kabloonamiut, and some of the Kabloonamiut women excel at the traditional womanly crafts.

With a few exceptions, the confirmed Kabloonamiut we encountered at the settlement have been long-time residents of either the Baker Lake or some other settlement in the Arctic. A comparison of the family histories of these household heads with other family histories reveals some significant differences. Unlike the majority of household heads in the region, the Kabloonamiut household heads were either born outside the Baker Lake region or have lived for lengthy periods outside this district, particularly in settlements along the west coast of Hudson Bay. Two were born at Repulse Bay and are *Aivilikjuarmiut* in origin; four were born in the Tavani region; four were born at Baker Lake but spent considerable periods of time as permanent residents of coastal locations before moving back to the Baker Lake Area. Some moved with their *Kabloona* employers when these were reposted; others moved in search of a more satisfactory livelihood. This characteristic of mobility extending outside the Baker Lake region also occurs in the background of a few household heads whom we have classified as "marginal Kabloonamiut."

As a result of this mobility, people in this grouping are part of rather far-flung networks of friends and relatives, in contrast to the Nunamiut whose networks are more concentrated and localized in a particular area. To illustrate, Louis Tapati, a prominent Kabloonamiut who was born in Repulse Bay, has relatives who remain there; he also has relatives and close friends in the settlements at Chesterfield Inlet and Rankin Inlet. To the latter place, his daughter and her husband have recently moved. This man and his family try to visit at least two of these other settlements every summer, travelling by boat down Chesterfield Inlet and into Hudson Bay. Illustrations of similar networks of friendship and kinship (extending far outside the region under discussion) could be given for five other Kabloonamiut households.

In none of the other works consulted are the mobility patterns in the family histories of settlement dwellers spelled out, but we can infer from references made to settlement dwellers in at least two other communities that at least some of them come from afar. For instance, the Hudson's Bay Company Interpreter and Clerk at Port Harrison is from Labrador; traders, helpers and special constables at Eskimo Point are *Aivilikjuarmiut* from distant locations up the west coast of Hudson Bay. It seems reasonable to suggest that Kabloonamiut with the histories of pronounced mobility will not identify strongly with a particular region and with a sub-culture within a particular region. This does not mean, however, that they have only a weak identification with the settlement they live in.

Another characteristic in the histories of some Kabloonamiut families in the Baker Lake region is the existence of something like a patron-client relationship with a Kabloona person. By this we mean something more than simply an employer-employee relationship. Traditionally the Kabloona patron, whether Hudson's Bay Company trader, missionary, or Royal Canadian Mounted Police, showed diffuse interest in their Eskimo employee and his family, doing special favours for them, offering them advice, scolding them for untoward behaviour, even where this had nothing to do with the job. In five of the eleven confirmed Kabloonamiut households, the heads are the offspring of parents who were themselves linked with some Kabloona person, such as missionary, Hudson's Bay Company manager, the Royal Canadian Mounted Police, in a patron-client relationship. We can envisage the acculturation process as being mediated originally through the Kabloona patrons or sponsors. Today the clients themselves are the mediators between the Kabloona society and the Nunamiut.

Do the people classified as Kabloonamiut form a distinct *stratum* in the community? At Baker Lake they do. Numerous social bounds link Kabloonamiut with one another. With the exception of two household heads in this group, the Kabloonamiut are more linked with one another by kinship and by affinal ties than they are with the Nunamiut in the surrounding hinterland. Thus interaction based on shared membership in kinship groups and on in-law relationships tend to set off the Kabloonamiut from other Eskimos for certain kinds of social action. Besides, there is a pronounced tendency for the Kabloonamiut to arrange and encourage marriage of their offspring with the offspring of other settlement dwellers rather than with land dwellers. It is interesting to note that the practice of arranging marriages from birth or even before is still carried on by Kabloonamiut families in the settlement, whereas it has been abandoned among many people in hinterland camps. We know of nine pairs of children from twelve Kabloonamiut families in Baker Lake who are promised to each other. We know also of four Kabloonamiut children at Baker Lake who are promised to settlement dwellers at Chesterfield and Rankin Inlet. Future marriages of this nature, both within the settlement and between settlements, will serve to crystallize the now rather amorphous stratum of Kabloonamiut, setting it off as an even more distinctive grouping than it is at present.

What we are witnessing is the emergence of a socio-economic class system among the Eskimos of the Baker Lake region. Economically, a class system exists where a *stratum* of people possesses a larger share of wealth than other *strata*, and where there is unequal access to the facilities and resources which are economically valuable. At Baker Lake almost half of the cash income flowing into the eighty households from all sources goes to the households of fifteen settlement families. These include ten of the households which we have classified as Kabloonamiut. If full-time jobs are to be considered a scarce but valuable resource, then these families have a kind of monopoly on that resource. The development of a money economy makes it possible for people to accumulate wealth in a manner which was hardly possible in the traditional society. While no Eskimo family would be considered wealthy by standards of the south, the gap between the average Kabloonamiut family and the average land family is very wide. As one Kabloona official put it, "If things don't change around here we'll have two kinds of Eskimos – the haves and the have-nots."

The growth of economic disparities within Eskimo communities in other parts of the Arctic is noted by several of the authors consulted.

Between settlement and land there is differential access, not only to cash income, but to other class-linked facilities as well. For instance, the basic education required to manipulate the changing social and economic environment is distributed unevenly among settlement and land people. At Baker Lake, all eligible children in the settlement attend the new federal school full-time. Although all the camp people consulted want their children to attend school, only about half of those eligible are able to attend because of shortages of school space, teachers, and living accommodation for land children. From Port Harrison, Willmott reports that only settlement children go to school. Thus, the ground-work for future increases in differentiation between settlement and hinterland people is being laid now.

In terms of status, a class system exists when a stratum of people who interact and intermarry much with one another receive more prestige than others and where people in that stratum exert a larger measure of influence and leadership than others in the community. It is difficult to make conclusive statements about prestige allocation among the modern Eskimos, first, because of the confusion in the literature on the modern Eskimos between prestige, esteem, and liking; and second, because there is a lack of general consensus as to who among them and outside their own kinsfolk are most deserving of deference and respect.

We use prestige here to mean the deference and respect received in face-to-face relations, and esteem to mean the admiration and applause received. To cite a distinction which has become familiar in anthropology and sociology, prestige goes with certain statuses in a society, while esteem attaches to role performances. For instance, the position of doctor is a prestigious one in our society. A person can be an average or perhaps slightly-below-average doctor and still receive the deference and respect, not to mention the material rewards, allocated to doctors as compared to, say, carpenters. Esteem, on the other hand, is accorded someone who performs well at some task. For instance, a good carpenter, a good football player, indeed a good pick-pocket, are admired and in some cases applauded for their above-average performance, without the positions they occupy in the social system being particularly prestigious. We realize that this is not an entirely satisfactory distinction, but feel that it is useful in trying to sort out what is happening in the re-ordering of relationships and the normative system among the Eskimos.

As to the confusion between prestige and liking, this is less excusable. We find in three reports consulted the claim or the implication that Eskimos who work for the Kabloona are unpopular with the other Eskimos, that the latter do not like the former. One is led to believe that the authors of these reports share this dislike, for they apparently conclude that those who work for the Kabloona are insignificant in the social system and so can be dismissed from further consideration. This is, of course, a methodological *faux pas*, because the Kabloonamiut have a key role to play in the process of social change, a role which is discussed later in this report.

This question of liking leads us to consider another aspect of current Eskimo attitudes which has something to do with status distinction but which is partly independent of it. This is a distaste expressed for a way of life different from one's own. Some Eskimo at the Baker Lake settlement refer to land people as backward and behind the times, in the same way as some city people might refer to those from remote regions of the countryside as "hicks." This bias on the part of settlement dwellers is reported from Port Harrison, Great Whale River, and Rankin Inlet. The reverse attitude, that is, the distaste for those who live in settlements and work for wages or live on government funds, is reported from Great Whale, Sugluk, and has been expressed by a number of confirmed Nunamiut in the Baker Lake region.

If we leave this matter of liking and distaste and consider the allocation of prestige and esteem, we are on surer ground and a higher degree of concensus can be detected. There appears to be general concensus among the Eskimos that people who live in poverty are to be pitied and looked down upon, whether they live in settlements or not. In the traditional society, both prestige and esteem were given to those who had mastered the skills of living off the land and sea. These people were also the wealthiest in terms of equipment, food, dress, and symbols of status, although the disparities between them and their fellow-men may not have been wide by our standards. New criteria of evaluation are entering the scene: the mastery of such skills as those required to mix easily with both the Kabloona and the "traditional" Eskimo; command of the English language; ability to perform work which is highly valued by the Kabloona, such as the operation, maintenance, and repair of machinery – in short, criteria pertaining to the mastery of both the social and physical environment. Persons who are high on these criteria and who are comparatively wealthy certainly receive deference and respect from fellow Eskimos in the Baker Lake region – although some of them are not liked.

We would venture the following generalization on the basis of our own field-work and the perusal of the literature. The highest ranking Eskimo in the community is probably that person who has the highest income and who gains it as an entrepreneur. Where this is feasible, such as in those places where sea-mammal hunting with Peterheads or other large boats is profitable, the boat-owner is probably the highest ranking person in the group. This position is enhanced if he also lives in the settlement and is regarded by the Kabloona as a spokesman and leader of his group. Such appears to be the case at Sugluk and Povungnituk and, perhaps, at Tuktoyaktuk. However, where entrepreneuring is not feasible, we appear to have two systems of ranking: one for the settlement and one for the land.

There is some support for this suggestion from Baker Lake. It should be pointed out that in this region there are few opportunities for people on the land to amass objects, food, income, and other status differentia because of the relative paucity of caribou and the instability of the fur market. However, a few of the twenty land camps usually have a satisfactory year and periodically enjoy a year of abundance. The heads of these camps enjoy considerable prestige. It is interesting to observe that in the most successful camp the leader keeps well abreast of modern technology. In 1959 he purchased a motor toboggan, which he uses to great effect in patrolling his fox traps. When this man comes to the settlement, he is treated with considerable respect, although he is not particularly well liked. At the settlement he interacts with some of the marginal Kabloonamiut but rarely with the highest ranking Kabloonamiut. The wealthiest Eskimo at the settlement is also much respected and imitated, his innovations have mainly to do with style.

While it may be true that there are currently two systems of prestige ranking, we have the firm impression of a trend towards the ranking of settlement people on a prestige scale, the ranking of land people on an esteem scale. Successful land people may be admired, but they are finding it increasingly difficult to find spouses for their sons, there being a tendency for girls on the land to seek a settlement living, and a definite tendency for girls in the settlement to refuse to marry young men on the land, no matter how admired are the families of the young men. We may expect this trend to gain momentum, the more young people are exposed to the settlement and particularly to the education which will soon be universal.

Given the system of ranking statuses by whatever criteria, there still remains the question of the extent to which people who are equal in rank form strata which cut across the community. We have already mentioned the tendency for settlement people to form a stratum in Baker Lake and to channel marriage within the settlement or between settlements. Within the settlement patterns of interaction in sociability tend to go along status lines. Moreover, most of the marriage arrangements noted were between families of roughly equal rank. To illustrate, two of the children of one special constable are betrothed to two of the children of the other special constable. The son of the wealthiest Kabloonamiut, a skilled worker for the Department of Transport, is promised to the daughter of the maintenance foreman of the Department of Northern Affairs installation.

The adopted son of the Anglican catechist, who is also an independent building contractor of some means, is promised to the daughter of the only Eskimo minister in the Arctic, at Rankin Inlet. The latter case, and others like it which could be cited, foreshadow an extension of strata across community lines and the emergence of status groupings which are pan-Eskimo rather than specific to given communities and sub-cultures.

It may be that the emergence of such community-transcending status groups is most likely to occur in those areas where band and extended family solidarity is weakest or non-existent. In these areas a condition of organic solidarity or integration should more quickly replace a condition of mechanical solidarity or integration.

Until very recently in many arctic localities where people depended on sea-mammal hunting, a group of extended families making up a hunting camp, band, or deme, numbering from thirty to sixty people, formed a corporate group for many purposes. These groups more or less duplicated one another in economic and social function, although some might be more highly regarded than others. These groups were differentiated internally, of course. For instance, within a band rights over scarce large boats were vested in the leaders of certain families, rights which were inherited. For the Canadian Arctic, this pattern has been reported as traditional for Tuktoyaktuk, Sugluk, and Povungnituk.

In these places, segmentation into relatively large, similarly structured groups, implies that solidarity is channeled at the level of the band, camp, or deme. The more autonomous and solid the band, the less likely it is that horizontal stratification cutting across the boundaries of bands will emerge.

The evidence from studies consulted points to a lessening of band autonomy and a definite tendency for bands and extended families to become economically differentiated or specialized. Thus, at Tuktoyaktuk, one extended family group is now specializing in boat-building, another in hunting, another in reindeer herding. In Sugluk, two bands specialize in sea-mammal hunting, owning their own Peterheads, another specializes in working for wages at the Kabloona installations; another tends to specialize in trapping. This kind of specialization is going on within settlements, and is a process well worth observing, step-by-step, as it develops.

In the Baker Lake region and in other parts of the Arctic where, at least in recent times, the band system was not prevalent, where camps were smaller, and extended families less demarcated than in the regions mentioned above, there is no traditional groupings into large units beyond the simple extended family which might form the basis of ordering relations in the settlement.

As far as we can discover, at no time since the history of sustained contact began did the Eskimo in such settlements as Baker Lake, Rankin Inlet, and Eskimo Point divide into sizable segments, each more or less duplicating the other in social and economic function. As suggested earlier, the absence of a previous band structure, as described for some sea-mammal hunting locations, is a condition favourable to the rapid development of socio-economic strata which cut horizontally across the whole Eskimo community at a settlement. However, even where this band structure exists, the tendency is towards a condition of organic solidarity.

Another interesting development which accompanies the movement into settlements is the working out of relationships between Eskimos of different regional origins. As pointed out earlier, the Eskimos were traditionally differentiated into sub-cultures which some earlier authors referred to as tribes. Let us for the sake of convenience refer to these sub-cultural groupings as ethnic groups. In many settlements there is considerable ethnic mixing. At Baker Lake, one finds among the permanent residents *Utkuhisalingmiut, Harvaqtormiut, Quernermiut*. At Rankin Inlet, *Aivilikjuarmiut* from the North rub shoulders with *Ahialmiut* and *Padlermiut* from the south.

We do not yet have adequate data on interaction among people in these different groups, intermarriage rates, and so on, but from personal observations and reports ethnic identification among the Eskimos has always been weak, compared, say, with the kinds of traditional identification characteristic of some Indian people. Many young people encountered at Baker Lake and Rankin Inlet did not know the ethnic origin of their parents and themselves showed little interest in this matter.

One way in which ethnicity is used should be reported, for it has some bearing on class and status differentiation. On several occasions in our experience, ethnicity has been brought in as an explanation for differences between people. For instance, at Baker Lake a person explained that one group of brothers were superior travellers and dog-handlers because they were *Utkuhikhalingmiut*. During a conversation about one family group which had a rather high rate of deviance in its history – such as incest, fighting, mental disorders – one Eskimo offered the explanation that they "are *Harvaqtormiut* and these people are very backward and stupid." At Rankin Inlet an Eskimo informant told a joke which discredited the *Netsilikmiut*. When we pursued the question of just what was the matter with the *Netsilikmiut*, the informant finally summed it up by saying, "They don't have anything!" By this he meant that they were poor. This led us to inquire into the link between the uses of ethnicity and low rank. Our findings so far indicate people of high rank do not speak of themselves in terms of ethnic membership (except as Eskimos), and presumably do not identify strongly with a regional ethnic group; nor do they speak of people from other regions who are also of high rank in the community as being from such-and-such an ethnic group. However, when they express feelings of superiority over the people who are of low prestige, they are likely to formulate explanations of why this is in terms of ethnicity. To cite another illustration from Rankin Inlet, in 1960 we were discussing a group of people who had been relocated in 1957 from the Interior Keewatin where they had survived a famine. Even after a year and a half at the mining settlement, many of these people were on relief, were disheartened, apathetic, and so on. A prominent settlement Eskimo in the gathering pointed out to us, assuming that we did not know it already, that, of course, these people were *Ahialmiut*, and what can you expect of them? It suddenly occurred to us that two of the household heads from the interior migration were doing very well materially, working regularly, living in a wooden house, eating and dressing well, taking part, and in some situations a leading part, in Eskimo community activities. I asked the informant, "But aren't X and Y *Ahialmiut*? From his reply I gathered that he did not think of these men and their families in ethnic terms at all.

As in the surrounding society, there is an ethnic dimension of social class, in at least some settlements. Ferguson talks of how the Mackenzie Delta Eskimos, who were the wealthiest in Tuktoyaktuk, look down upon migrants from Alaska and from the Coppermine region. To some extent the invidious comparisons between these regional ethnic groups have to do with recency of settlement, and the status of newcomer. It is too early to say to what extent these ethnic sub-divisions will be perpetuated, or how long ethnicity at the regional level will be used explain low status position and deviance. However, it is worth documenting what little we have been able to gather in this matter in the hope of prompting some research into this interesting form of differentiation.

Other new forms of differentiation in Eskimo society should be mentioned. There are two forms of sorting-out and grouping which are familiar to us, but without precedent in Eskimo society; the division into religious denomination and the emergence of something like age sets, manifested particularly in middle and late teenage gangs in the larger settlements. These forms of groupings are not dealt with in this report because they are less directly related to status differentiation than are the settlement-land and the ethnic distinctions, and my focus of interest here has been in class and status differentiation.

On the basis of what has been documented here, it appears that we are witnessing the emergence of social and economic classes which will, before long, cut across community boundaries in the Arctic, linking people in a pan-Eskimo grouping. We do not predict the rapid passage of the Eskimo into the Canadian class system. This is not the place to go into the matter of relations between the Kabloona and the Eskimos in Arctic communities. On this matter we say simply that these groups form demarcated sub-systems or sub-communities in every settlement for which we have information. Because of the barriers between sub-systems, we may expect that the Eskimos will not simply "pass" into the larger society in any substantial numbers. Articulate Eskimos are already claiming to speak for all Eskimos vis-à-vis all Kabloona. These articulate Eskimos are Kabloona-miut by our definition and the products of either settlement living or lengthy stays in Kabloona institutions, such as hospitals and residential schools. In cultural terms, they are much closer to the Kabloona than they are to the traditional Eskimos. However, for many of them, their identification with the Eskimo reference group is growing increasingly intense. Parallels from the literature on Indians are relevant here, in particular the literature on the role of and characteristics of leaders of nativistic movements. My closing suggestion is that if pan-Eskimoism does emerge and crystallize, the peculiar conditions promoting the development of Eskimo social classes will have been to a large extent the determinants.

The Economic Situation of the Eskimo

DIAMOND JENNESS

To the pre-European Eskimos trade meant only the simplest barter, and in Canada even that occurred but rarely. A man expected to support his wife and children by his own efforts from the sea and the land around him. Food he obtained by hunting and fishing; with his own hands he made all his tools and weapons. Snow, hard-packed by the wind, furnished the building blocks with which he erected his winter dwelling, and the skins of caribou and seals supplied the covering for his summer tent. The same skins or furs, carefully cut by his wife and stitched together with sinew-thread from the back of the caribou, provided clothing for himself and all his family. For food, clothing, and shelter, therefore, he depended on no man; he was completely self-supporting, as no European has been since some of our ancestors 15,000 years ago crouched for warmth and safety in the caves of central France during the closing centuries of the Great Ice Age. Once or twice in his life-time, perhaps, our Eskimo exchanged his home-made knife for a soapstone cooking-pot, or a strip of white fur from the belly of a caribou for a long wooden pole that could serve as a fish-spear handle; but to a degree that we today can hardly comprehend he was free and independent, master of his own fate, as far as any living creature can be master of its fate in this our imperfect and ever-changing world.

Today they are free no longer. The first white men who gave them guns and ammunition, steel knives, and metal cooking-pots in reward for their services or in payment for their furs destroyed their independence by creating needs that could only be satisfied by association and trade with the outside world. The Eskimos saw and craved numberless things from that world

SOURCE: Diamond Jenness, *Eskimo Administration: Canada* (Montreal: Arctic Institute of North America, Technical Paper 14, 1964), pp. 99-119. Reprinted by permission of the author and publisher. Title supplied by the editors.

which seemed to make life easier or more pleasant, and little by little they lost the skills and the knowledge which their fore-fathers had acquired under the stress of isolation, and handed down to generation after generation of their descendants. When Europeans brought them guns, steel axes, and steel knives they gave up the art of chipping stone, of making three-piece bows of driftwood backed with twisted sinew, of setting snares for caribou and hares, and of stalking to within harpoon-range wary seals that basked uneasily in the spring sun on the surface of the ice. It is an old, old story the world over. How many white women in Canada today have learned from their grandmothers to make soap and candles, or to spin wool, weave on a loom, and clothe their families with garments made entirely in the home?

We cannot revert to the life of our forefathers before man discovered electricity, erected steel-rolling mills, and invented diesel and gasoline engines. Neither can the Eskimos. Once they forgot the lore and lost the skills of their ancestors they could not survive in the Arctic without a continuous inflow of goods from the outside. That meant trade, or rather barter, since no money circulated until quite recently, save in the Mackenzie Delta, where the Eskimos acquired more knowledge of English and of writing than other Canadian Eskimos through their close contact with Alaska, and with a dozen or more white trappers and traders who settled in or near the Delta and married native women during the first decade of the twentieth century. In this barter all advantages lay on the side of the white man. The Eskimo could offer him nothing but his labour, which the white man hardly needed, and the furs of the fox, the polar bear, and (in the Mackenzie Delta) the muskrat, luxury articles of fluctu-ating value which civilization can always dispense with. The Eskimo himself, on the other hand, could no longer wrest a livelihood from his barren home without the weapons and tools, the boats and other goods which the traders brought in from the world to the south; by some means or other he had to obtain those goods or perish. He knew no world except the Arctic, and dared not try to move his family outside it, even if he had been given the opportunity. So it was the white man who called the tune, and the Eskimo who danced to the music. It was the white man who decided where to set up the trading posts, what goods he should bring into the north, what prices he should demand for them, and how much (in money or credit) he should pay the Eskimos for their labour and their furs. And the Eskimos had no choice but to submit.

Today the tune has changed. Its melody, cheerful when the civilized world was prepared to pay high prices for white-fox furs, has moved into a sombre key darkened with notes of gloom. The profits of the fur trade no longer cover the expenses of the trading stations: only a few years back the Hudson's Bay Company had to close its posts in northern Labrador. Styles in the world of fashion change rapidly, and the white-fox fur has to compete with the furs of other animals, many raised on special farms, and with the new synthetic furs that are cutting into the sales of the natural product. Were this merely a temporary phenomenon, like a glut in the supply of wheat, it might benefit the Eskimos (and our northlands) if the government set a floor price on white-fox furs; but Cantley, who studied this expedient in 1950, rejected it as ineffective, and a more recent investigator supports his opinion. As a foundation on which to build an enduring economy in the north, the fur trade has proved no more stable than shifting sand. This holds particularly true for the trade in white-fox furs, because that animal resists domestication and in the wild state fluctuates greatly in numbers, obeying an irregular cycle that averages roughly four years. In a year when the foxes reach their peak, an Eskimo may often trap as many as one hundred, whereas in a lean year he may catch only ten. The cycle's irregularities, and the wide differences between the fat years and the lean, make prediction of a trapper's catch more uncertain than the prediction of a prairie wheat harvest; and they immensely complicate the problems of the trader who may be obliged to outfit him on credit.

Let us balance the fat years with the lean ones, and estimate how large an income the average Eskimo family has been earning from his furs since the war years. The amount will differ from place to place, of course, since the fox population is not spread uniformly over the Arctic. Very rarely, too, does every household in a district now spend the winter on its trapping-ground, but one or more families remain in the settlement, either through ill-health, or because the head of the household has steady wage-employment. Cantley, who also took an over-all view, has provided us with an estimate for the ten years 1940-50. Assuming for those years a mean price for the white-fox fur of $10, he calculated that trapping had yielded the average Eskimo family $360 in a peak year and $100 in a poor one, giving a mean income of about $200. . . .

Local studies in several small settlements give similar figures for more recent years. On Southampton Island the average annual return per family from white foxes and polar bears during the ten years from 1949 to 1959 amounted to only $330; and at Eskimo Point only about $400. Marjorie Findlay, who studied the Fort Chimo Eskimo in 1945, says that their trapping yielded at best $200-$300 a year; and Willmott in 1958 calculated the separate incomes from trapping for three groups among the Port Harrison natives at $72, $240.40, and $276.22, respectively. From the Western Arctic we have similar figures. At Tuktoyaktuk, near the mouth of the Mackenzie River, where the family income in 1957 approximated $1,850, substantially more than in any other arctic settlement, Ferguson reckoned that 60 per cent was derived from wage-employment, permanent and casual, 22 per cent from government allowances of one kind and another, only 11 per cent (i.e. about $200) from trapping, and 1 per cent from handicrafts.

From time to time one hears a rumour – which may be true – that a certain trapper and his family have captured in a single season, on Banks Island perhaps, over 1,000 white foxes, whose furs, at $10 apiece, would have brought him an income exceeding $10,000. Instances of such large catches have occurred in the past, and may occur today; but they are counter-balanced by the very much larger number of cases in which the trapper and his family have captured no more than five or ten. This can be demonstrated quite clearly from some statistics recently released by the Game Management Service of the Northwest Territories (Canada, Department of Northern Affairs and Natural Resources). During the ten years from 1952 to 1961 inclusive, trappers in the Northwest Territories, nearly all of whom must have been Eskimos, captured a total of 328,000 white foxes, which they sold for $4,395,000. The Eskimo population during those ten years averaged 9,800, of whom approximately 8,000 lived in the Northwest Territories, the remainder in northern Quebec. Reckoning the average Eskimo family to contain 4.8 individuals and assuming that every family trapped (which of course was not the case), then each would have caught an average of 20 foxes yearly, and derived from their furs an annual income averaging about $264. If only three-fourths of the population engaged in trapping, the contribution of fox furs to the income of each trapping family would have averaged about $352.

Nearly fifty years ago I spent the greater part of a winter with two families of Eskimo trappers on the arctic coast of Alaska one hundred miles east of Point Barrow, its northernmost cape. Throughout October and early November, my hosts set their nets in a lake about eight miles behind their seashore cabin, and hauled in several hundred whitefish weighing, on the average, from four to six pounds each. After allowing the fish to freeze they stored them in bags outside their cabin on a high wooden platform beyond the reach of the sled dogs. On this same platform, shortly before I joined them, they had cached two seals and five or six brant, all shot in the late autumn when open water still lingered near the mouth of the Colville River, and some of the birds that had nested on the tundra during the brief summer had not yet returned to the south. In the first days of November, before they had laid out their lines of fox-traps – at that period the north Alaskan trapping season began on November 15 and ended on March 31 – their nets ceased to yield the usual quota of fish and hung empty, why I do not know, for an Eskimo near another lake seventy miles away, I discovered later, was netting a few fish right into February. Whatever the reason, our nets had become profitless, and there was nothing we could do save pull them out and store them on the platform until spring. From then on, my hosts devoted all their days to trapping. Every morning when the weather permitted they left the cabin before dawn, and returned at dark, or an hour later, after completing the round of their traps. Both families, my Eskimo interpreter, and myself, lived on the fish and meat they had cached away, and on the flour, rice, and other European foods we had bought in the trading store at Barrow;

and once a day we fed our dogs with a fish or half a fish apiece. Before the New Year, however, our supplies became so low that it was necessary to conserve the fish, and chop frozen chunks of meat for the dogs from a whale carcass that had stranded on the seashore twenty miles away: at the same time we sent a sled to Barrow to bring fresh supplies of food for our own use. Only twice down to the end of February, when I retreated with my interpreter to the Barrow trading post, did we come upon the tracks of a polar bear near our cabin; never once did we see the hoof-prints of a caribou; and only twice, as far as I can remember, small flocks of ptarmigan. The coast all around us seemed lifeless, save for the numerous fox-tracks, and for the solitary raven that haunted our neighbourhood and once cawed mockingly at me as it rose in the air and flew away. It is true that our excursions did not carry us more than about ten miles from our cabin, except when we visited our nearest neighbours almost three times that distance down the coast, because from mid-November until mid-February the sun never rose above the horizon, and only the bright moonlight and the flashing aurora ever relieved the intense darkness that enveloped us from three o'clock each afternoon until nine o'clock the next morning. Nevertheless, even within our ten-mile radius I had expected many more signs of life during the six hours of twilight, since the basin and mouth of the Colville River had been one of the richer game areas in arctic America less than fifty years before.

I relate this episode because it illustrates the utter incompatibility of an efficient trapping régime with a life based on hunting and fishing. Before the white man introduced the fur trade into Arctic Alaska the grandparents of my Eskimos had hunted with inefficient bows and arrows in the area where I spent that winter, and had successfully raised families there; but the herds of caribou had not then been massacred with high-powered rifles, and the hunters had been free to move about as they wished in search of game, not tied down to one small locality as we were by trap-lines. My hosts would have starved to death had there been no trading post within reach, because being inlanders, they had never learned to track down and harpoon the seals in winter at that mammal's breathing-holes. They had lost the independence of their grandparents and were bound hand

and foot to the fur-trade economy imposed on them by our civilization. Our Canadian Eskimos are in the same condition. It is criminal folly therefore to suggest, as is often done, even today, that we should encourage them to take up again the life of their forefathers, and endeavour to recover their independence by hunting and fishing in regions where game has not ceased to be plentiful. Hunting and fishing may still provide them with food and even clothing, but it cannot bring in the income they need to buy rifles and ammunition, boats and outboard motors, and all the other articles of civilization without which they would perish almost as rapidly as we would. Through no fault of their own, trapping has ceased to provide that income. . . .

Cantley, more than ten years ago, suggested the introduction of small industries or handicrafts, a suggestion that the government has taken up with vigour. Before we review the results of its efforts, however, let us enquire how large an income an Eskimo family requires today to become economically self-supporting, and at the same time relatively content.

Actually, it is not possible to calculate such an income with any pretence to accuracy, because conditions vary so widely from place to place in the Arctic. Some families are able to procure more fish and game than others, at little or no expense beyond their own labour. They live where seals are plentiful, where schools of white whales enter the estuary of a river, or shoals of char migrate upstream to spawn in inland lakes; or perhaps, as on Southampton Island, close to some locality where a herd of walrus gives birth to its young. These families will spend far less on store food than the Tuktoyaktuk native who worked on the D.E.W. Line, and whose food bill at the local Hudson's Bay Company store ran as high as $1,000 yearly. We must consider, too, the cost of clothing for a family, no great sum for the few Eskimos who still find numerous caribou in their neighbourhood and can dress in fur garments patterned after those of their forefathers, but an appreciable item in the budget of a Port Harrison or Southampton Island native who has never seen a live caribou. Housing presents another variable item, particularly since the government began to subsidize it and encourage the Eskimos to set up small prefabricated dwellings of special design. One type, measuring 12 feet x 20 feet, costs about $1,500 erected, of which amount the government donates $1,000, writes off $250 as the value of the buyer's labour in putting it together, and gives him a ten-year loan to cover the remaining $250. The payments on such a house may be negligible, but its heating during the long winter, with fuel oil that sells (at Cape Dorset) for $28 a drum, and in remoter settlements for double that figure, costs from $200 to $700 yearly. In contrast, an Eskimo of the Mackenzie delta can still avoid all housing costs, if he wishes, by erecting a cabin of driftwood, and by heating it with driftwood in a homemade sheet-iron stove. Finally there are the transportation costs of the Eskimo who wishes to hunt and fish and visit his neighbours – as all of them still do. At Coral Harbour in 1961 a 22-foot canoe cost $625, a whaleboat $4,000, a "Peterhead" schooner $10,000, and a 7½ H.P. motor to drive the canoe or the whaleboat $275. Many Eskimos today cannot afford even a small flat-bottomed dingy at $300, but must share a boat and outboard motor with their neighbours. However, a boat and motor, like a rifle, lasts for several years, whereas food is consumed almost immediately and must be constantly renewed: and now that many Eskimos are spending most of their days in the settlements, it is the food bill that often heads the list of a family's expenses. The D.E.W. Line worker at Tuktoyaktuk in 1956-7 was spending 55 per cent of his wages on store food, whereas at Cape Dorset four years later the average family expenditure on food hardly exceeded $300. But in the latter district 60 of the 75 families were living during the greater part of the year on the land, at a considerable distance from the settlement, and there they were obtaining most of their food by hunting and fishing, which still left them spare moments for carving small figurines from soapstone to sell in the world's art markets.

It is clear, then, that the factors on which we must rely to calculate the minimum income an Eskimo family requires vary so greatly in different regions of the Arctic that our estimate can be no more than an informed guess. I myself would suggest about $1,500, in cash and kind, as long as the prices of the essential goods – rifles, boats, cloth, flour, and tea – remain at or near their present level. Should these prices rise even slightly, however, my guess would jump to $2,000. In many places the Eskimos could still survive, perhaps, on as little as $1,000, as they did at Fort Chimo in 1954; but Canada dare not again consent to such wretched conditions as prevailed during that period there and at other places in Ungava Bay.

A statistician, Dr. P. S. K. Murty, recently calculated that on December 31, 1960, the Eskimo population of Canada (including northern Quebec) numbered 10,751. Of that total 3,521 (1,774 males and 1,747 females) fell into the age-group 15 to 34, and 1,808 (976 males and 832 females) into the age group 35 to 54, giving a possible labour force of 5,329 (1961). He estimated further that only 307 individuals in that force, or approximately 6 per cent, had enjoyed steady wage-employment during 1960. A much larger number had been intermittently employed on such jobs as stevedoring, freighting supplies, and carpentering, for periods lasting from a few days to a few weeks; but the majority of the 5,329 Eskimos between the ages of 15 and fifty-four earned no wages at all, and the males could have been listed in a labour register as unemployed

How, then, did they manage to pay their way? How did they retain their credit at the trading store, if they required an income, in cash and kind, of at least $1,500? They could no longer obtain all their food by fishing and hunting, as their forefathers had done before the coming of the white man; nor all their clothing; nor the weapons, tools, and cooking utensils they used every day of their lives. These they had to buy at the trading stores from the money they earned by their labour, and from selling such furs as they had gathered during the winter; and the latter, as we saw, never brought an income averaging more than $300. Seeing that about 90 per cent of the labour force was unemployed, that is to say, earned little if any wages, how did they succeed in buying what they needed and remain solvent?

Cantley supplied an answer in 1950 when he reported that the Eastern Arctic Eskimos of his day were earning from their labour and their furs only 40 per cent of the money they were spending at the trading stores, and that the government was supplying 60 per cent through pensions, family allowances, and various hand-outs. Since his day government activities in the

Arctic, and the operation of a small nickel mine (now closed down) at Rankin Inlet, have given steady work to a somewhat greater number of Eskimos, but otherwise there has been little change in the employment field. Perhaps a dozen communities have increased their incomes from handicrafts and from fishing; and trapping has yielded higher returns in some years and lower returns in others. But the number of Eskimos receiving relief payments virtually doubled between 1957 and 1959, and in the latter year comprised nearly half the total population. The economy of a people must be extremely sick when half of them, year in and year out, are driven to line up for relief chits.

A little help has reached them lately from the embryonic industries and the handicrafts which Cantley had counted on to invigorate their economy, and which the present administration has promoted with the utmost energy. These have proved successful to a degree, but utterly inadequate to compensate for the underdeveloped condition of the Arctic today and the poverty of its known or at least utilized resources. Both the Hudson's Bay Company and the government itself had previously experimented with some of these "industries" and abandoned them; but each new generation hopes, not unnaturally, that its greater knowledge and technical skill will bring success where an earlier generation failed.

. . . Several years before the outbreak of the Second World War, Dr. A. E. Porsild successfully established for the government a small domesticated reindeer industry in the Western Arctic. The single herd of 2,370 animals that had arrived on the east side of the Mackenzie River Delta in March 1935, increased steadily until in the 1951 round-up the mother and daughter herds together mustered 8,412 deer, despite heavy losses through straying, sickness, wolves, and other causes, and the slaughter of a considerable number for their meat and hides. They were grouped at that time into three herds, the largest, containing 5,559 deer, under direct government control, the two others, numbering 796 and 2,057 deer respectively, owned and managed by Eskimos, but still under government supervision. On the planning board a third herd was to be cut out and placed under Eskimo ownership; and the authorities were dreaming of a day when reindeer in large numbers would be grazing near every Eskimo encampment, patiently serving all the needs of their masters. In 1952, accordingly, they cut out the third native herd, and in 1954 a fourth, although for at least ten years they had been encountering great difficulty in finding young Eskimos willing to apprentice themselves as herders.[1] Then in 1956 the bright prospects of wage-employment on the D.E.W. Line stations which were being erected in that part of the Arctic brought on a crisis. One after another the owners of three of the herds surrendered their animals to the government and moved away, leaving only one native herd numbering less than 2,000 deer, and one government herd swollen now to about 6,000. Ottawa then decided to split its own herd into two and place their management in private hands. The curtain has not yet fallen on the final act of the drama, but it would seem quite clear that as an economic enterprise reindeer herding has already vanished from the Canadian stage.

*   *   *

The Arctic's oldest industry, of course, was whaling, the pursuit of the huge bowhead whales for their baleen, their oily blubber, and their meat; but this ceased at the beginning of the twentieth century, after baleen had lost its commercial value. Before it declined, the Hudson's Bay Company, which had been disappointed by the fur trade at its newly founded post at Fort Chimo, began to exploit the belugas or white whales that fre-

---

[1]Overhead, and the returns in production, are set forth in the following table, taken from an interim report of the Reindeer Committee (Canada, Department of Northern Affairs and Natural Resources, 1957):

Expenditures from 1926 to 1957

Purchase of 2,370 reindeer	$ 154,830.00
Preliminary investigations and establishment of the Reindeer Station, 1926 to 1935	139,040.00
Cost of maintaining Reindeer Station, 1935 to 1957	871,640.00
Total Expenditures	*$1,165,510.00*

Production 1935 to 1957

Meat produced: 12,054 carcasses weighing an average of 120 lb. apiece	1,446,480 lb. meat
Hides distributed in Eastern Arctic	4,647

I suspect that these figures do not include the quantities of meat and hides used by the reindeer herders and the supervisory staff, or donated to the police post and the two mission hospitals at Aklavik.

quent the estuaries of several rivers in northern Labrador and south Baffin Island, and the salmon and char that migrate up the Koksoak, the George, and the Whale rivers of Ungava Bay. The beluga fishery too declined quickly, probably because the rate of slaughter exceeded the animals' reproduction rate, although Low in 1903 attributed it to their increasing wariness of the nets which the hunters stretched across the estuaries at high tide. The Eskimos, however, continued to hunt them for their own use; and from time to time officers of the Hudson's Bay Company tried unsuccessfully to revive the commercial industry. So too did the government in Cumberland Sound, about 1930; and a commercial company in 1949 at Churchill, where the Department of Fisheries imposed on the catch a limit of 600 animals yearly, and prohibited any slaughter by sportsmen. In 1951 Eskimo, Indian, and white fishermen killed at the mouth of the Churchill River 584 beluga, each measuring about ten feet long and weighing approximately 900 pounds; and they shipped 3,200 pounds of beluga steaks, carefully wrapped in one-pound packages, to Winnipeg, where they sold on the open market without difficulty. During the first half of the following season, the hunt opened so well that the Department of Fisheries raised the permissible quota to 700 beluga; and the actual catch totalled 699, of which one Eskimo hunter alone killed 283. But only one year later the catch dropped to 599; and it continued to decrease until 1955, when the export of meat apparently ceased. Between 1957 and 1960 local hunters, mainly Métis or Indians of mixed descent, killed annually about 400 animals, from which the oil, though not the meat, went south; but the extraction plant fell into disrepair and suspended operations in 1960, whereupon beluga fishing as a commercial enterprise passed out of existence.

More lasting, and also more profitable than the Hudson's Bay Company's beluga fishery, was the salmon and char fishery in Ungava Bay, although this too in the end suffered the same fate. Beginning in 1881 on the Koksoak River, it netted during its first four seasons forty, twenty-four, thirty-eight, and slightly under forty tons in rapid succession, all of which the company shipped to England on a small vessel equipped with a dry-air freezing plant. From 1884 onward, the company worked the George and Whale rivers in addition to the Koksoak, but at the end of that century Low reported that the fishery had declined everywhere, and in one season, 1897, had practically failed. We hear very little about it during the first three decades of the twentieth century, and what we do know has been summarized in an earlier passage. The industry closed down altogether about 1931, and remained forgotten until the summer of 1954, when a commercial air pilot tried to revive it. He bought from the Eskimos around the Chimo air-base 2,584 pounds of salmon at 17 cents a pound, boxed it, and shipped it by air, on aircraft that would otherwise have travelled empty, to Roberval, where it was repacked and sent on to Montreal. The report on the first shipment, we are told, was not entirely favourable, but a later shipment received a better reception.

Meanwhile, in 1950, the Arctic Services Branch of the Department of Resources and Development had set up an experimental fishing station at Port Burwell to stimulate a fuller harvesting of the cod and seals in that district where the Eskimos were almost destitute. The experiment proved only partly successful, one reason being that the natives displayed little liking for salt cod. Then Ottawa tried other methods of expanding the economy of the Eskimos and making them more self-sufficient. It promoted small boat-building plants at Lake Harbour in the Eastern Arctic, and at Tuktoyaktuk in the Western; but both these enterprises languished. Recalling then an experiment by its Wildlife Service during the 1930's on the north shore of the Gulf of St. Lawrence, it attempted to create an eider-down industry at Cape Dorset and in Payne Bay similar to the flourishing Icelandic one; but that too failed to take root, perhaps because the handling of wild birds as carefully as domestic poultry lay outside the realm of Eskimo experience. Undismayed, the government landed at Fort Chimo in 1955 ten sheep from the Central Experimental Farm at Ottawa, hoping that those animals might thrive as they have in the southernmost fiords of Greenland and replace the vanished caribou; but the half-starved sled dogs quickly wrote *finis* to that experiment. Ottawa then decided to investigate the possibility of exploiting the char that migrate up so many arctic rivers; and in the summer of 1958, the Department of Northern Affairs and National Resources sent out from Frobisher, by air, a trial shipment of 1,500 pounds of char, which it distributed to a number of the best restaurants in Montreal and Toronto. Within a few days it received a repeat order for an ever larger quantity, indicating that, if carefully handled and processed, this fish could find a ready market in southern Canada, and also in the United States.

Eagerly the department went into action, not on the char alone, but over a much wider field, attacking in the beginning those arctic districts where distress seemed greatest, and employing methods and principles that had been evolved in building up under-developed regions in other parts of the world. In the first summer season it sent in experts to assess the natural resources, and in the second it sent in other experts to help the Eskimos develop such resources as seemed capable of exploitation. Behind the experts stood the department's administrators, ready to finance the Eskimos with small loans from a fund – the Eskimo Loan Fund – which parliament had approved a few years earlier. In essence, therefore, the scheme was a "little Colombo" plan for arctic Canada, but with this difference, that the experts were permanent employees of the Canadian government, and their surveillance was more intense than would have been possible had they been working in a foreign land. The department had no desire to spend money and effort on palpably uneconomic enterprises, or in areas that were lacking in economic resources. On the contrary, it demanded that every enterprise it supported should become, if possible, self-sustaining, and that the natives who operated it should stand in due course on their own feet and no longer need outside support. In that way, it was convinced, the Eskimos would gain not only economically but socially and psychologically, while the government too would benefit from the reduction in its expenses for straight relief.

The districts in which the department has conducted economic surveys since 1958, when the program first took definite shape, are all, or nearly all, districts in which the local Eskimos had been living near the starvation level. Some useful results have already flowed from these surveys, and from the new or increased activities that they have stimulated. Thus the char fisheries at Port Burwell, George River, Frobisher Bay, and Cambridge Bay have added thousands of dollars to the incomes of the local Eskimos. At George River alone they lowered the government's relief expenditures from $40,000 in 1957 to only $40 in 1960. And in this and other districts the morale of the Eskimos, which had sunk to very low depths, began to show symptoms of buoyancy again.

Unhappily, the situation fails to inspire optimism. None of the measures the government has yet taken, nor all of them combined, have turned the tide of distress in the Arctic. They have not won the economic struggle. Some government officials recognize this, and look upon any increased exploitation of the region's biological resources as a mere stop-gap, a useful palliative pending the discovery of a permanent cure for its economic ills. Every year, indeed, it is becoming more and more clear that neither char, nor salmon, nor any other fish or mammal in the Arctic, swarms in numbers large enough to withstand the drain of large-scale commercial exploitation; that very few districts contain sufficient food resources to maintain their present human populations, and can certainly not support their increase; that beyond the tree-line there are no other exploitable resources except perhaps oil and minerals, which the Eskimos themselves are unable to develop because they lack both the knowledge and the capital; and, finally, if we may trust the opinions of some of our scientists who study world-mineral resources, that there is little prospect of any considerable oil or mineral development in arctic or subarctic Canada within the very near future, except perhaps on the north and west coast of the Labrador Peninsula.

*   *   *

It appears equally certain, too, that the government's efforts to help them make fuller use of the Arctic's wildlife, and in that way earn the money to pay for their necessities, have failed to produce significant results outside of two or three localities, because the wildlife is not plentiful enough to sustain heavier exploitation than it is undergoing at the present time. Art-lovers, however, have discovered a new resource. Nature has endowed the Eskimos (and indeed human beings everywhere) with an innate desire for beauty, even though they can no more define what beauty is and means than we can; and in the era when our British and French ancestors were still painting their bodies with woad and shielding themselves from winter's cold fogs with the skins of wild animals, Eskimos were carving delicate figurines of seals, polar bears, and other animals on the ivory tusks of the walrus, and decorating them with concentric circles and other curvilinear designs. Their artistic skill has come down to their descendants, as we can see in the bird figures, the toy sleds and dog-teams, and the many other ivory curios that our museums have collected from modern Eskimos in Alaska and Labrador.

*   *   *

Unhappily the market for art and handicraft objects is fickle, as both we and the United States have found with Indian baskets, beadwork, totem-poles, and silver jewelry. The successful art and curio dealer must unerringly sense the public's changing whims and try to provide new objects to whet its flagging interest. Houston has done this at Cape Dorset by fostering the making of prints from carefully selected Eskimo drawings, and, with the instinct of a business man, preserving their uniqueness and value by restricting their reproduction to fifty copies each. The prints too have found a bull market in the south, and with the carvings that Cape Dorset continues to produce have drawn that settlement's 330 inhabitants, for a time at least, out of the Slough of Distress and Despondency into which they had fallen on to the Hill of Self-Sufficiency and Self-Respect. In 1959 prints and carvings together poured into the settlement $22,000, a substantial sum that, evenly distributed, would have added $300 to each family's income. This revenue almost trebled in 1960, and when the final returns for 1961 came in, the total reached nearly $100,000.

Notwithstanding Houston's remarkable success with handicrafts, the cold analytical administrator will not let his imagination take flight, but will hold it firmly down to earth with dry, hard facts and figures. Cape Dorset is only one small Eskimo settlement in our Arctic, and it owes its relative prosperity to the driving qualities of one unusually capable man. No other settlement, except possibly Povungnituk, has attained equal success with its handicrafts, or seems likely to do so in the future; and even at Cape Dorset they have not brought affluence, but only freedom from distress and from dependence on government relief payments. To enjoy real affluence a man must possess an income that exceeds his expenditures on what he holds to be necessities, or near necessities, and that the Cape Dorset Eskimos have by no means obtained. Furthermore, no one knows whether the market will turn sour on Eskimo handicrafts, and if so, how soon. It may be difficult to maintain their present high quality if the art extends too widely; for many craftsmen are not artists and not all Eskimos are even craftsmen. Foreign imitations, again, may cut into the market. I have seen a store window in Yokahama filled with "American Indian Totem-poles" that had never felt the British Columbia sun; and many a Canadian housewife may derive as much satisfaction from the "Hummel" figurine she bought in a 15-cent store as the sophisticated connoisseur from his genuine article. The art trade is beset with so many uncertainties, so many pit-falls, that beautiful prints and attractive soapstone carvings are not a safe base on which to build a people's economy; and they can never become such a base, indeed, though they may lighten the poverty of a few individuals and support to a small extent a base that is already established.

We have seen how steady work on the northern airfields during the 1940's brought unexpected prosperity to a number of Eskimo homes, raised their standard of living and their morale, and perhaps improved their diet and their health, at least temporarily. The construction of the airfields, however, was a fleeting task that lasted two or three years only; and because their subsequent operation demanded skilled personnel, it did not prevent the Chimo and other Eskimos from lapsing into destitution again. The same "temporary boom and bust" conditions resulted from the construction of the D.E.W. Line in the 1950's, although in that instance a force of over 90 Eskimos was retained for maintenance work; and similar conditions would have followed the government's construction programs at Inuvik in the Mackenzie River Delta, and at Frobisher on Baffin Island, had not these new administrative centres opened up a number of minor jobs for Eskimos in the government service. Even the Eskimo colony at Resolute Bay, in the arctic archipelago, to which place the government, in

1953, removed three destitute families from Port Harrison – along with one Pond Inlet family to initiate them into their new environment, making in all twenty-one Eskimos, a number that through immigration had increased by May 1961, to eighty-three – even that settlement does not derive its present prosperity, and the contentment of its colonists, from the relative abundance of game in the vicinity. It derives them from the employment obtained by several heads of families at the airbase, from the amenities that the base's proximity has made available to them, and from the close links it maintains with the outside world for purposes that only incidentally include the colonists' welfare. It would be correct to maintain, I believe, that the economic prosperity (but not necessarily the social prosperity) of an Eskimo community today is roughly proportional to the amount of wage-employment it obtains, and not, as formerly, to the wildlife resources that exist in its neighbourhood.

Sooner or later every period of construction must come to an end, and most of the unskilled workers who have toiled on the structures must lay down their tools and give place to others who will occupy and use the finished buildings. In the Arctic that time seems to be approaching:

> The employment opportunities for local labour, created by the construction of the Distant Early Warning line, the move of Aklavik, and other government construction programs have provided some much needed additional income for a number of those who were formerly dependent upon fur trapping for a livelihood. These and similar opportunities will occur for several years, but only a relatively small proportion can be counted upon to continue for longer than that. They therefore cannot be regarded as a cure for the problem of economic distress in these communities but merely as a short-term palliative. Full use must be made for the respite thus provided to develop more permanent sources of employment for a substantial number of those now engaged in trapping.[2]

The Department of Northern Affairs and National Resources, after analysing current employment trends, estimated in December 1956, that there were 1,270 jobs, half of them skilled and half unskilled, which might be filled by Eskimos within the ten years from 1957 to 1967. About 20 per cent of those jobs, it anticipated, could be expected from private concerns, mainly the Hudson's Bay Company and mining interests; the remaining 80 per cent would be openings in the government service. The Department of Transport might use 200 Eskimos as radio operators and 150 as meteorological assistants; the Department of National Health and Welfare could use a considerable number of young women as nurses and nurses' aides; and the Department of Northern Affairs and National Resources would require teachers for the many new schools it was erecting in the Arctic, and janitors to take care of the buildings and to repair simple defects in the plumbing, the heating, and the electric lighting.

The ten-year period has now passed its mid-term. Will the department's estimate of 1,270 jobs for Eskimos be fulfilled? It seems unlikely. Murty's figures for 1960 show this breakdown of the 307 Eskimos who, by his computation, had been steadily employed during that one year.

Employer	Number of Eskimos Employed
Depts. Northern Affairs and National Health	45
Dept. Transport	22
R.C.M.P.	11
Dew Line	17
Federal Electric Co.	69
Rankin Nickel Mine	58
Missions	2
Hudson's Bay Company	3
Miscellaneous	80
Total	307

Independent sources give higher figures for certain items in this table, perhaps because they interpret the term "steady employment" more broadly, or include Eskimos working for

[2]Canada, Department of Northern Affairs and Natural Resources, *Annual Report, 1955-1956* (Ottawa: The Queen's Printer, 1956), pp. 101-102.

agencies whom Murty may have overlooked. Nevertheless there seems no doubt that the total number of Eskimos continuously employed during the last few years, has at no time reached 600, and that eighty Eskimo workers at the North Rankin Inlet Nickel Mines lost their jobs when the mines closed down toward the end of 1962.[3]

It must have been deeply distressing to the government that out of the 1,270 jobs in the Arctic which it hoped might be filled by Eskimos before 1967, only 549 (by the highest estimate) had materialized by late 1961; and in the meantime the Eskimo labour force of over 2,000 males had been growing larger year by year. To watch 15 per cent of those jobs evaporate during 1962 must have added to Ottawa's anxieties.

Why should these jobs evaporate? Why should employment be so scarce? And why cannot the Eskimos fill all or most of those jobs that are even now available?

Jobs are scarce because the Arctic is still an undeveloped region inhabited, in the main, solely by Eskimos, by government officials, and by the traders of the Hudson's Bay Company. Its only exploitable resources (apart from handicrafts, furs, and a few fish) are minerals; and as yet these are little known and completely neglected, save for the nickel deposits once mined in Rankin Inlet. Remoteness from markets, transportation difficulties and a very severe climate make it an unusually high-cost region, even on this continent, and whatever oil and minerals it possesses must compete with similar oil and minerals from such low-cost regions as Venezuela, Africa, and the Middle East. . . .

In 1956 the Department of Northern Affairs and National Resources was looking, not to the mining industry alone, but to trade, which meant in practice the Hudson's Bay Company, to open up a number of jobs for Eskimos during the next ten years. These trade jobs may still be available, indeed, if the company can find natives capable of filling them. But the situation in the north has changed with the increased costs of goods and labour, and with the collapse of the high prices the world was once prepared to offer for arctic furs. Today the fur trade alone no longer covers the expense of maintaining a chain of trading posts in the far north, and the "forts" of the Hudson's Bay Company have become general stores that derive less profit from the traffic in pelts than from the sales for cash of general merchandise.

> *Price changes will, of course, vary according to the goods selected. However, it does seem abundantly clear that price changes do not explain the sharp upward trend in sales figures in the north in recent years. People across the north in total and on the average have much more money to spend than they ever had before, and they are buying more things with it than ever before.*
>
> *I think there is little doubt but that the income in kind — the food and clothing from land and sea to which I referred — has declined, at least in relative importance. Certainly it has gone down sharply in proportion to the growing population. It is apparent, however, that that decline is being offset by the steady increase in the goods that are bought for cash*[4]

This statement by the Commissioner of the Northwest Territories holds true both in the Mackenzie River Basin and along the shores of the Arctic, where the predominantly Eskimo population is obtaining its cash from three sources: wage-employment; the sale of furs, handicrafts, char etc.; and government grants. In 1950, when Cantley, grouping the first two sources together, credited the Eskimos with contributing only 40 per cent of the cash they were disbursing and assigned the other 60 per cent to government grants, much less cash was circulating in arctic communities, fewer Eskimos were working for wages, and neither handicrafts nor fish had become important money-earners. Today when handicrafts are flourishing, and the white-fox fur is selling at a slightly higher price than the average in Cantley's day, we can hardly be far wrong if we rank the three cash sources as roughly equal.

*　　　　*　　　　*

---

[3]Twenty-two of these eighty were taken on by the government for the maintenance of buildings previously serviced by the mines. The most reliable estimates of the permanently employed Eskimos that I have been able to obtain are:

1956-57	1957-58	1958-59	1959-60	1960-61	Late 1961
560	590	590?	?	?	549

[4]Opening Address by Gordon Robertson, Commissioner of the Northwest Territories, at the Twenty-first Session of the Council of the Northwest Territories, Fort Simpson, 10 July, 1961, p. 4.

The ignorance of English, and lack of education and training, which prevent the hiring of Eskimo clerks by the Hudson's
Bay Company, also prevent the natives from receiving any but
unskilled jobs from the government. Yet there are many government posts in the Arctic today filled, at great expense, by white
civil servants, who seldom stay there more than one or two
years and then must be replaced. And replacement costs are
high.

*   *   *

Ours is a mechanical age, fast becoming an electronic one
that will have little use for illiterate and unskilled labour. The
key then to our Eskimo unemployment problem, as of unemployment in many other parts of the world, is education and
training. Italy discovered two years ago that the thousands of
unemployed and only semi-literate peasants in the Mezzogiorno,
the region from Naples south, whom she was hoping would
quickly find jobs in southern Germany and other labour-short
areas within the Common Market, were not receiving the
welcome she had expected because they lacked the necessary
education, and she immediately initiated a crash educational
program to remedy the situation. Here in Canada the nickel
mine at Thompson, Manitoba, which employed 150 Indians
during the construction phase, now employs only about 20 on
a casual basis and 10 permanently, not because there was any
racial discrimination against Indians – for the ten skilled men
who have been retained on the permanent staff are acceptable
to management and labour unions alike – but because all but
these ten were unskilled. The iron centre of Schefferville, in the
heart of the Labrador Peninsula, witnessed the same phenomenon; very few of the 110 to 150 illiterate or semi-illiterate
Indians whom the mining company gladly employed during the
construction period have steady jobs today. And should the iron
ores of Ungava, or of the Great Whale River District, be
exploited within the next decade, as seems not impossible, scores
of Eskimos and their families will doubtless congregate there
and earn good wages during the first few years; but unless they
can be educated and trained in the interval, they will fall by the
wayside again as the mine enters full production, and become
an even heavier charge on the public purse than they are today.

The Flexibility of Eskimo Social Organization

W. E. WILLMOTT

In a recent paper, Professor Honigmann has discussed "flexibility" as one element of the Eastern Arctic Eskimo ethos.[1] He defines flexibility as "a relaxed mode of procedure and tolerant attitudes toward demands of living." He is particularly interested in the ideational implications of this aspect of ethos, the Eskimo's "passive resignation toward disasters" and lack of elaborate theories of causation, which he relates to child-rearing practices that reinforce a flexible approach to the problems of living.

The present paper will amplify this point by giving examples of flexibility in social organization and by discussing its practical and theoretical implications. The material for this paper was gathered during the summer of 1958 at Port Harrison, P.Q., a community on the east coast of Hudson Bay where most of the 340 Eskimos live in small local groups of thirty to fifty individuals in six to ten households.

In an article in the *American Anthropologist*, Professor Embree has suggested that "loose integration" is a functional aspect of Thai culture. It is possible to make a similar case in Eskimo culture for the equivalent concept, flexibility. Rigorous life in the Arctic, where subsistence itself is a never-ending challenge to man's ingenuity, demands a high degree of inventiveness and at the same time prevents the establishment of large, permanent local groups where patterns may become formalized and endowed with value.

To say that flexibility is functional does not, of course, explain its presence as a part of Eskimo culture. No attempt is

SOURCE: *Anthropologica*, vol. 2 (1960), pp. 48-57. Reprinted by permission of the author and publisher.

[1] John and Irma Honigmann, "Notes on Great Whale River Ethos," *Anthropologica*, vol. 1 (1959), pp. 106-121.

here made to explain its origin, but only to describe and discuss it as it exists today. The following sections will deal with flexibility in the areas of family organization, kinship terminology, community organization, and recreation. The implications of flexibility for the acculturation of the Eskimos to majority Canadian patterns will then be discussed, and the paper will conclude by raising some theoretical questions arising from this concept.

Family Organization

If it is possible to speak of a basic social unit in any society, as Professor Leighton suggests it is, the household is such a unit for the Eastern Eskimo. Most activities of both men and women take place for or in the household. Nevertheless, many of its functions are variously fulfilled for its members by other households in the local group, and even its membership may change from time to time.

A new household may or may not be established by a marriage. Depending on expediency, a newly married couple may live with the parents of either spouse or may build their own snow house or tent. Locality can be described as flexible.

The normal form of marriage is permanent monogamy. This is so, not because of strong moral or ritual circumscriptions that would tend to make marriage a rigid form, but because monogamy is the best adaptation to the cultural-ecological circumstances: a man cannot live without a sewer-cook-boot softener, and each woman must have a hunter-trapper. The attempts of the missionaries to make a value of permanent monogamy have not succeeded. This is evidenced by the large number of marriages without benefit of church (almost two-thirds of the sixty couples) and by the other forms of marriage in the area: two polygynous households, two households in which the women provide for the economic needs of several brothers, and two cases where men have sent unsatisfactory mates away and taken new wives, although the first marriage had been in the church in each case. The form of marriage could be described, therefore, as flexible monogamy.

Although the household normally provides for the daily needs of the individual – food, sleep, clothing, sexual satisfaction

– these needs may be satisfied in any household in the local group. Young boys may sleep in various tents if it is convenient, for instance, and a person may eat as much as he likes anywhere. When the fish are brought in from the nets, everyone around may partake of raw fish. Similarly, prayers involve whoever is in the tent at the time. From the point of view of function, then, the household can be described as a flexible unit.

The household is rendered flexible in membership by the mechanism of adoption, which distributes children between households more equitably than does nature alone. Where infant mortality is high (294 per 1,000 in the past decade) and epidemic and starvation are likely to wipe out several individuals at a time, adoption aids group survival. Death, sterility, or old age need not be reasons in this society for a couple to lack children so long as there are children in the area.

Adoption is much more prevalent among Eskimos than among other Canadians. Of the 175 children under fifteen in the area of study, twenty-eight are adopted, or 16 per cent. In most cases, the child is adopted because the adopting couple want a child rather than because the child does not have a home. Very few of the adoptions are registered with the Royal Canadian Mounted Police, and several of them involve re-adoption by other parents.

If family forms are as flexible as here suggested, one could expect a high degree of variation and a wide range of types. This is in fact the case, for the sixty-five households range in size from two to thirteen individuals; twenty-one include more than one nuclear family, whether paternal relative, another nuclear family, a lodger, or the child of an unmarried daughter.

Kinship Terminology

Eastern Arctic Eskimo kinship terminology is quite specific, distinguishing between affinal and consanguinal, male and female, younger and older, and often between agnate and distaff. For instance, the term for father's brother, *akkak*, is different from the term for father's sister, *attsak*, parent-in-law, *sakiak*, or mother's brother, *angak*. The system of terminology could be described as bifurcate collateral.

But the use of these terms as observed in the field does not stick to their meanings as given by an interpreter. For instance, *ningaut*, daughter's husband, may also be used for cousin's husband. I found nine terms in use between cousins, none of which distinguished anything but sex and relative age. And *akkak*, father's brother, was found in use variously to describe father's brother, father's brother's son, father's sister's son, husband's brother, husband's brother's son, father's sister's husband, and mother's brother's son. Other terms are used with similar flexibility.

In fact, kinship terms appear to be used with little regard for their literal meanings, although these meanings are recognized by the Eskimos as specific. Rather, they are employed as they seem appropriate to the nature of the personal relationship between the two people. If a man looks on an older male cousin as belonging to an older generation, the term *akkak* may seem more appropriate than the literally correct term, *qatanguk*, first cousin.

Kinship terminology is also used between unrelated individuals in the same local group, especially among children. Social relationships are given kinship status in order to cement the local group together. Thus, all children of similar age in a camp may call each other *qatangutik*, a term that was variously described to me as meaning "first cousin," "any relative of the same age," or "someone born in the same camp."

Community Organization

In the area of Port Harrison, there are seven local groups. The largest of these, comprising eighteen households, is located at the white settlement, where, according to a rule established by the local Royal Canadian Mounted Police, only those families may settle one of whose members is working for the whites. The other six local groups are camps from five to fifty miles from the settlement, made up of from six to ten households each.

As far as we can determine, the traditional Eskimo local group was a small, flexible, nomadic band without clearly defined leadership roles, and whose membership varied somewhat from year to year as different families decided to camp together after each summer gathering. This pattern has changed under the impact of varying contact situations. Around Port Harrison there are three quite distinct patterns of community organization today: 1) the organized camp, 2) the loosely conglomerate camp, and 3) the settlement. These can best be described through a historical review of their origin.

With the advent of the fur-trader – about fifty years ago in this area – camps became more stabilized in both membership and location because of the establishment of individual traplines that were maintained from year to year. The trading companies found it efficient to work through one spokesman for each group, and this man's position of leadership was assured by the policy of presenting Peterhead boats and whaleboats to spokesmen in order to assure their loyalty. Since these boats then became the primary means of summer transportation and hunting, the owner controlled the movements of the camp and assumed a position of considerable power. Three of the six camps around Port Harrison have powerful leaders who own large boats, and each has a stable population with a strong feeling of differentiation from the other camps.

As the fur trade declined, many Eskimos moved into the settlement and lived on relief, sharing the food of relatives who were employed. This centripetal tendency, which has been observed throughout the Arctic by students of Eskimos, was brought to a sudden halt in 1957 by a local Royal Canadian Mounted Police order that all Eskimos not employed in the settlement should relocate in camps. This order reduced the Eskimo population of the settlement from twenty-seven households to thirteen, from about one hundred and thirty-five persons to seventy-five. Those who left the settlement moved about five miles away, where they established two loosely organized camps that fragment in winter and come together for early summer. Another camp, whose leader died without logical successor, has also become a loose conglomerate of households. These three camps appear to be the most similar to pre-contact patterns of community organization.

Those households that remain in the settlement itself are held there by the existence of the white establishments, not by indigenous community organization. There is no recognized leader of the Eskimo community, although the Hudson's Bay Company interpreter acts as a middleman whenever orders are given or requests received by whites.

Although private ownership of the tools and product of the hunt was recognized in the traditional band, weapons and tools not in use by their owner could be used by anyone in the band, and food was shared to assure that no one in the band would starve as long as there was supply. These patterns were maintained during the rise of the fur trade, and are still maintained today in regard to the hunt. Wages, however, are not shared, primarily because they are part of a new economic pattern that includes majority Canadian ideas of private property. Also, they are not in a form that can be readily shared, since they are paid as credits at the Hudson's Bay Company store and turned into goods as the wage-earner requests it. Similarly, earnings from trapping and soapstone carving are not shared but belong to the individual.

Since the camp depends on the hunt for half its food, patterns of sharing make households more interdependent than the households in the settlement, where each lives primarily from wages. Hunting is undertaken by settlement Eskimos only as a supplement to their diet, and sharing is therefore only incidental now to new pattern that is replacing it.

Eskimo community patterns have been able to change several times in a few short decades, each time adapting to the changing economic situation. The existence of several patterns within the same area and within the lifetime of these Eskimos indicates that these patterns are flexible, without strong values attached.

Recreation

What might be considered a trivial example of flexibility, but one that nevertheless makes the point clearly, is recreation. Aside from the traditional forms of recreation, the most important of which is visiting, the Eskimos have adopted various new ones from traders and other agents of civilization. From the point of view of this paper, the interesting thing about these borrowed forms of recreation is that they become less formal and more flexible, although highly structured in their original patterns. Two examples will indicate the de-structuring of games among the Eskimos.

The Eskimos in the camp I studied played cards every night. The women preferred a type of 500 rummy, although the men played five-card games that were entirely new to me. The rules of 500 rummy changed from hand to hand, the person next to the dealer determining the winning score, the wild cards, and the number of cards to be dealt on the first hand. On subsequent hands the revolving dealer decided how many cards to deal, depending on her own advantage, so that every hand became a different type of game.

Checkers are played by some Eskimos. As with other gambling games, the rules change after each game, depending on the alternate choice of the two players. Some of the observed variations were: pieces may move only forward but may jump backward as well, kings may move the entire diagonal of the board, kings may jump the entire diagonal of the board, pieces may jump backward only as the second jump of a double jump that has started forward.

Perhaps the best example of a formal pattern of recreation that has been de-structured by the Eskimos is the square dance. Learned originally from whalers and traders, Scots and French-Canadians, the dance has changed to allow any even number of couples instead of the originally prescribed four. Individuals may use a shuffle or a jig-step, and the figures follow each other according to the whim of the lead couple rather than by the original plan of the dance.

Each aspect of Eastern Arctic Eskimo social organization exhibits flexibility. The four examples given here are intended as an illustration of this characteristic, not as proof of the proposition. Its implications to the acculturation of the Eskimos and to social theory remain to be discussed.

Flexibility and Acculturation

There is no doubt that flexibility had much to do with the fact that white contact with Eskimos has been relatively free of conflict at Harrison. Since action patterns were not rigid nor heavily value-laden, they could adapt to the changing situation without the Eskimo feeling an overwhelming sense of loss. Changes introduced by whites were not viewed as threats to an Eskimo way of life, but rather as a factor of environment to which the Eskimo must adapt with the same approach he has always used in adapting to a hard and capricious physical environment.

The Eskimo's attitude toward the environment is summed up in the word *"arunamut,"* which literally means, "because nothing can be done," and implies "therefore we must face the situation without regret." Ever since the white man entered the Arctic, the Eskimo has said *"arunamut"* to all his incomprehensible antics. White economy, then white religion, and finally white political authority have penetrated Eskimo society, wrought far-reaching and irrevocable changes on it – often without the understanding of the Eskimos involved. Yet these changes have not been overtly opposed by the Eskimos. Rather, the social organization has adapted to the changes as it would adapt to a natural disaster or an environmental change.

The *arunamut* attitude has resulted in the unfortunate consequence that the Eskimo now accepts as an environmental axiom much that in democratic society is considered an individual's prerogative and duty. For instance, the right to choice of religion, the right to choice of residence, the duty to work, the right to bargain as a free agent, and the right and duty of education for children do not involve individual choice among Eskimos in this area.

But if this flexibility has led to domination of Eskimo society by various white agents, it may also abet the process of acculturation that the Eskimo is still undergoing. For even rapid social change need not produce conflict in a society where behaviour patterns do not appear as rigid values, where the social organization is suited to easy adaptation. The problem facing the administrator in such circumstances is not one of gradualism to avoid conflict, but rather the destruction of relationship with whites that involves the acceptance of white authority as an incontrollable part of the environment, and the reassertion by the Eskimo of control over the areas of culture that have been in white hands. Fundamental in this process will be the realization of economic independence of the Eskimo local group, its ability to act as a free agent in economic matters.

Theoretical Significance

The flexibility of Eskimo society provides interesting theoretical problems for the anthropologist, which are ultimately of practical importance as well. Firstly, it raises the question of the integration of each social unit in the society. For if patterns of behaviour are not standardized as values and defined to include deep emotional content, what produces solidarity and integration in the society, in the local group, or in the family?

The question of family integration is one for particularly fruitful speculation and research by social scientists. The family, or household, is the basic unit of traditional Eskimo society. One would therefore expect it to be highly integrated, with strong interdependence not only on the economic level, but on the personality level as well. But the relative ease with which children are passed from one family to another, and the apparent lack of personality damage to children resulting from even repeated adoptions, indicates that ties between parents and children are easily broken, easily made. This would suggest that neither parent nor child feels an overwhelming sense of unique relationship.

But if this is so, and since we know that personal identity is learned from relationships, how does the child gain his sense of personal identity? How does he learn to understand his status and, consequently, his relationship with other members of the society? It has been assumed by social scientists interested in socialization that this personal identity comes from the unique relationship between parent and child, especially mother and child. Is it possible that personal identity may develop without such a unique relationship that is defined as endowed with extraordinary emotional intensity? These are only preliminary queries that come to mind on what is obviously a highly complex subject.

The question of the integration of the local group provides another area of profitable research for the anthropologist. It seems evident that kinship is not the primary mechanism for integration of the organized camp, but rather the economic co-operation of the households, primarily in the use of a large boat. These camps appear to persist, however, in places where they have ceased to function as economic units. The historic evolution of the status of leader and its present demise offers an interesting developmental study of status.

Secondly, the relation between flexibility and integration provides interesting theoretical speculation for the functionalist. Flexibility "does not mean that the society is poorly integrated," Embree states:

> On the contrary, the loose integration is a functional one, allowing not only variation in individual behaviour, but also in national behaviour. [In Thailand] it had a survival value which may well go back to the early days of extensive Thai migrations and which has served the nation well to this day.[2]

Embree points out that the functionality of flexibility in this case raises the theoretical question of whether it is possible to find a one-to-one correlation between "needs" and structure. Although he does not mention Malinowski, this appears to be a suggestion that Malinowski's functionalism needs restudy in the light of these findings.

Malinowski has stated that function is defined "by showing that human institutions . . . are related to primary, that is biological, and derived, that is cultural needs. Function means, therefore, always the satisfaction of a need."[3] By this definition, and by reading Malinowski on acculturation, one gets the impression that in his view, specific needs are satisfied by specific social units, which change under impact from functionally equivalent units in another society.

But in Eskimo society it is often difficult accurately to define the functions (by Malinowski's definition) of any social unit, for they change in different circumstances. One might go further and suggest that the four-fold description of function proffered by Parsons does not produce fruitful results in a situation where institutions are not clearly defined and their functions vary according to circumstances.

Summary

Eskimo social organization is characterized by what Honigmann has called flexibility – a lack of rigidity and value associated with conventional ways of doing things. The flexibility may be seen in family organization, in the loose definition of the form of marriage, in the casualness of adoption, and in the informal approach to functions. It may be seen in the non-literal use of kinship terminology, which emphasizes the personal nature and closeness of the ties between two people rather than their actual kin relationship. It may be seen in the various patterns of community organization and the ease with which one changes into another. And it may be seen in the recreation patterns that become de-structured when practised by the Eskimos.

Flexibility has allowed acculturation to proceed with relative lack of conflict, and it may do so in the future. On the other hand, it produces the problem of lack of control by the Eskimos over many aspects of their society – education, religion, political authority, and especially economic organization – that are today entirely in the hands of whites.

Finally, the flexibility of Eskimo social organization raises the interesting and researchable theoretical questions of the integration of various social units and the functional approach to institutions of Malinowski and Parsons.

[2]John F. Embree, "Thailand – a Loosely Structured Social System," *American Anthropologist*, vol. 52 (April, 1950), p. 191.
[3]Bronislaw Malinowski, *A Scientific Theory of Culture* (Chapel Hill: University of North Carolina Press, 1944), p. 159.

Two Attempts at Community Organization among the Eastern Hudson Bay Eskimos

ASEN BALIKCI

The decrease of the useful fauna in many parts of the Arctic has created new problems in the acculturative process of the Canadian Eskimos. In areas where Euro-Canadian establishments were developed, inter-ethnic tensions and various disfunctional processes have appeared. Almost everywhere the dependence of the natives on the local trading posts has increased. Many solutions to the "Eskimo problem" have been suggested. One hears about relocating south the native populations of the Canadian Arctic, or concentrating them around a few mining centres, or various rapidly developing cottage industries. More conservative observers feel that the Eskimos, with the help of some Euro-Canadian agencies, may develop new forms of ecological adaptations and establish satisfactory symbiotic relations with the Euro-Canadians. It appears, however, that these objectives can be realized only if new and superior forms of social organization are established among the Eskimos. This paper attempts a description of such efforts in two Arctic locales, Great Whale River and Povungnituk (Eastern Hudson Bay). The data presented here have been collected during two summer trips to these regions, in 1957 and 1958 respectively.

Great Whale River

Three major acculturative phases can be established for the Eskimos living in the area between Cape Jones and Richmond Gulf.

SOURCE: *Anthropologica*, vol. 1 (1959), pp. 122-135. Reprinted by permission of the author and publisher.

1) The first and middle part of the nineteenth century were characterized by contacts of varying intensity with the whalers and the Hudson's Bay Company outpost at Little Whale River, leading to the gradual increase of trapping, the introduction of metal tools and firearms with some important changes in the sealing, fowling and caribou hunting techniques.

2) During the last quarter of the past century until the 1950's, the Hudson Bay Company's activities in the area grew in importance aiming mainly at the stabilization of the fur trading system. While whaling for commercial purposes came to a stop, trapping was steadily developed. The large caribou herds were soon exterminated with the help of the newly-acquired firearms. This brought to an end the seasonal inland migrations of Eskimo hunting groups. The Eskimos came to rely increasingly on the various commodities imported by the Hudson's Bay Company, such as foodstuffs, clothing, tent material, tools, etc. The role of the local trader was important; he controlled the debt system, encouraged trapping and provided occasional employment. Conversion of the Eskimo to the Anglican faith meant a quick rejection of the traditional beliefs and curing, and adoption of the Eskimo syllabary.

3) During the 1950's, extensive changes took place in the ways and the organization of Eskimo groups. Several new agencies entered the area and paramount among these were a construction enterprise and officers of the Department of Northern Affairs and National Resources. In the following paragraphs, a picture of the relations between the Eskimos and the various Euro-Canadian agencies during the summer of 1957 will be presented. This description is essentially limited to the symbiotic relations of the two ethnic groups. Contrary to Keesing's cultural definiton of a symbiotic situation which refers to borrowing of traits where two cultural systems maintain contact, the term is used there to denote all social interactions not motivated simply by the desire of sociability.

Prior to the development of an important construction program at Great Whale River, the Eskimos traditionally inhabiting the coast between Cape Jones and Richmond Gulf lived in small isolated groups usually at the mouths of the larger rivers. Most, if not all the members of such a group, were bound by kinship ties, and in several communities a headman, usually an older and successful hunter, enjoyed considerable prestige. He directed the seasonal movements of the camp and had the last word in the use of the boats. Among some groups, however, no hunter with outstanding prestige was to be found. In winter, the trading post was visited regularly for supplies and for a few weeks in summer all the groups concentrated at Great Whale River. Trading was conducted individually by each hunter and never through the headman. In the camps important patterns of collaboration existed during some collective hunts and in sharing food. While members of different groups visited occasionally, no significant intergroup collaboration existed, except during starvation periods when food gifts were made.

During the summer of 1955, numerous employment opportunities were made available to the Eskimos at Great Whale River. This led to the concentration of all regional Eskimo groups near the trading post. A large number of natives were hired individually as labourers. Soon after, for various reasons, many of the labourers abandoned their jobs and returned to hunting. Thus the large Eskimo community was split into two occupational groups: labourers and hunters. The marked differences in income produced some mild tensions between the two occupational groups. Hunting decreased rapidly and fresh meat became scarce. Certain prostitution practices and some epidemics allegedly brought by the Euro-Canadians were instrumental in creating a feeling of hostility directed against the white workers. Soon a Northern Service Officer was appointed to cope with the many administrative problems originating in this complex acculturative situation. He acted as an employment agent and an accountant for the natives, distributed relief and family allowances, and was kept informed about the activities of the hunters. He was faced mostly with individual cases, and when dealing with collective problems, addressed an assembly of most, if not all adult, male, Eskimos. The Royal Canadian Mounted Police constable looked after the actual distribution of the relief, kept the vital statistics, and also acted as an adviser to the natives on many occasions. The male nurse regularly visited the Eskimo tents tending the sick and encouraging individual or family sanitation practices. The Anglican missionary conducted services in the local church supposedly for the whole Eskimo community. He also practised small group and individual preaching, while trained catechists conducted group prayers in the tents.

The increased monetary income of the native labourers stimulated the sales for cash at the counter of the trading post. Trading became increasingly anonymous and was conducted generally between the Eskimo women and the store's clerks. The contacts between the trader and the Eskimo men became less intense, the debt system was partially abandoned, and the status of the trader was considerably diminished.

To sum up, these interactions reveal that the Euro-Canadians considered Eskimos either as individuals or as family heads, but very rarely as representatives of a larger grouping. Two examples may suffice. The headman of a group of hunters tried to obtain some ammunition on relief on behalf of his people only to be accused by the latter of not sharing the supply equitably. Another headman voiced an opinion regarding the activities of the prostitutes, considering himself as spokesman for the whole community. A further investigation revealed that he was representing only himself together with a small circle of relatives. Cases like these led the administrators to call all the adult Eskimos when problems of collective interest were to be discussed. The headmen, however, continued to exercise their traditional and limited authority over their groups in regard to the use of the boats and the seasonal migrations in the case of the hunters.

Different factors led the Northern Service Officer to encourage the creation of an elected Eskimo Community Advisory Council. Principal among these factors was the necessity to institutionalize a system of communication between the Administration and the Eskimos. While the former could easily call on individual natives, the discussion of collective problems was a difficult matter and it was hoped that a Community Advisory Council could more easily sound the natives and bring already prepared answers to the Administrator. Furthermore such a Council was to evolve gradually into a sort of self-government, able to take decisions concerning all the Eskimo groups at Great Whale River. Thus a superior level of socio-political integration was to be achieved in the native society through the democratic process. For some time, however, the functions of the Council were to remain only advisory and consultative. The administrator retained all executive authority.

Summoned by the Administrator, the Eskimos cheerfully elected six individuals – three headmen, one interpreter, and two natives of some prestige. Of the six only two had any authority over their groups. One group was represented by two councillors while several others had no representative at all.

After its constitution the Council had been apparently consulted on various subjects such as control of dogs, choice of foods to be served in the mess hall, over-time pay, and income tax. The main test took place in a few weeks, on a problem of dog-food distribution. The Council was asked by the Administration to organize the equitable distribution among all the Eskimo families of the considerable kitchen refuse thrown out daily by the Euro-Canadian mess. The refuse was used as dogfood. The mess managers have been throwing the refuse in the community dump where it was individually collected by the Eskimos according to their needs. The managers felt that it was preferable to have the refuse removed directly from the kitchens at regular hours. The Council decided that P., a representative of a large group, should be in charge of the removal and distribution of the refuse. P. immediately chose two of his relatives for the execution of the task. Soon after, the Eskimos noticed that, instead of sharing the dog-food, among all the tents, the two men stored it in the camp of P. Objections followed and the Council modified its decision. Two groups were to perform the task alternately. For a few days the program operated smoothly. Two boys of each group regularly removed the refuse. Soon, however, one of the boys went hunting and did not arrange for replacement. His companion was unable to proceed alone and the whole operation was first temporarily, and later, completely dropped. The Community Advisory Council never met again. What were the factors instrumental in the failure of the Council?

a) The Council was created first in a shallow frame, without any specific function or a longe range program of activities. Only a quick explanation by the Administrator preceded the election of the councillors, and a year later the few Eskimos who still knew about the Council were unable to give any information about its objectives. These informants perceived the Council as an artificial creation of the Administrator who called the sessions at will and only whenever he had a problem to discuss.

b) The problems the councillors had to deal with were either not understood or of little interest to them and the solutions were obviously to the advantage of the Euro-Canadians.

c) The Administration was apparently ignorant of the absence of any symbiotic inter-group relations among the natives. The Great Whale River Eskimos show essentially a family level of integration with some important forms of collaboration at the group level such as sharing food and the use of imported boats. Division of labour, except along sex and age lines was unimportant and, whenever present, due to Euro-Canadian influences. The dog-food distribution program called for a certain amount of economic specialization and inter-group collaboration. It was naive to believe that this could occur within the Eskimo community without the supervision of an Euro-Canadian agency. The program might have succeeded if certain remuneration of the dog-food collectors was envisaged. No such measures aiming at the development of some organic solidarity among the Eskimos were considered.

d) The loose character of the headman-group and the headman-headman relations were equally misunderstood by the Administration. Traditionally the headman derived his prestige from his superior hunting and trapping skills and his knowledge of the ecological conditions of the country. In a wage economy he found himself to be just another labourer, and sometimes not the best one. In the acculturative situation prestige became attached to income and possessions and the already loose authority of the headman suffered. As one informant described a headman, "P. speaks only for himself." The recent unequal distribution of wealth produced new jealousies and tensions between individuals, headmen, and different occupational groups. This reduced the possibility of inter-individual and inter-group collaboration in the Council and in the community.

e) The representation of the groups in the Council was unequal. This stimulated arrangements benefiting one group, led to the objections of the other groups, and discouraged planned collaboration.

Povungnituk

The history of the Eskimo-European relations in the Povungnituk area falls into four interactional periods.

1) The first period, roughly similar to the corresponding phase at Great Whale River, lasted a quarter of a century longer. The influence of commercial whaling on the ways of the Povernitormiut remains uncertain. The trading post at Little Whale River was visited only once a year, in spring, and trapping did not seem to have been intensively practised. Firearms largely replaced the bow and arrow and the long spring harpoon late in the nineteenth century. The conversion to Christianity of all the Eastern Hudson Bay Eskimos took place almost simultaneously around the 1880's.

2) The second or adaptive period covers the end of the last and the first three decades of this century. A trading post was established in the area, trapping was intensified, the decrease of the caribou herds produced some important changes in the seasonal migrations and increased the dependance of the natives on the trading post. The role of the trader became very important. He interfered in the migrations, encouraged trapping, acted as petty justice officer, gave medical treatment, helped during starvation periods, procured some wage employment, and through the individual debt system, controlled the prestige structure of the community.

3) The third period was one of crisis and ended with the beginning of the present decade. The almost complete disappearance of the caribou, together with the decrease of the other useful species, reduced considerably the supply of fresh meat. Trapping was not sufficiently productive, it failed to increase the cash income and stimulate consumption of larger quantities of imported foodstuffs. Periods of hunger became more frequent. Messianic beliefs appeared, reflecting an atmosphere of crisis due to the decrease of the caribou and the seals.

4) This last period of social reorganization extends to the

present time. It is characterized mainly by the concentration of almost all Eskimo groups around Povungnituk Bay, the development of soapstone carving for commercial purposes, the increase of government relief under various forms, the creation of group accounts, and the arrival of a Roman Catholic missionary. In the following paragraphs, a more detailed picture of the symbiotic interactional system at Povungnituk will be presented, drawing from data collected by the author during the summer of 1958.

The natives remembered vividly the difficult pre-war and post-war years when people died of starvation in the northern and central camps. Trapping provided them with a very irregular income, pelts worth only $3,222 were sold to the trader in 1951-52, while two years later their total income from trapping amounted to $39,361. An Euro-Canadian informant remembered that as late as 1955, the natives were begging for food and seemed intensely preoccupied with the possibility of starvation. In recent years, family allowances and relief to the needy families and individuals distributed by the Federal Government through the local trader, made available to the natives larger amounts of ammunition, clothing and imported foodstuffs. The economic conditions of the community, however, were radically changed by the development of carving for commercial purpose. Stimulated by the trader, the Eskimos increasingly devoted themselves to the carving of small animal or human figurines of soapstone representing mostly traditional subjects. All carvings were priced and purchased by the trader. Soon carving became the dominant activity in the area, the total sales of carvings increased from $740 in 1952-53, to $38,000 in 1955-56. Povungnituk came to be known as a "carving community." The Eskimos were freed from the necessity of intensive hunting. They did not have to remain any longer near their traditional hunting and trapping grounds and settled around the post. Most of the groups had headmen and formed compact clusters of tents. As at Great Whale River, the group collaboration patterns inherited from the traditional and the fur-trading periods, continued to function (food sharing and common use of boats under the supervision of the headman). A reasonable supply of fresh meat had to be assured and most of the poor carvers continued trapping. Povungnituk Bay was not a good hunting or trapping area and the hunters and trappers had to travel long distances, in summer or winter, to their traditional hunting grounds. This necessitated a larger number of sea-worthy boats powered by motor engines and an increase in the amount of supplies necessary to the trapper along the trail. Individual hunters could not easily face these new expenses. A collective solution to the problem had to be found. The local trader suggested and succeeded in establishing the following program. The seven or eight Eskimo groups who lived in relative isolation along the coast prior to their concentration at Povungnituk, were to establish group accounts at the trading post. A fraction of all earnings was to go to the group accounts. With the funds thus accumulated some larger goods for collective use such as boats and new engines could be obtained. Only elected group leaders had authority to spend the funds. No community, supra-group account was envisaged.

The system worked successfully. Following many informal consultations, many of the headmen who enjoyed some prestige among their kinsmen and others were elected. Soon several canoes, new engines, and larger motor boats were acquired. The contribution, freely accepted by the group-members, fluctuated from 5 to 35 cents for each dollar earned by the members, depending on the importance of the goods to be purchased. The system was flexible and allowed for larger or smaller savings. Under the control of the group leader, some funds were used to purchase gasoline, ammunition and supplies for the needy trappers. Needless to say, through their supervision of gasoline purchases, the control of the group leaders over the boats was strengthened generally. The Eskimos had to ask permission before using the boats. Soon tensions occurred between headmen and some hunters who were refused supplies from the group accounts. Another headman who monopolized the use of a boat was bitterly criticized. Similar tensions brought the splitting-up of a group with two separate camp accounts and the formulation of plans for acquisition of personal canoes by some Eskimos. It should be noted, however, that these tensions never endangered the functioning or the existence of the system which was perceived by the natives as highly beneficial. While minor purchases were left to the discretion of the group leader, any major decision concerning the group accounts was taken after many informal consultations and discussions. No formal meetings of the group members took place. This fitted well into the traditional Eskimo pattern of group decision-making. No explicit attempt was made by the Euro-Canadians to organize a community council of group leaders. Occasionally the group leaders were called to meetings and asked to answer questions of interest to most of the members. It is relevant that numerous Eskimos were present at these meetings and replied individually. Outside the sphere of group accounts the group leaders had little or no authority over the other Eskimos, except in traditional situations.

Conjointly an attempt was made by the trader to establish an exchange system between carvers and fishermen. The system was intended to provide a compensation for the continual gifts of fish by the hunters to the specialized carvers. The fish was to be purchased by the trader and later sold to the carvers. Thus the traditional sharing patterns were to give way to formalized inter-Eskimo trade relations, reflecting the recent occupational differentiation within the community. The system functioned successfully for some time under the close supervision of the trader. When his control was relaxed, the natives quickly reverted to their traditional sharing practices.

A third organizational project was invented by the local Missionary. Under his leadership a carver's association was founded. This new co-operative intended to sell carvings directly in Southern Canada, with the help of the Mission. Some intermediaries could be eliminated and the profit margin to the Eskimo increased. The members showed a great interest in the new institution, assembled once a week and collectively priced each carving. All carvings were examined, discussed, and individual styles compared. Good sculptures brought considerable prestige to the carver and some competitive attitudes appeared. A successful carver, himself a group leader, was chosen as president. He failed to exercise any authority and during the group deliberations behaved as an ordinary member. Odd jobs connected with the carving trade were regularly remunerated with the funds of the association.

In the following paragraphs, the factors which contributed to the success of the previously described organizations will be listed.

a) The new forms of collaboration connected with the group accounts were at the group level with some similarity to the interactional patterns developed during the fur-trading period for the acquisition and use of imported vessels.

b) Both the group accounts' system and the carvers' association were created in view of very specific objectives. Far from constituting shallow structures, they existed only in function of their aims which were executive rather than consultative. Furthermore, these objectives were perceived by the Eskimos as highly beneficial to them.

c) The group account system was flexible. It allowed for the formulation of either immediate or long-range projects and variable contributions. The initiative for these projects came from the Eskimos and not from the Euro-Canadians. The natives felt that the group accounts were "their business" and took keen interest in them.

d) The objectives of the new structures (acquisition of boats, providing the needy families with imported supplies, sale of carvings at reasonable prices) were of central importance to the Eskimos, solving problems of economic relations with the Euro-Canadian agencies that the simple traditional structures of Eskimo society could not face.

e) The group account system was suggested to the Eskimos at the end of a period of crisis when the natives were willing to accept changes. It was a timely answer to their pressing desire to acquire imported goods.

f) The new structures were not only initiated but continually supervised by the Euro-Canadians. The trader, however, controlled the system as such, without interfering with the projects formulated by the Eskimos.

Conclusion

Three recent organizations described above can be presented very schematically as follows: (the charts refer to the actual functioning of the systems and do not include normative elements).

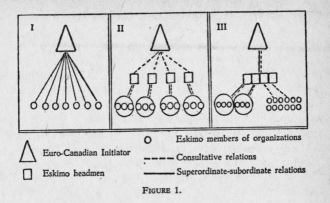

△ Euro-Canadian Initiator

□ Eskimo headmen

○ Eskimo members of organizations

- - - - Consultative relations

———— Superordinate-subordinate relations

FIGURE 1.

Comparing the three, it is clear that they represent systems of increasing complexity. System I is simple enough, it reflects superordinate-subordinate relations between the Euro-Canadian initiator and the members of the Sculptors' Association. System II indicates the Trader's roles as community accountant and stimulator, the general absence of formalized inter-leaders' relations, and both the consultative and superordinate-subordinate relations between leaders and group members. System III is characterized essentially by a formal grouping of community representatives, which is a step in advance over system II and represents an integrative effort at a higher level, and by the consultative relations between some councillors and a large portion of the Eskimo community.

Certain normative statements concerning the functioning of these organizations can be listed:

1) It is assumed that the Eskimos of these two communities cannot create by themselves any supra-group structures or spontaneously establish formal group-headman relations. Thus the catalytic activity of an Euro-Canadian organizer seems necessary. A superior type of organization may succeed better if, during an initial period, it is closely supervised and stimulated by the initiator. Within the established framework he should allow for the formulations of projects by the natives. His role should become increasingly permissive, without completely abandoning control over the functioning of the system. The

nature and the duration of the control exercised by the initiator should depend on the complexity of the system. Complex organizations necessitate a strong leadership and supervision.

2) New structures, representing a superior level of socio-political organization, have better chances of success when created for the achievement of specific tasks and when these tasks are well understood by the natives and concern some vital local problems, perceived as such by the Eskimos. Paramount among these, appear the Eskimo–Euro-Canadian economic relations. Thus the trader seems to be an ideal organization initiator. He is the local link between the Eskimos and the Euro-Canadian economy and the "vertical" integrator of the community. (The initiator should direct his efforts both along the "vertical" and "horizontal" organizational axis as distinguished by Dr. R. L. Warren.)

3) Before establishing the chart of the projected institution, the homogeneity of the traditional groups, the headman-group relations and the recent occupational differentiations should be realistically analyzed and taken into consideration. In localities where a higher level of socio-political integration is necessary, some gradual development of the planned institution may be appropriate. Thus after the natives have been thoroughly familiarized with system II, it is possible to conceive the success-ful creation of a formal grouping of headmen characteristic of system III.

People under Tutelage

JOHN J. AND IRMA HONIGMANN

"Those who come after us will gradually come to do the
work now done by white men – we will be able to do some
because the whites are good teachers. The whites, most of
them, do not get angry with the Eskimos. . . . We Eskimos
want to do the same as the whites so that our children and
children's children may survive."

Anakudluk, *councillor and lay reader*

At almost every turn, the town exacts learning by Eskimos
as the price of surviving in their town roles. The purpose of
this paper is to treat the results and circumstances of tutelage
fostered by town life in Frobisher Bay. . . .[1]

Our account up to this point surely demonstrates that
Eskimos have successfully, often easily, learned much new
behaviour, many tastes, and increasing responsibilities. They
have accepted a plethora of new goods that town life brought
forth. Tutelage is of two kinds. In one the Eskimo, confronting
features of town life that need to be mastered, devises adequate,
hitherto unavailable, responses, perhaps imitating Euro-Canadians' example. Such learning is relatively undirected, unguided,
unstructured, unsupervised, and more subject to trial and error
than the second. In the second, tutors encourage him to respond

SOURCE: John J. and Irma Honigmann, *Eskimo Townsmen* (Ottawa:
        Canadian Research Centre for Anthropology. University of
        Ottawa, 1965), pp. 157-227. Reprinted by permission of the
        authors and publisher.

[1]In 1963 Frobisher Bay contained about 900 Eskimos, who had
come there from various parts of Baffin Island and elsewhere, together with about the same number of non-Eskimos (overwhelmingly Euro-Canadians). The town originated in 1941, in which year
the United States Air Force built an installation near the present
site, but attracted most of its Eskimo population only in the late
1950's, when the DEW line created abundant economic opportunities. Despite its size and heterogeneity it is a remarkably integrated place, and contains, in effect, three sub-communities.
(Editors)

in certain definite ways, advise and teach him, withdraw support if he deviates from what they deem appropriate, and reward him if he attains the goal as they see it. In this important type of learning, the Eskimo assumes new roles while Euro-Canadians observe, correct, reward, and punish. Many people act as tutors including Government officials far off in Ottawa as well as in Frobisher Bay; the clergy in preaching, work with church councils, and counselling; public health nurses; Euro-Canadian on-the-job supervisors, policemen, judges, and, of course, schoolteachers. Sometimes Euro-Canadians move Eskimos physically to promote faster or more intensive change; for example, the church sent a catechist to Cape Dorset for six months to receive ministerial training, a few youths have gone South for vocational training, and some Eskimos live in close proximity to Euro-Canadians at the Air base.

*   *   *

...The town's dual ethnic division, in which Euro-Canadians monopolize power and initiative, affects tutelage. Euro-Canadian-set laws and administrative policies are among the foremost conditions that call forth learning. For example, a series of legal and administrative acts brought alcohol within Eskimos' easy reach, thereby initiating a vast educational situation.[2] A Government-sponsored housing co-op led more than a dozen families to change their style of life, and official sponsorship of a consumer co-op would similarly alter buying habits. Not that Eskimos are wholly passive; we merely emphasize the vital role of laws and policies in guiding Eskimo townsmen. Since Euro-Canadians apportion many desirable rewards of town life, they also possess powerful means of sanctioning learning. An Eskimo who will not acquire correct work habits loses his job; if he doesn't pay his bill, the company disconnects his telephone; not to register a new baby means no family allowances; his child's excessive absence from school cuts off family allowances for that youngster; if he acts boisterously in the tavern the waiter will bounce him, and so on, Euro-Canadians also pose as models; their way of life has been the object to be emulated. Eskimos in varying degree emulate them in school, on the job, in the Community Council, and at play.

*   *   *

For all its broad front, tutelage goes on unevenly, some areas of life being relatively neglected. Experience teaches the Eskimo how to act in court, but nobody instructs him on his legal rights. No sanctions are put on the putative fathers of babies born out of wedlock to make them assume financial responsibility. Although the Rehabilitation Centre tried to teach one unemployed man, not a Rehabilitant, to drive, for formal driving instruction – a valuable town skill – one must go South. Individuals, too, learn at different rates and then go in different directions. Few, if any, women know how to drive or, for that matter, possess the other technical skills of employed men. Young women between sixteen and twenty-five, compared to their male peers, speak English better and more readily, are far more sophisticated in dancing and habits of dress, and show greater ease in meeting whites. When girls of this age group have also had opportunity to live in the South, they emulate flawlessly many tastes of Euro-Canadian girls of the same age.

Youth correlates with the furthest modernization. Schooling helps even young children to outdistance their parents in familiarity with some things in Euro-Canadian culture, including English. Full-time hunters lag behind steadily employed families in modernization. Not unexpectedly, those who have already penetrated quite far into the new culture find it easiest to move further. Familiarity with English, especially, facilitates new learning, particularly of subtle things.

If we speak of Eskimos changing readily and learning eagerly, it is necessary to bear in mind that the town accommodates apathetic individuals, including some too old to care about novelty, as well as ambitious, energetic people, including self-

---

[2]Regrettably, space limitations required the omission of lengthy sections dealing with the authors' interesting account of government-directed resocialization programmes, such as are carried out by the Frobisher Bay Rehabilitation Centre and the local School. In keeping with the authors' theme that living in town is in itself a major educational experience for the Eskimo, we have included only their observations on less directed and structured aspects of community life. These include movie attendance, participation in co-operative commercial ventures, as well as participation in the democratic process at the community and national levels. See authors' article, "Learning to Drink", pp. 197-217 of this volume (Editors)

taught Anglican lay readers, and a forty-eight-year-old woman employed on wages in the Rehabilitation Centre, who complained that the cook wouldn't teach her how to cook professionally, though she wanted badly to learn.

*   *   *

Movies, the major spectator activity for Frobisher Bay Eskimos, undoubtedly exceeds any other mass medium (except possibly school books) as an effective medium of tutelage. In contrast to films, the radio seems practically nil in its educational impact. The significance of motion pictures struck us one evening in an Eskimo home when the owners' seven-year-old granddaughter and her friend each received a glass of fruit juice. Before they drank they clinked glasses, a practice which, they shyly volunteered, they had learned from the screen. Many local movies present the polite society's side of American life but many also present violence, often the violence of bygone, western, frontier life. Eskimos undoubtedly prefer fast action films in which the activity carries the story, obviating reliance on long dialogue scenes such as most people find hard to follow (we did, too, when the sound track or electronic system was defective) (see Table II, page 000). In the I.O.D.E. hall[3] we saw children grow increasingly restless and adults walk out during drawing-room comedy. On the other hand, we have heard people animatedly describe movies packed with excitement and saw the audience remain fixed in the hall till the picture finished. Eskimo projectionists, when they order films from catalogues or borrow them from organizations in town, act on their knowledge of what other Eskimos like. The Rehabilitation Centre ordering films for the Aurora theatre at the Airbase, forbade southern distributors to substitute titles if a requested picture could not be sent. The distributor should rather send the picture next on the schedule, in that way avoiding films that might bore the local public.

TABLE 1: *Types of Films Shown in Aurora Theatre and attendance, April, May, June, 1962**

CATEGORY	NUMBER OF PICTURES IN CATEGORY	PERCENT OF ALL CATEGORIES	AVERAGE DAILY ATTENDANCE	PERCENT OF ADULTS	PERCENT OF CHILDREN
Adventure and westerns	22	59	100	68	32
Music and comedy	8	22	66	68	32
Drama and other	6	16	65	65	35
Science fiction	1	3	138	66	34
Total	37	100	92	67	33

*Taken from tabulations prepared by the Rehabilitation Centre.

A careful investigation of films' tutorial influence remains to be done. We base our generalizations on more or less casual data plus some interviews with a fifteen-year-old English-speaking informant, a school drop-out, who possessed a good knowledge of movie stars. We worked with him to learn what he recalled from films he had recently seen. Here are some of his précis:

> *May 6. The picture last night was about Oklahoma [title, "Oklahoma"]. It was a long time ago when I first heard the music: I was in the hospital here in Apex to have my appendix out and I used to play the records. [What is the picture about?] It is about singers; two men want one girl, and the other man tried to kill the other man with what looks like a telescope. When you press the button, a knife comes out and hurts his fingers. He tried to do that and it didn't happen. They were having a square dance. They were having sales too [i.e., an auction sale]. Two men were trying to get a beautiful basket for a girl. They bid high, up to $50, and the younger man for $53 won the basket. They got married, the older, fatter man burned the hay with those*

---

*The hall was donated to the town by the Imperial Order of the Daughters of the Empire, a national voluntary association. (Editors) *two persons on top. The woman jumped down. The fellow who tried to burn the hay had a knife in his hand. The younger man tried to jump on that man, the man with the knife. He killed himself by accident.*

The boy's age may account for his failure to recognize more of the film's romantic theme. He also ignored or overlooked the status differences between the rivals, one a rancher and the other a farmhand.

May 13. [*Informant much enjoyed the film last night.*] *It was about dinosaurs and cave men. They were under the water frozen solid, and they took them from under the water, two dinosaurs and one cave man. A little boy wasn't afraid of these. He had a friend. They tried to kill that dinosaur with dynamite and gasoline, but they couldn't. The cave man went into the house at night. He didn't know anything [reported with much amusement]. He saw a mirror and thought there was a man inside, and broke it. And a radio! He tried to eat an apple, but it was wooden, and grapes. He went on a bed. The boy came in and thought Miss Betty was there. The cave man ran away when he saw Miss Betty, because he was scared of her painted face. Lightning woke up the frozen beasts. A bulldozer fought the beast and killed it. The cave man died when rocks fell on him. He was trying to save the girl's life when the beast tried to take her.*

May 16. [*The informant described "The Big Land."*] *They had cows and put them on the ranch. They put the cows in cars. When they got to another land, the cows went out. They put them in a ranch. The bad guys scared them away. They killed the watchman and scared the cows. They laid a fire to scare the cows and the cows began to run away. The man tried to get the cows back and the little boy was on the wagon, on the street, and the horse was scared, and the wagon rolled. The cows came closer. The good man goes in front of the cows and saved the boy's life. The good man and two bad men, they drawed after this. The good man, I think, killed them. Those two men killed the good man's partner, so the good man started to be mad. That's why he killed them. [Anything more?] They tried to build a town but the bad man burned it up. [He rated the picture "very good," better than the previous Sunday's film about revived prehistory.]*

The informant's next film happens to be one we, too, had seen. We learned from our interview how many gaps remain in the youth's account.

May 22. [The movie had been "Flight from Zahrein," but the informant had forgotten the title.] They had a truck. They stole it from the hospital and they travel on the land. The army tried to get them, but they can't. They run out of oil [gasoline]. [Then?] They walk to the machines and they get oil from there and food. And they get to another land. In the desert they got to an oasis. Soon as they get there, the airplane come and shoot the truck, and the truck blew up. But the people came out and went to the oasis. And that young boy got shot in the stomach. They get another truck in that island. It had no battery. So they got battery from the other truck. The truck started to move through the desert. Two army trucks were coming and a sandstorm. They were going through the sandstorm. They fight. One army truck blew up and the other one too. Then the sandstorm was over and they found other houses.

We are, of course, not much concerned with whether members of the audience correctly follow the fictional narratives or not. We seek to gauge what they learn from movies. As we said in connection with school (p. 000), what a youngster learns in the movies may well reinforce his learning in school. It may also augment what he learns in town, for example, about the significance of batteries in motor vehicles, the fact that batteries may be transferred from one vehicle into another, and the importance of fuel. We believe that from these films our informant obtained a more concrete meaning of deserts, oases, and sandstorms; the importance of pasturage for cattle, and the meaning of heroism and treachery. Movies allow adults and children to sample more of the world's cultural and geographical variety than they could otherwise experience. Most of the people have by now attended too many movies to see much for the first time, but that doesn't wholly obliterate the educational significance of motion pictures.

Although we emphasize the growth-promoting side of films, people themselves attend for the recreational value. Audiences show little interest in documentary pictures, according to people who have tried to show them, unless they depict Eskimos. A small audiences left in the I.O.D.E. hall one evening paid steadfast attention when some visitors unexpectedly showed a film about Greenland Eskimos, and reacted with still more pleasure when home-movies of Frobisher Bay itself flashed on the screen.

Now we will sketch, or at least mention, other areas where conspicuous tutelage either had occurred prior to our field work, allowing us to see only the end product, or where it currently occurred. As far as possible we hope to avoid repeating things already mentioned earlier about Eskimos learning to dance, dress, use cosmetics, carve and market stone figures, hold jobs, appreciate a clean town, assume leadership, use telephones for local and long distance calls, live in relatively complicated houses, drive cars, freeze game in refrigerators, organize co-operatively, and similar topics. They, however, all represent innovations, sometimes radical ones, in town-dwelling Eskimos' lives.

After only a few days in Frobisher Bay, we confronted our first situation richly informative about learning possibilities for Eskimos, the Arctic Co-operative Conference, which met in the I.O.D.E. hall. At this point we will appraise this assembly not for providing us with information about Eskimo co-operative enterprise, but for what it could teach the Eskimo delegates themselves, and for how it demonstrated D.N.A.[4] officials tutorial role.

The conference gave Eskimos experience with an agenda (conveniently mimeographed in Eskimo syllabics), arranged by date and hour. That the meeting fell behind the agenda may well have taught delegates how hard it is for conferences to discipline themselves. They also learned that an agenda needs to be approved and can be revised before a meeting begins. They agreed to a short set of procedural rules specifying, for example, that no man could talk more than once on an issue (a rule the chairmen ignored). The hall's physical arrangements, with the neatly placed tables forming a rectangle open toward the stage where more tables laid end to end accommodate chairmen, interpreters, secretary, and other speakers, could hardly have struck Frobisher Bay Eskimos as wholly novel. Some of them had been to Community Council meetings or attended sessions of the Community Association's board of directors, where tables also help to organize participants. The flag on the stage cast an air of national significance over the conference. Local delegates came appropriately dressed in business suits with ties; they tended to wear better fitting clothes than Eskimo delegates from elsewhere. . . .

About a month after the co-op conference, we attended an evening meeting that implemented the official support of co-operative endeavour. In his Apex Hill home, the local co-operative officer met with thirteen men who, as he put it, had expressed interest in starting a second housing co-operative society in Apex. We don't know what originally motivated the men. The meeting provided us with an intimate view of the educational role of the regional co-operative officer and of tutelage in action.

After waiting 40 minutes for the interpreter finally to show up as he had promised (he was located and phoned in the pool hall), the co-operative officer announced that Ottawa had approved of as many more three-bedroom co-op houses as the community could afford. Such houses would go only to men with jobs, who alone could pay for them. People assembled at this meeting had shown a desire to own their own homes. Tonight they had come together to form a co-operative. He explained the value of a housing co-operative. First, by working together the men would get cheaper houses than they could otherwise afford. If one person went to buy such a house, it would cost six or seven thousand dollars. Second, a co-operative was advantageous because modern houses were too complex for one man to build alone. Several men working together in a co-op could do the job expeditiously. If people thought it took too long to build the present co-op houses, let them remember

---

[4]Local usage for government official of the Department of Northern Affairs and Natural Resources. (Editors)

that they were the first and the men had made mistakes. In the future it would not take as long. Third, co-ops would help weld into a community people who had come from "all over the place." A co-operative would make them feel that Frobisher Bay is their home. Something they need, better housing, would bring them together. Here, in fact, is the most important reason for a co-op. Fourth, a co-operative resembled the way Eskimos have been living for thousands of years. White men thought of co-ops only a few hundred years ago, but what they have formulated is exactly the same as the Eskimo way of life, and the best way to live.

Less systematically the official argued that a family was economically better off paying for a house than renting it. After he had finished, he invited the men to speak. One Eskimo explained that he hadn't been to many of the group's previous meetings because he had on occasion been ill and sometimes busy. But he has heard that some of the houses will have four bedrooms; he would like such a house. In his reply the co-operative officer adhered to a firm line. It might be too late for four-bedroom houses now. The group had spoken only about three-bedroom buildings. Houses for the Eskimos have been getting a little better every year, from matchboxes to this, and further improvement could be expected. Who knows what ten years would bring? The Eskimos might be living in houses like this, he said, referring to his two-story home. Probably no man in the group found himself puzzled by the idea of an unlimited future marked by constant progress.

Did the assembled company want to form a co-operative to build houses? By consensus the answer seemed to be that they did. The officer explained that joining the co-operative would cost them little; they need only pay fifty cents each for an incorporation fee. Then they could borrow money from the Government and apply for a thousand-dollar Government subsidy on each house. After he moved in, each man would pay $35 monthly to repay his share of the Government loan. As the meeting concluded, the officer gave the men another inspiring message. The Eskimos, he said, for the first time are their own bosses. Too often in the North the white man is the boss and pushes the Eskimos around. But in a co-op like this, the Eskimo is the boss and he can tell the white man what to do. *You* (speaking to the interpreter) know this. You (speaking to the group as a whole) are now in a co-op. These words assured Eskimos of their autonomy, just as the co-operative conference did.

Co-ops are hardly as traditional as the official suggested. If they were, they might require much less encouragement and advice. Through them, as through the Community Council and Community Association, Eskimos have gained experience working together in highly formal groups. Eskimos have learned, at least partially, that in some respects such groups even take priority over individual aspirations and kinship loyalties. In a dramatic instance of organizational thinking, the Sisi Housing Co-operative expelled a defaulting member, though the group contained two of his brothers. The fact that members waited several months before they finally took such action, which the co-operative officer had probably advised, suggests that they found it an unpleasant and difficult thing to do.

*   *   *

Eskimos, belonging to a nation that values the democratic process, have had abundant experience with balloting. They employ the secret ballot in connection with church, to choose representatives for the Community Council, to select persons to direct the Community Association, and to elect officers in the Rehabilitation Centre. Twice they have voted in Federal elections. We observed their participation in the Federal election of April 8, 1963. Both condidates appeared at dances in the I.O.D.E. hall, their local Euro-Canadian managers not only sponsoring the dance but also paying for free doughnuts and coffee. Managers and candidates made political speeches interpreted into Eskimo. In the case of Mrs. L. J. Hardie, the Liberal incumbent, her manager blamed the Progressive-Conservative government for Eskimos losing jobs in Frobisher Bay and for the threat of even greater unemployment following withdrawal of the U.S. Air Force. He accused the party in power of "fighting with the Americans." The Liberals, he said, "gave you" pensions and family allowances and brought the profitable Dew Line to the Arctic. He minimized the number of Eskimo homes that the Progressive-Conservative candidate had visited when he had been to Frobisher Bay (probably more than his candidate had been into). "White people" will vote for Mrs. Hardie, his candidate, he assured his predominantly Eskimo audience, because she knows the Eskimos. She has even travelled by dog team. People there in the hall had seen her dressed in a parka and mukluks. The Eskimos, too, should vote for her.

Eskimo voters, however, preferred her rival, Eugene Rheaume, probably partly because of his manager's much greater personal popularity in town, where he had once worked for D.N.A., and partly because of his more strenuous campaigning. Rheaume's picture on a poster bearing an English and Eskimo legend (the latter in syllabics) peered down from many electric poles and even hung in Eskimo homes. Up to the eve of the election, his manager persistently made home-to-home visits.

Both in 1962 and 1963 the Federal elections brought out a large Eskimo vote, over 80 per cent of the predominantly Eskimo populations of Apex and Ikhaluit. More Eskimos voted in proportion to Euro-Canadians, and their greater strength twice carried Rheaume to local victory. (In 1963 he also carried the rest of his district and won a seat in Parliament.) In heavily or wholly non-Eskimo polling areas of Frobisher Bay . . . Mrs. Hardie either outdistanced her rival or received a much larger proportion of the total vote cast than in the predominantly Eskimo polling areas.

Our information doesn't permit us to conclude that the Eskimos who voted in the 1963 Federal election did so with careful regard to issues and policies. Like many voters in the United States and Canada, they voted for personalities. That Eskimos twice so definitely chose one way rather than another and turned out to vote in such large strength testifies eloquently to the way they have learned to respond to a hitherto unfamiliar experience presented to them in town.

Tutelage is socialization. Eskimos learn either through being confronted with opportunities that challenge them to master new behaviour or through teachers' personal direction and encouragement. Doubtlessly, personal attention proves more effective than unsponsored, trial-and-error learning. Some Eskimos occupy positions more advantageous than others to receive Euro-Canadians' personal attention and help. They are men and women who have impressed a Euro-Canadian with their ability, dependability, ambition, intelligence, or other approved, personal qualities. The white man, moved by his ideal of promoting the Eskimos' progress, responds to the promise held out by those qualities and confers special attention on his protégé, thereby creating a most efficient learning situation.

*   *   *

One still hears judgments deploring the outcome of change. Many non-Eskimos convince themselves that the Eskimo, by having accepted the white man's leadership, adopted roles in Euro-Canadian society, and turned to the aids, amenities, or simple baubles of Kabloona culture, struck a bad if not fatal bargain. Or, more likely, they see the unhappy outcome having come without Eskimo ever having chosen. They then view him as having been victimized by an unsuitable life forced on him by people more powerful than he. Eskimos themselves aren't quite so unrealistic or dogmatic in evaluating what has happened in their culture, though they perceive that with new benefits they have also inherited perplexing choices. Even when, like Symonee of Ikhaluit, they choose by turning their backs on the town, they won't abandon the new culture's conveniences and religious values.

The Educational System
in the Western Arctic

CHARLES S. BRANT AND CHARLES W. HOBART

The educational system in the Western Arctic is characterized by these features: continuous use of non-native teachers, in the past dominantly clergy, changing to lay teachers today; throughout its history, instruction given wholly in English; establishment and heavy utilization, from the beginnings, of residential schools, with latter-day emphasis upon large units; curriculum almost entirely oriented to the southern Canadian culture and value system; and minimal attempts to produce text materials appropriate to the Arctic.

The history of Eskimo education in Canada has throughout involved confrontation of generations of pupils by wholly non-native teachers. The earliest schools in the western Canadian Arctic were established by the Oblate Fathers at Fort Providence in 1867, by Anglican missionaries at Hay River in 1918 and at the mouth of the Mackenzie Delta in 1929, later by both groups at Aklavik on the Mackenzie River. The white teachers who staffed these schools maintained, to quote Diamond Jenness, "religious kindergartens that hardly deserve the name of schools," and provided an education that "taught nothing and explained nothing."[1] Some had little appreciation of Eskimo psychology and discipline was frequently maintained by the liberal use of corporal punishment. The traumatic effects of this were yet evident in the way our adult informants recalled their school experiences, thirty and more years later, when we interviewed them.

The last decade and a half has seen the retrieval of educational responsibility by government from the missions and a vast increase in school facilities and in percentage of school-age

SOURCE: "Eskimo Education, Danish and Canadian: A Comparison," *The Canadian Review of Sociology and Anthropology*, vol. 2 (May, 1966), pp. 47-66. Reprinted by permission of the authors and publishers. Title supplied by the editors.

children in attendance. But the "new look" in Eskimo education is in major respects only an ungraded and extended replication of the mission program, with religious aspects suitably played down.

We will comment especially on (1) exclusive use of Southern Canadian teachers, (2) English language instruction, (3) Southern Canadian curriculum materials, and (4) use of very large boarding schools. All of these features were characteristic of the mission organized schools: their perpetuation under the federally administered educational system justifies the designation of this as an upgraded mission-type educational program.

(1) Both the mission and the federal schools have made exclusive use of Southern Canadian trained teachers, who in virtually all cases have been whites. Under the federal program there has been an upgrading of these teachers in terms of their formal qualifications. However, it can be argued that the net effect of this changeover has been negative as far as education is concerned. The mission teachers, although formally less well qualified, were characterized by a missionary commitment, which meant that their period of Arctic teaching tended to be relatively lengthy. As a result they came to know the Eskimo children quite well, far more frequently than do lay teachers today. Thus, despite the criticism of them made earlier, they more often came to discover which motivational and teaching procedures were most effective with Eskimo children. By contrast, the federally employed teachers sign a two-year contract to teach in the North, and they may resign after one year if they are willing to pay their return fare to their southern Canadian homes. The rate of contract renewal is so low that the teacher turnover rate is about 30 per cent annually; a teacher who has more than two years of Arctic teaching experience is considered

---

*The authors devote a substantial part of their paper to an account of the educational system in Greenland, their purpose being to compare the Canadian Arctic educational system with it. Unfortunately, limitations of space and a stress on Canadian Arctic content led us to exclude that portion having to do with Greenland. (Editors)

[1]Diamond Jenness, *Eskimo Administration: Canada* (Montreal: Arctic Institute of North America, Technical Paper 14, 1964), pp. 47, 48.

a veteran. The result is that a sizeable proportion of Eskimo children are taught by "green" teachers, and this seriously affects the educational process.

It takes the average teacher from the South, suffering from culture shock, isolation in an unusual environment, and the handicap of over-training in the culture-bound precepts of professional pedagogy, at least one year to discern the particular problems in teaching his shy and unsophisticated Eskimo pupils and to devise ways of coping with them. The arrangements of teachers' housing and provisioning characteristically tend to seal them off socially from the native communities. In Inuvik they live in the "serviced" white area of town, and teachers all over the Arctic annually receive a large shipment of provisions from southern Canada to last them all year. Thus they are independent of the people and the land as far as food is concerned. Their life outside the classrooms is overwhelmingly that of participation with other resident whites – fellow teachers, Hudson's Bay Company and Department of Northern Affairs personnel, policemen – in a caste-like situation.

A variety of consequences of this teacher-staffing situation were encountered during the field work. In one remote community Eskimo informants were plainly still shocked, two years after the original events, at the fact that a teacher had frequently shouted or screamed at the children. In some communities, despite the esteem in which education was held, the rapport between teachers and pupils, and between teachers and families, had so broken down that families made little effort to get their children to school, and teachers complained of the regularity with which they had to go out and "round up the children."

(2) The exclusive use of English as the language of instruction among children understanding little or none of this language, by teachers knowing nothing of Eskimo language – who thus cannot explain any difficult English concepts, or grammatical usages in Eskimo – creates a number of difficulties. The first year or two of classes must, of course, be given over almost entirely to the teaching of English, with the result that two years of grade retardation is usual. The retardation is aggravated by the fact that many of the children are over-age when they enter school, miss a year during the course of their

schooling, or both. It was precisely to minimize an unnecessary increase in this kind of retardation that the Special Navajo Education Program, devised in the United States, made provision for teaching a number of subjects in the Navajo language. This was done in order to avoid tying educational advancement in all spheres to mastery of English, and also to provide children in new and strange educational situations with the emotional support of some "official" use of their native tongue.

Not only is instruction exclusively in English, but the tendency of children to use Eskimo among themselves is so effectively discouraged that it is virtually never heard among children on boarding school premises. For boarding school children two negative consequences of this situation deserve mention. The first is that during the summer vacation periods at home the child's communication with parents and kinsmen is hampered by a growing value and attitude gap resulting from his tendency to view everything Eskimo, language included, as being of little worth, since it is not worth recognition in the school curriculum. The second is that the exclusively English nature of the school situation and the almost exclusively Eskimo nature of the home situation tends to increase the child's problems of integrating these overwhelmingly dissimilar facets of his life, and to give to the school an air of unreality and irrelevance to life as he and his family experience it. The school situation appears to be a kind of unique "game" to the child, which he learns to play when he is in the appropriate situation, but does not play elsewhere. As a result there is little carry-over from the school to the home situation. For example, when children past grade three are instructed in school to draw a house, they portray a two-storey house, surrounded by trees, with a flagstone walk leading up to the door: in short, a "schoolbook" house which they have never directly seen and which is unrelated to the houses they know.

(3) All of the text materials used by Eskimo children in the Western Canadian Arctic were devised for southern Canadian children. The only progress which has been made toward the production of Arctic-related material consists of two experimental Curriculum Guides, one a Social Studies Program, and the other a Language Arts Program, produced in the Mackenzie

District. For neither is there specially prepared accompanying text-book material. The most obvious consequence of the use of southern Canadian material is that many of the objects and concepts with which southern children are familiar, such as fences and farm life and city life, are completely strange to the Eskimo child. Teachers who were interviewed frequently complained of the problem they encountered in trying to explain these irrelevancies to their classes. Thus valuable time is wasted in trying to explain things to the Eskimo child which are useless for him to know. The fact that much of the content is meaningless to him increases the irrelevance and the "never-never-land" game aspect of the education process for the child. Furthermore, since education as such is seen as important, and since the distinctive aspects of Eskimo life and culture are completely ignored, the only possible conclusion must be that there is nothing in native lore or tradition which is worth learning. Thus this curriculum tends to be destructive of respect for Eskimo values and for father, mother, and others highly able in native skills but not formally educated. Moreover, when the child is removed from home, from the age of six or seven to fifteen years, for education in a hostel school where none of the native skills are taught, it is clear that the consequence of this education is to render him unable to return to his home community, since he has not had the opportunity to learn the values and the skills which are prerequisite to living there.

(4) Some idea of the emphasis upon residential schools in the Mackenzie District of the Canadian Arctic is provided by figures for the 1963-64 school year. There were then 818 Eskimo children between ages six and eighteen attending schools operated by the government in the area between Pelly Bay and the Alaskan border. Three hundred and fifty-three, or 43 per cent, attended residential schools, and three hundred of the three hundred and fifty-three were in one large institution, the Sir Alexander Mackenzie School, at Inuvik.

The large present-day residential school, in material terms, presents an enormous contrast to those of the past. In construction, equipment, furnishings and comfort, it ranks with the best schools of southern Canada. In the Inuvik school, Eskimo children experience a standard of living superior in every respect to that in their home settings.

The social and cultural environment of the large residential school is something else, however. From the age of six, children are annually air-lifted from the little communities along the Arctic coast, with their warm, kinship-based, inter-personal environments, to the large efficiency-oriented, under-staffed, strange, impersonal surroundings of the residential school hostels.

The large turnout at departure time in late summer is not to be explained by any wholesale or unqualified enthusiasm on the part of the parents for sending children away. In most settlements the choice is between residential school education and none at all, and Canadian Northern Service Officers have done a persuasive job of selling the importance of education. Teachers reported that there was relatively little crying and complaining by pupils in their presence, but this should not be taken at face value. Parents commonly reported that in accord with Eskimo tradition, they counselled their children to contain their emotions lest they make the white people at school feel unhappy. Most of the school personnel mistake the rather mask-like smiling faces surrounding them as evidence of good adjustment on the part of the children of a supposedly innately cheerful and happy people. Most of the children do appear to cope with the separation experience very well, probably because their early childhood training is nearly ideal, and thus they do not react neurotically to the separation. But significant symptoms of trauma of separation from family and familiar surroundings, such as bed-wetting, nightmares, and quiet crying in bed, are not uncommon. Many of these go unremarked by the overloaded staff; others are explained away in folk-common-sense terms. The emotional deprivation which is suffered by the Eskimo mothers of young children, out in the settlements, is entirely beyond the field of perception of the school personnel.

The modern residential facilities of the boarding school provide the Eskimo child with an experience of physical comfort and convenience which is commonly dysfunctional for the intercession periods and the post-school life of the pupil back in his home community. The demands of the school for participation in the tasks of maintenance are minimal and light. Everything is provided and life is rather effortless: plentiful and well-prepared food is automatically ready at mealtimes; hot water is at hand at the turning of a faucet; clean clothes return from the laundry at regular intervals; clean warm bedding is provided; and the interior environment is always at a constant warm temperature comfortable to whites. For the Eskimo child, accustomed from an early age to taking part in the constant, arduous tasks of household maintenance, and hardened to the rigours of the Arctic climate, residential school life is experienced as a very "soft" life indeed. And, as might be expected, he tends to develop a marked distaste for conditions at home after experiencing the sharp contrast between the two environments.

What are the consequences of this residential schooling experience for Eskimo children? Particularly among the less acculturated Eskimo children from communities such as Gjoa Haven, Spence Bay, Coppermine, Holman Island in the central Arctic, and the bush areas of the Delta, our interviews show that a coherent pattern of problem behaviour emerges in children as a result of experience in residential schools. It is the picture of an unhappy, dissatisfied, unadjusted child – almost always described by the word "cranky" by informants who could speak any English. In contrast to the obedience, respectfulness and helpfulness typical of Eskimo children in "unspoiled" communities, such children were disobedient, complaining, disrespectful, and reluctant to undertake chores spontaneously or at the indirect hinting of parents in the way which is traditional among Eskimos. They were unable to amuse themselves in a self-contained manner or be contented.

Especially marked was the children's loss of respect for parents, which has several sources. For one thing, they discover that there are many good things in life which are apparently taken for granted in the white world. They come to appreciate some of these luxuries while at school, and to disdain parents who may never have heard of them and in any case cannot provide them. This loss is also rooted in the school curriculum, which is almost exclusively oriented to the white man's culture, with no distinctly Eskimo content at all, as noted earlier.

Other behavioural consequences of schooling include jealousy and fighting. The returned child, deprived at the age of six or seven of his mother's love and care for ten months of the year, becomes greedily demanding of it and resentful of another child's becoming the object of her attention. The traditional Eskimo internalized controls on aggressive behaviour tend to break down in the competition-oriented school subculture, and this is aggravated by the experience of frustrating physical privations to which children are suddenly returned at home. Other consequences mentioned by Eskimo parents are lying, stealing, and sneaky behaviour, all of them offenses against traditional Eskimo morality and virtually unheard of in the more remote settlements.

To be sure, Eskimo children learn much of the material they are taught in the schools, and even if there is no one else in camp to whom the child might speak English except himself – and such an instance was observed of a child carrying on an English conversation with himself – his abilities are prized by his parents. Should a white man turn up in the community, he will be quickly and proudly summoned to act as interpreter. But it can well be asked: To what extent do children generalize what they learn? Girls do well in Home Economics at the expensively and modernly equipped vocational school at Yellowknife. Put such a girl into a job such as housekeeper at a nursing station and she will apply her skills excellently, preparing fine meals for the patients and keeping a spotless kitchen. But look inside her home and you will get the impression she learned nothing at school. Such a two-response or "two-game" pattern is what one would expect of the children in these circumstances. Writing of the *day* school at Baker Lake in the Eastern Arctic, Vallee notes: "For the most part, the day school is a purely Canadian agency, an envelope of Kabloona society and culture in which the child is sealed off from the traditional Eskimo milieu. If the child were put on board a rocket each morning, then whisked within minutes to some school in the South, then whisked back to Baker Lake again in the afternoon, the contrast between his school milieu and that of his home would not be much greater than it is at present."[2] This separation between education and environment is even more sharp where the child's living arrangements during the period of the school year are purely Canadian. Thus residential school children experience completely different worlds in their home communities and in the residential school. About the only tie between the two is an airplane ride. In the two worlds, they speak different languages, wear different clothes, eat different foods, live in different facilities, have different associates, follow different schedules, experience different disciplines, enjoy different recreations. The parents of children from outlying regions know nothing of the children's life in the school, and the school personnel know almost nothing of life in the camps from which the children come.

Obviously, much of contemporary Eskimo education in the Western Canadian Arctic is inappropriate, and perhaps even dis-educative from the standpoint of preparation for the life children will lead as adults. But educational and other officials are often quite candid in stating one of their goals to be the weaning of children away from traditional Eskimo community and culture. They justify this in terms of the high rate of Eskimo population growth and the increasing availability of more advanced types of employment in Arctic industrial centres for well-trained, sophisticated Eskimos – employment which will enable them to live richer, more interesting lives.

In response to this position, several replies may be made. First, the assumption of great increase in advanced types of employment is open to serious question, indeed has been questioned by experts in economic development and even by the Deputy Minister of Northern Affairs in a 1961 publication. The second would challenge the right of planners to decide what kind of communities and cultures should survive and what kind should become extinct. Articulate Eskimos in Alaska have expressed themselves rather eloquently on this point. The third is that there is evidence that often it does not work. Where the effort is one of cultural replacement there is always the possibility that the product may "fall between two stools," may be unfitted to return to the traditional life of his father, having experienced a softer, "better" way, but may not acquire the motivations and internalized disciplines which are presumed in contemporary wage employment. Most Arctic settlements have examples of this wastage, drifters who are unable to adapt to the loneliness or the employment conditions of the town, but who despise traditional employments, and live parasitically off the sharing patterns of the community. Claremont has documented the widespread existence of this pattern among young Eskimos aged twenty to thirty-five in the Mackenzie Delta, most of whom were products of church residential schools.

We do not wish to imply that the education of Eskimos should be primarily oriented to fitting them to continue living the current pattern of life of the settlements from which they come: clearly the rapidly increasing size of the Eskimo populace and the speed of change of life in these communities as well as the broadening range of opportunities in the world today make that both impossible and undesirable. However, we do maintain that the regimen and the diet in the hostel, and the curriculum in the school, which are oriented only toward the southern Canadian way of life, are equally unrealistic, and often tragic in their consequences. The ideal would be an educational program similar to that in Greenland, which would keep open two possibilities – fitness for training for southern-type wage or salary employment, and for returning to the life of hunting and trapping on the land – just as long as possible. We advocate this for two reasons. The first is that there are some who will never acquire the skills and the motivations to make a very successful adjustment to wage employment. If they are able to return to life in the settlements their lives will be happier, more productive, and more law-abiding than if they are condemned to a "hanger-on" way of life around some community like Inuvik, Aklavik, or Cambridge Bay. The second is that if young people are not early alienated from either way of life, their chances will be maximized for integrating both ways to some extent within their own personalities. Only thus can they avoid the confusion of identity, and the covert but endless seeking for home that is characteristic of those taken too early from home and weaned

²Frank G. Vallee, *Kabloona and Eskimo in the Central Keewatin* (Ottawa: Department of Northern Affairs and Natural Resources, Northern Co-ordination and Research Centre, 1962), p. 162.

to a boarding school way of life lacking the warmth and the relationship satisfactions which only home can provide.

At the outset, we suggested that the contrasting conceptual models of cultural continuity and cultural replacement, as defined, were applicable to the Danish and Canadian systems of Eskimo education, respectively, when they are viewed in long-term historical perspective. The purport of our data and interpretations for both systems have been that, while the direction of change has been towards cultural synthesis, the magnitude of such change has been very great in the Danish case and very slight in the Canadian one. The transition to a synthetic system in Greenland, greatly accelerated in the past decade, has not occurred without seriously disruptive effects, some of which might have been avoided or minimized by different policy decisions. Such decisions might have been indicated by a more carefully considerad forecast of probable effects of alternatives.

However, it is evident that the administration in Greenland is non-ethnocentric, planning-minded, and self-critical; moreover, that it has seriously encouraged and utilized social research as an aid in the formulation and periodic modification of policies and programmes. In Canada, while there are occasional signs of development of such orientations in northern education and administration, the emergence of a policy of cultural synthesis, as we have defined the concept, seems very problematic. The main thrust of the programme remains directed towards cultural replacement.

Learning to Drink

JOHN J. AND IRMA HONIGMANN

So far we have spoken about tutelage as it occurs in organized groups, guided by teachers of one kind or another. However, we began . . . [by] saying that practically every situation in [Frobisher Bay], particularly those departing from precedent and tradition, encourages Eskimos to learn appropriate behaviour. We now propose to analyze other, conspicuous topics and contexts that have called forth learning, . . . [particularly the use of] alcohol. It is certainly true that we did not observe learning to drink as an on-going process, for Eskimos had adopted styles of drinking before we arrived in Frobisher Bay. We studied the point that Eskimos in 1963 had reached in learning to use (or avoid) alcohol and also reconstructed how drinking habits changed following the legal introduction of alcoholic beverages to these people in 1960.

Prior to January 19, 1960, Frobisher Bay Eskimos saw or heard of their Euro-Canadian military and civilian neighbours using alcohol, but only illegally could they themselves possess or consume it. Then practically overnight, in consequence of a far-reaching court decision that freed all Canadian Eskimos from discriminatory injunctions concerning drinking, they acquired precisely the same privileges as the white man. They can go to the counter of the Territorial Liquor Store on any of several afternoons and evenings weekly, show their permit, and order wine, rum, whiskey, gin, or beer (including ale) for delivery three weeks later, paying with their order. Almost any evening they can sit down in the Rustic Room, a tavern in the East Coast Lodge hotel, and drink beer or hard liquor, hoping that the waiter won't take it into his head to detect drunkenness and refuse to serve them before they are ready to leave.

SOURCE: John J. and Irma Honigmann, *Eskimo Townsmen* (Ottawa: Canadian Research Centre for Anthropology, University of Ottawa, 1965), pp. 196-215. Reprinted by permission of the authors and publisher.

We are bound to rely mostly on hearsay and police records for what happened when alcohol at not too steep prices became legally available to Eskimos in Frobisher Bay. Eskimo and Euro-Canadian spokesmen both agree that a number of Eskimos, both men and women, embraced the new opportunity with the same alacrity and enthusiasm they have shown for other promising, new experiences. They purchased mostly beer and apparently drank it without full awareness of its consequences, lacking a tested pattern of drinking that would have regulated the speed and amount consumed at any one time. We did not try to secure figures for 1960 but in 1962, drinkers in a population of approximately 380 adults consumed 6,588, 5,520, 3,516, and 4,200 cans of beer from the liquor store alone, in May, June, July, and August respectively, plus sixty-five ounces of spirits in May and twenty-five ounces each in July and August. Then, in September, 1962, the three-week waiting period already in force for spirits came into effect for beer as well. In that month beer taken from the store fell to 540 cans but liquor remained the same, twenty-five ounces. In the following three months Eskimos consumed only 864, 1,188, and 1,140 cans bought at the store; spirits rose to 245, 750, and 565 ounces. . . . As might be expected, drinking between January, 1960 and September, 1962 fostered heavy public drunkenness and allegedly contributed to considerable fighting and many other offences. Police estimated that 90 per cent of all offences heard in court in some way involved the excessive use of alcohol, mostly by Eskimos. Most arrests, in fact, represent offences against the Liquor Ordinance. Between 1959 and 1960, total convictions (Eskimo and non-Eskimo) jumped from 53 to 155, and in 1961 reached 190; a very large proportion of persons arrested must have been Eskimos.

This historical review, we know, sounds wholly negative and reconstructs the Eskimos' experience with legal drinking in terms of community problems. Our sources leave us no alternative but to take this stance; that is how the vocal part of Frobisher Bay today views the beginning of legal drinking. In similar terms these people evaluate contemporary drinking.

The town took various measures to curb excessive drinking. Police vigilance, fines, and jail sentences constituted pressure to control alcoholic indulgence. A social worker, however, reports that the Eskimos failed to learn from punitive measures. When he tried case work with people who drank heavily, he found it to be effective only for short periods of time. Also each Saturday afternoon a small number of men who drank heavily attended group meetings at which, sometimes, a doctor spoke on drinking or the men played cards and checkers. However, the welfare officer questions the effectiveness of those meetings. Townspeople also received literature written in Eskimo describing difficulties that could arise from excessive use of alcohol and explaining the relationship between drinking and offences committed against the law. Sometime before March, 1962 the superintendent of the Rehabilitation Centre helped produce six radio plays in Eskimo, many of which dealt with drinking and its connection with violence and other social problems. [The local] radio station CFFB aired the tape-recorded plays, Euro-Canadians receiving copies of the scripts translated into English. The plays presented drinking with an unequivocally moral tone, giving drinkers and the tavern a disreputable air. We will refer to these plays again when we describe the ideology that surrounds drinking today. Efforts like these to combat the Eskimos' enthusiastic response to alcohol proved discouraging, but two measures administratively introduced in September, 1962 proved more effective. The tavern could no longer sell beer to be taken off the premises, and at the liquor store customers had to wait three weeks before they could pick up their paid-for beer or any other alcoholic commodity. Although unpopular with some local Euro-Canadians, who recently circulated a petition to repeal the waiting period on beer, these measures have greatly pleased officials and police with the way they slowed down Eskimo drinking. Reportedly public drunkenness declined. Offences against the Liquor Ordinance, which totalled ninety-six from December, 1961 to August, 1962 dropped to forty-two between December, 1962 and August, 1963. Criminal offences also fell, from twenty-six in the first period to eleven in the second period. Police and others connect these drops to the decline in excessive drinking. We saw drunks abroad relatively rarely, so that the few intoxicated men who came late to the Saturday night dance (after an evening at the tavern) proved noteworthy. Yet Euro-

Canadians remain vigilant and keenly attentive for behaviour
. . . [which] in a white context might go unnoticed. Their
apprehension was keynoted by a D.N.A.[1] officer who, speaking
of the twice-weekly dances at which police showed up regularly,
said, "We are always alert for signs of drinking." The image of
Frobisher Bay's disorganization, painted for us before we ever
reached Baffin Island, stems from such traumatized attitudes
held by Euro-Canadians.

Undoubtedly Eskimos have altered their use of alcohol,
partly as a result of an administrative act, partly through their
decision not to take advantage of the extended waiting period.
We will now describe the current style of Eskimo drinking,
pointing out the cultural circumstances and attitudes that have
formed and maintained it.

Our thesis holds that drinking – the apparently simple
custom of downing alcoholic beverages – ties in with many other
parts of a way of life. Drinking constitutes part of a cultural
configuration, and assumes the form it does under the influence
of other elements in that configuration. A people's culture at
many points guides, controls, and gives meaning to drinking.
The dynamics that determine a given style of drinking, therefore,
reside in the total web of the activity itself, with the result that
eradicating a given form of drinking requires a revolutionary
readjustment of a way of life. . . .

. . . Tutelage with respect to drinking proceeds in the orbit
of Euro-Canadian control. Eskimos concerned about drinking
hold the Euro-Canadian responsible for what they deem to be
troubles promoted by alcohol. They expect him to use his power
and responsibility more than he has in fact done, in order to
correct conditions. They don't know that the decision making
alcohol legal for Eskimos sprang from a long-standing dilemma
in western society between salvationist and libertarian values. . . .

Unlike Kwakiutl Indians, Eskimos don't drink to assert
equality with whites nor do they flaunt scoff-law drinking at
them. Eskimos as a group don't have a seriously antagonistic or
competitive relationship with Euro-Canadians that would give
such drinking point, nor are they hostile toward the police (as in
the Mackenzie Valley), though such attitudes may be forming
in young men just quitting their teen-age years.

Alcohol compares with other sources of happiness that Eskimos can tap in Frobisher Bay. Their attitude toward it partakes of the same optimistic appreciation for town life that the people reserve for warm houses, movies, bingo games, the security of Rehab, and the white man's food, especially candy and soda. To be sure, regular drinking is less prevalent than indulgence in many of those other gratifiers. Eskimo informants put the matter similarly. People drink because it makes them feel good, or to become happy. Some drinkers, though, are spoken of as "never happy when drunk" since they grow angry and violent. We conclude that Eskimos drink to realize the effect of alcohol, to promote an optimal degree of intoxication, which instigates good feeling, relaxation, and a sense of gaiety. Behaviour of men drinking in the tavern confirms this use of alcohol. Some women also drink for the psychological reward that optimal intoxication fosters, but others come to the tavern simply to be with, and perhaps keep watch over, their husbands. We might at this point add that our data on Eskimo drinking seen in the light of drinking in other cultures, don't confirm theories entertained by knowledgeable D.N.A. officials about why Eskimos drink excessively. Two views frequently reiterated ascribe Eskimo drinking to boredom and to pressures imposed by town life and culture change with which people can't cope adequately and from which they seek escape. We see the Eskimos as far from bored in town. We do not believe that drinking is in general deficiency motivated, though we can see ground for this hypothesis when it is applied to a few chronic drinkers. . . . Officials also view Eskimo drinking as "impulsive," but that word describes rather than explains, though it well explains why store purchases of beer declined following the three-week rule.

While Eskimos drink for happiness, they ambivalently also conceive of alcohol as bad and drunkenness as dangerous. They share the North American's traumatized, puritanical attitudes toward alcohol, attitudes that picture drinking as noteworthy or special behaviour, not so much because of its capacity to dissolve inhibitions and promote gaiety but because it is fraught with

---

[1]Local usage for government official of the Department of Northern Affairs and Natural Resources. (Editors)

menace and connotes depravity. Extremists, of course, hold that any amount of drinking is sinful – and we met such people in Frobisher Bay – Euro-Canadians and Eskimos. More moderate people warn about the danger of alcohol to children, to drivers, and for addiction; they fear lest it unloose illicit sexual and aggressive impulses. In some degree, every moderate social drinker probably carries these attitudes. Presumably, they enable a moderate drinker to regulate the amount he takes at any one time.

We first noticed the Eskimo's traumatized attitudes to alcohol at the preliminary hearing conducted in March for an accused murderer. The defence apparently wished to elicit testimony from Eskimo witnesses that would establish the extenuating fact of the man's drunkenness at the time he committed his crime. Witnesses admitted seeing him at the tavern, but avoided saying outright that he had been intoxicated, as if that judgment would have offended or slandered him. At other hearings before the justice of the peace we also heard defendants minimize the amounts they guessed they had drunk. Eskimo supervisors gave unhesitating, direct evidence of their opinion that drinking is unwholesome. They unfavourably appraised workers and rehabilitants who drank regularly. They claimed that drinking undermined good work habits. An intelligent Eskimo informant blamed the deaths of a man and his wife within the year on the lethal effects of too heavy a use of alcohol. In the tavern one night a man reported that a friend, a professional hunter, had warned him that after ten years or so of heavy drinking his hands would become too shaky to hold a gun steady and so he would have to cease hunting. One night in the tavern, Eskimos relaxed by considerable beer described somebody as "a very good man," one reason being that he never drank. A stereotype in Eskimo ideology connects drinking with violent aggression, an attitude that heavily colours alcohol. At a meeting of the Community Council in June, 1962, Simonie [a young local Eskimo] described excessive Eskimo drinking as the worst problem confronting Frobisher Bay. Others confirmed his view that before the white man came bringing alcohol, people had been happy and gotten along with each other, but since then they have quarrelled with each other as they never did before.

(Incidentally, Simonie drinks socially. At his 1962 Christmas party, to which he invited many kinsmen and of which we saw movies, he served champagne.) It is unlikely that the unfavourable view of drinking grew up only since the Eskimos assembled in Frobisher Bay. More likely, attitudes based on contemporary experiences integrate with teachings disseminated on Baffin Island much earlier by Protestant missionaries.

Some of the radio dramas in Eskimo, prepared with the assistance of the superintendent of the Rehabilitation Centre and enacted by Eskimo men and women over radio station CFFB, reinforced the sentiment that drinking is dangerous and depraved. In the series' opening play, Teekerk, one of the two main characters who appears in all six dramas, after securing his wife Oomut's family allowance money, goes to the tavern with his friend Kudloo. There they begin to quarrel drunkenly and are thrown out. Returning home, Teekerk finds Ittikak visiting with Oomut. Teekerk accuses them of intimacy, to which his wife responds, "You are always accusing me of things. I never bother with other men. You are the one who runs after all the women when you are drunk." Then, angered by the baby's wailing, Teekerk beats the child. Reproved by Ittikak and Oomut, he whips out a knife and threatens to kill both, but Ittikak holds him fast until a policeman, summoned by Oomut, arrives. The second drama opens with Teekerk in court, charged with assault. (Actually it opens with the announcer saying: "Last week you heard how Teekerk got drunk and was put in jail.") Unlike defendants whom we heard in court, Teekerk is eager to speak in his own behalf. He tells the judge that "before the white man came we were happy. We didn't get drunk. It is not our fault. We don't understand the white man's ways. We are Eskimos, liquor is not a thing of the Eskimos but a thing of the white man." Teekerk is interdicted, legally deprived of exercising his right to drink. In the fifth play a policeman, whom Teekerk and Kudloo guide over the country by dog team, in turn guides Teekerk through the rationale of liquor legislation. The white man has brought many new things to the Eskimo people, including cars, movies, stoves, liquor, and rifles. "Many of these things are not completely understood by the Eskimos. In order that these things help the people rather than hurt them, there are many things which one must learn to do, and many things that people must not do when using these things. It is the policeman's job to see that the rules for using these things are kept." This incident symbolizes a premise of the Euro-Canadian philosophy with respect to tutelage: the white man's responsibility of guidance. As one official put it, when a white man comes into the country and wants to live on the land, he depends on the Eskimo to show him how to survive effectively. Here in Frobisher Bay, the Eskimos are in a strange situation. They might get hurt without guidance, so it is the white man's duty to teach them to adapt effectively in the town. Kudloo asks, "What about if somebody drinks so much that he didn't know what he was doing and tried to hurt somebody else. If he was really drunk he could try to kill somebody else." The policeman seizes the opportunity to point out "that is why there are laws about liquor." For that very reason the judge interdicted Teekerk. The policeman tells Teekerk and Kudloo that Eskimos received the legal right to drink after they asked for the right. The last assertion at least corresponds to local opinion. One informant told us that people spoke of a prominent local Eskimo who had gone to Ottawa to press for the equal right of Canadian Eskimos to drink. The man referred to also described himself as being a spokesman for his people, who wanted the right to drink. Now, our informant continued, some persons blame that spokesman for what has happened to Eskimos in Frobisher Bay.

Unfavourable attitudes toward alcohol, reinforced by fear of arrest and by the undisguised reproaches with which some Euro-Canadians greet Eskimos who drink too much, help Eskimos to regulate their own drinking. A frequent drinker, who is also a member of the Community Council, told us that he drinks only until he is a little happy, but doesn't go beyond that. Then he goes home. He added that drinking beyond a safety point results in violence. A Western Arctic Eskimo said he directly encourages more men to adopt such self-regulation. People in Frobisher Bay, he explained, haven't had a chance to observe the style of drinking that goes on "at the Lord Elgin" (a popular hotel in Ottawa) but only the kind that construction workers do. Still, he thought, conditions in Frobisher Bay were hardly as "rough" as those in the Western Arctic.

Even moderate drinkers risk arrest for public drunkenness. To avoid that danger, men who drink to intoxication rely on the taxi to carry them safely to their door.

As part of Eskimos' more general readiness to allocate responsibility to Euro-Canadians, most Eskimos quite willingly allow Euro-Canadian to regulate their drinking. They accept the waiter's refusal to serve them with more beer once they are already intoxicated. No Eskimo openly disapproved of the three-week waiting period for beer, and some drinkers approved it. An Eskimo explained that the three-week period didn't matter very much. When a man wants to drink he goes to the tavern where he can't drink too much because the waiters control what he gets. (The same night, after coming home drunk, he got into a fight with neighbours and police had to be called.) A few persons have even asked the welfare officer to inform the tavern owner not to serve them when they went there. One Eskimo employee allows his white supervisor to give him a note to the innkeeper on nights when he need not go on duty. There are also Eskimos who voluntarily appealed to the court for interdiction.

We doubt that Eskimos fully understand addiction, yet we heard of drinkers who realize drinking is bad for them and want to quit but "can't." Our observations suggest that perhaps two or three men verge on alcoholism, in that they drink heavily several times weekly. No Eskimo we know is a compulsive, daily drinker.

Eskimo drinkers secure practically all their alcoholic beverages from two local outlets, the territorially-owned liquor store – from which no beverage moves except to a permit holder – and the Government-licensed tavern. In addition a few Eskimos occasionally drink while they eat in the restaurant that opens off the tavern, and drink in the Canadian Legion hall at the Airbase. Since the Legion hall serves primarily members, ideally nobody but a quota of invited guests whom Legionnaires sign in are allowed to enjoy the hall's relatively low prices. During our stay, loose observance of this rule annoyed the police and brought about tighter regulation of the hall by the liquor inspector. Very low prices prevailing in the United States Air Force clubs didn't benefit any Eskimo, for they weren't at all admitted to the Air Force's social rooms.

Despite organized opposition to opening a retail liquor outlet by a pressure group, in which Eskimos like Simonee of Ikhaluit aligned themselves with a few Euro-Canadians, the Territorial Liquor Store began business in September, 1961. For a year it made only beer available for immediate delivery; then, in September, 1962, beer joined wine and spirits under a rule that permitted delivery of any alcoholic beverage only three weeks after the order had been placed and paid for. Extending the waiting period to beer unquestionably reduced Eskimo patronage. We have comparable data on the number of Eskimo permit holders (all male) in the four months from April (when new annual permits become mandatory) to July 31, 1962 – before the waiting period had been extended – and from April to July 25, 1963, after the waiting period. In the former four months, seventy-eight Eskimos received permits from the liquor store; in the second, only thirty-two. Apparently most permits are applied for close to the beginning of the permit year, that is, soon after April 1. We conclude this from the fact that between August 1, 1962 and March 31, 1963 only nine new permit holders joined the seventy-eight who had received theirs between April and July, 1962. Presumably an equally small proportion of permit holders will be added to the thirty-two who got theirs prior to July 25, 1963, indicating a drop in store patronage by Eskimos. Only four rehabilitants held permits in 1962-63 and only one had gotten his by July 25, 1963. Eighty-seven permit holders in a total population of 209 men over twenty-one (most of whom are eligible for a permit, not having been interdicted), indicates that just a bit more than one-third of the eligible men intended to deal with the liquor store before the waiting period covered beer sales.

Most permit holders actively use their permission. Seventy-two out of eighty-seven used their permits in 1962-63 and all thirty-two who had received theirs by July 25, 1963 had done so by that date. Especially do they use permits to buy beer. The significance of extending the three-week waiting period to beer may be gauged from the fact that only thirty – or 42 per cent – of the seventy-two Eskimos who used their permits in 1962-63 bought any wine and spirits (and hence waited three weeks to pick up their paid-for orders); seventy-one out of the seventy-two permit users bought some beer. Up to July 25, 1963 only thirteen of thirty-two Eskimos with permits (about the same proportion) bought wine and spirits and thirty bought some beer.

Why have Eskimos not continued to patronize the Territorial Liquor Store to the same extent after the waiting period began for beer as they did before? A western Arctic Eskimo couldn't explain why drinkers didn't order beverages three weeks in advance of delivery. He simply treated the idea as preposterous when he said people want to drink when they want to drink. In other words, for many Eskimos drinking is highly spontaneous. When it comes to alcoholic beverages, they don't anticipate wanting to drink three weeks hence. Unlike some whites, most Eskimos don't keep liquor on hand, for example, to entertain guests. Such behaviour with respect to alcohol can't be generalized too far and ascribed to an inability to plan or a reluctance to project wants into the future, for Eskimos who leave town do shop in the Hudson's Bay Company for the future and even in town families buy enough at a time to last for several days. Also some Eskimos have bought alcohol for delivery three weeks hence and continue to do so; undoubtedly more will learn to shop in this fashion, if they wish to drink at home or give a private party.

Table I shows that extending the waiting period to beer brought a big drop in the amount of money Eskimos spent at the liquor store, especially for beer. The sale of wine and spirits rose somewhat after September, 1962 and for the next eight months continued to remain up, suggesting that in this way the waiting period had a tutorial consequence, slightly altering drinking habits.[2] But we need more data to verify this hypothesis.

Table I also indicates how Eskimo liquor buying fluctuates from month to month and, apparently, from season to season. We are not sure why. For one thing, Eskimos may lack a firm pattern of social drinking which would keep fairly steady the amount consumed from month to month. We list other possible reasons under the column headed "Remarks" but cannot at this time defend any of those hunches with concrete data. We

---

[2] Note how beer sales dropped after the extension of the waiting period while wine and spirits sales rose.

entertained the hypothesis that if November buying was indeed
a consequence of the approaching holiday season, then heavy
sales would cluster toward the end of that month. Available data
for wines and spirits bear out the hypothesis. Mainly, though it
turns out that a few sophisticated individuals, who undoubtedly
had Christmas in mind, did much of the wine and spirit buying
at that time. One young man spent $20 on four bottles of
champagne and another $46 for assorted wine, whiskey, rum,
and liqueur. We lack precise enough data to test the hypothesis
with beer buying.

TABLE I: *Purchases by Eskimos at the Territorial Liquor Store
by Month, from July, 1962 to July, 1963*

MONTH	REMARKS	WINE AND SPIRITS	BEER	TOTAL
1962				
July		$ 6.00	$ 952.25	$ 958.25
August		6.00	1,137.50	1,143.50
September				
	Waiting period extended.	6.00	146.25	152.25
October		59.05*	234.00*	293.05
November				
	Purchases for Christmas season?	169.35	321.75	491.15
December				
	Purchases for Christmas season?	138.40	308.75	447.15
1963				
January		93.00	208.00	301.00
February				
	Murder occurred.	84.20	263.25	347.45
March				
	Effect of murder?	33.70	159.25	192.95
April		74.95	165.75	240.70
May		36.30	234.00	270.30
June		98.60	279.50	378.10
July				
	Summer migration to camps.	19.35	178.75	198.10
Total		$824.90	$4,589.00	$5,413.90

Between July, 1962 and July, 1963, seventy-four men spent
a total of $5,413.90 at the liquor store, an average of $73.16
for thirteen months.[3] Of course, many drinkers undoubtedly
frequented the tavern and spent additional money, of which we

have no record. Table II shows considerable variation among the liquor purchasers. Some men spent as little as $6.50 in the thirteen-month period; one went as high as $299.60 in his purchases. Analysis of Table II indicates that over half the purchasers spent below $50.

TABLE II: *Amounts Spent at the Territorial Liquor Store*
by Eskimo Purchasers from July, 1962 to July, 1963

NUMBER OF PURCHASERS	TOTAL AMOUNT SPENT
1	$275 – $299
1	250 – 274
1	225 – 249
4	200 – 224
–	175 – 199
2	150 – 174
4	125 – 149
5	100 – 124
11	75 – 99
7	50 – 74
19	25 – 49
19	6 – 24
—	
74	

If we categorize Eskimos as either high or low purchasers, and define a high purchaser as someone who spent above the average ($73.16), then we count twenty-nine high purchasers. We can match these with twenty-nine individuals selected because they fall at the opposite end of the scale, having spent the smallest amounts at the liquor store. The two categories diverge in certain social characteristics as Table III demonstrates. High purchasers, who may live in Apex, Ikhaluit, or at the Airbase, are most often steadily employed, wage-earning heads of families in their thirties and early forties. The community's leaders are well represented among high purchasers. Generalizing, we can say that the high purchasers are men who have closely assimilated town life; tutelage has made them familiar

---

⁸Total beverage sales in Frobisher Bay amounted to $180,735.85 in 1962-63 while in Inuvik in 1962 they reached $327,231.55, according to the *Annual Report, Commissioner of the Northwest Territories, 1962-63*, p. 19.

with the liquor store and even with deferred buying of alcohol. Note that in this category only six permit holders failed to renew their permits in 1963 while twenty low purchasers failed to renew their permits. High purchasers show somewhat better ability to drink and stay out of trouble. They have appeared in court less frequently than low purchasers. Although drinking undoubtedly encourages offences against the law (especially against the Liquor Ordinance), the fourteen high purchasers who have no offences recorded against them demonstrate that Eskimos can drink, and even fairly heavily, without committing offences that attract police attention.

Low purchasers manifest greater heterogeneity. Again heads of families predominate, but the category includes more young, unmarried men. Low purchasers have spottier employment records and enjoy steady employment less frequently, meaning they also earn less wages. Low purchasers include two rehabilitants and over twice as many men who received social assistance than appear among high spenders. Only one low purchaser ranks as a leader; he belongs to the Community Council.

Judging from these data (we repeat, they refer only to purchases at the liquor store and don't reflect liquor consumed at the tavern), alcohol consumption correlates directly with economic and social status; it is one mark of a full-fledged Eskimo townsman. We would expect that as employment opportunities and standard of living increase so will liquor consumption. After all, the same thing has happened in Europe and among Euro-Americans in Canada and the United States. Rehabilitants' lack of sufficient economic means limits them with respect to drinking, which no doubt accounts for the relatively small proportion holding liquor permits.

Many high purchasers at the liquor store also frequent the tavern, with at least one notable exception: the most sophisticated men in the community (for example, those who bought Christmas liquor), who also happen to be high purchasers, don't regularly frequent the tavern. Also whereas no woman holds a permit to buy at the store, women of all ages visit the tavern, though always there are many fewer women than men. We must also add that only one member of the Apex church council holds a liquor permit; he is one of the high purchasers, but drinks

TABLE III: *Comparison between 29 "High" and 29 "Low" Eskimo Purchasers at the Territorial Liquor Store from July, 1962 to July, 1963*

	HIGH PURCHASERS	LOW PURCHASERS
Status		
Heads of families	27	19
Unmarried men	1	8
Women	–	–
Other	1	2
Average age	36	29
Employment		
Steadily employed	20	8
Fairly steadily employed	1	2
Rarely employed	5	10
No employment record	3	5
Rehabilitants	–	2
No longer in Frobisher Bay	–	2
Social assistance		
Received welfare, 1962-63	3	7
Received liquor during months they received welfare payments	2	–
Liquor permit holders		
1962-63	29	27
1963-64	21	7
Law offenders (between Dec., 1961 and Aug., 1963)		
Under Liquor Ordinance	12†	19‡
Under Criminal Code	6†	6‡
No offenses	14	9
Neighborhood		
Apex	12	13
Airbase	3	–
Ikhaluit	13	15
No longer in Frobisher Bay	1	1

*High purchasers are men who spent more than the average of $73.16 in the 13-month period; they spent from $78 to $300. Low purchasers are men who spent the smallest amounts, from $6 to $36.

†Three people were charged under both the Liquor Ordinance and the Criminal Code.

‡Five people were charged under both the Liquor Ordinance and the Criminal Code.

socially and in moderation. No member of the Ikhaluit church council holds a permit. As far as we can tell, no church council member frequents the tavern.

Little happens in the Rustic Room, as the tavern of the East Coast Lodge is called, before evening. Weekend evenings, especially if they coincide with D.N.A.'s twice-monthly paydays, draw an especially large crowd. Beer forms the most popular drink, many customers ordering by brand name. The company distributes itself around a half-dozen long tables in the front part of the room, these tables becoming animated conversational groups as the evening goes on and more cans of beer are drunk. Usually peer groups of around the same age cluster at a table and become drinking companions. A table may include a taciturn, silent drinker who, if he listens to his stimulated companions, doesn't himself become animated. Women, perhaps because they drink somewhat more slowly than men, also hold back from participating in table talk even when, as frequently occurs, one is married to one of the group. The room rings with the shrill peel of the telephone; the popping, hissing sound of beer cans being punctured, and with repeated calls for "John," the principal waiter and a well-known, local, small businessman. On some evenings, if John works alone, he can't keep up with the demands for beer put forth in this part of the tavern and in the newer, adjoining part, where summer construction workers tend to congregate in the more comfortable chairs around smaller tables. Sometimes Eskimo clients flow across the low partition and into that part of the room. In summer, when trade is heavy, the tavern employs two waiters, plus a bartender who also serves the restaurant cum cocktail lounge next door. Occasionally an Eskimo kitchen helper brings out sandwiches, french fries, or other snacks that tavern customers have ordered. Drinking goes along with heavy cigarette smoking, so that a heavy veil of smoke hangs over the room or drifts out the door whenever it opens to admit a new guest, or the taxi driver to ask if anybody wants to go home. Young Eskimo men frequently receive calls at the tavern wall phone and the instrument also allows a customer to call the taxi when he wants to depart. The number of people in the Rustic Room brings up the volume of noise; Eskimos themselves don't as a rule talk loudly and rarely grow boisterous or disorderly. Presumably they have learned that too clear an indication of drunkenness will not only cut off service but will put a man out of the tavern. Sometimes when a patron is ready to go home, he staggers from his table to lean over other people to bid them drunken farewells. Finally he responds to the taxi driver's urging and leaves. Waiters are not too rigorous in refusing to serve intoxicated patrons; after all, it is no easy matter to gauge drunkenness if a man keeps his seat. At times a waiter arbitrarily cuts off service, as, for example, he denied a second whiskey to an Eskimo who had begun the evening by drinking whiskey with beer chasers. Waiters enforce other rules, sometimes quite rudely, though the Eskimos seem unaware of their discourteous treatment. They command a patron who persists in shifting from one table to another to stay in one place, otherwise he'll not be served anymore. A waiter explained this rule saying that only if a patron remains in one place can a waiter remember how much he has to drink. One evening a waiter told one of us that nobody at our table could order another drink unless everybody had first consumed what he already had before him. We demurred, since this rule forced us to keep pace with our Eskimo companions and, eventually, to drink more heavily than we cared to. The waiter then ignored the rule. So much regulation and caution once more express the Euro-Canadian's traumatized attitude toward alcohol and his constant fear that drinking will promote disaster, especially in Eskimos who, the stereotype says, don't know how to drink. Yet, some drunken Euro-Canadians in the Rustic Room seemed more conspicuous for their boisterousness, vile language, and aggressiveness than any Eskimo. Drinkers pay when served. At a table that has been welded into a group, each member in turn usually pays for a round plus a tip. Eskimos persistently treated us to beer at the tavern. However, some men hand over to the waiter only enough money for their own drink.

We counted sixteen Eskimo men and two women as people whom we identified as steady taverngoers. All the men are family heads. The women in question regularly accompany their husbands. Most of the men in this category also hold or held liquor permits, only two failed to renew in 1963. Men who frequently avail themselves of one liquor outlet also steadily utilize the other, twelve of the sixteen steady taverngoers proving to be high purchasers at the liquor store. As we would expect, since a secure income alone could support steady patronage of both liquor outlets, the steady male drinkers mostly hold steady jobs. One steady taverngoer has no regular source of income and another lives in the Rehabilitation Centre, where he earns auxiliary income through carving on his own account. Two of the steady male tavern visitors and one woman are elected members of the Community Council. Considering their record of court appearances, tavern data confirm the conclusion previously reached, that some Eskimos can drink frequently and, presumably, heavily without coming to the attention of the police. Between December, 1961 and August, 1963 out of eighteen steady taverngoers: nine have been charged under the Liquor Ordinance; four have been charged under the Criminal Code, eight have been charged with no offences. The total of offenders and non-offenders exceeds eighteen because three persons have been charged both with offences under the Liquor Ordinance and under the Criminal Code. . . .

We have already questioned whether heavy spending at the liquor store or steady taverngoing ties in with committing offences apprehended by police. Some Eskimos, we know, drink regularly yet don't get into trouble with the law. We count twenty-nine heavy purchasers and an additional six steady taverngoers, making thirty-five so-called regular Eskimo drinkers. Police arrested seventeen of these at least once in the twenty-one months from December, 1961 to August 24, 1963. The other eighteen show no arrest record in that period. Regular drinkers in fact furnish only a small part of the trouble with which police cope. Police apprehended a total of ninety-seven persons in those twenty-one months, seventeen of them being persons categorized by us in 1963 as regular drinkers. By our criteria, seventy-eight of the ninety-seven persons arrested are occasional drinkers. It is interesting that practically no non-drinkers got into trouble, but since most arrests were for offences coming under the Liquor Ordinance this discovery isn't really very surprising.

In Aklavik, E. Clairmont sees "excessive drinking" to be

"largely a problem among the younger settlement natives," i.e., those between sixteen and twenty-nine. This finding supports his belief that excessive drinking in Aklavik forms one delinquent sign of strain, that age category in E. Clairmont's opinion being particularly highly stressed.[4] We cannot readily identify "excessive" drinkers in Frobisher Bay, but if we take the regular drinkers, they do not mostly come from the age category in which Clairmont sees excessive drinking to lodge; they tend to be older.

*   *   *

TABLE IV: *Age Distribution and Arrest Record of Regular Drinkers**

AGE CATEGORY	NUMBER OF REGULAR DRINKERS	NUMBER OF REGULAR DRINKERS* ARRESTED BETWEEN DECEMBER, 1961 AND AUGUST 24, 1963
20–24	1	1
25–29	6	1
30–34	8	4
35–39	7	6
40–44	6	2
45–49	3	3
50–54	3	–
Over 55	1	–
Total	35	17

*Regular drinkers are defined as those who spent more than the average at the liquor store (See Table III) and/or visited the tavern frequently.

We observed intoxicated behaviour mainly in the tavern and at dances; for other information we relied on what informants told us. Although some Eskimos speak of drinking releasing aggression, they know that people who drink "too much" vary in their responses. Not all become angry and dangerous; some grow elated, and others wax sad, they say. Perhaps the

---

[4]Donald H. T. Clairmont, *Deviance among Indians and Eskimos in the Aklavik Area* (Ottawa: Department of Northern Affairs and Natural Resources, Northern Co-ordination and Research Centre, 1963), p. 58.

outstanding characteristic we noted was talkativeness. Shyness dissolved under alcohol and people, who next day froze stiffly in our presence, making their discomfort painfully evident, would relax to tell us anything we wanted to know, to the extent that language permitted. Toward the end of our stay tavern companions warmly assured us of how much they and other Eskimos liked our presence in town. However, one drunken young man, who had worked for another anthropologist, once became quite hostile, resenting our obvious and constant preoccupation with observation. Occasionally a drunken man demonstrates affection for other Eskimos, something that adults avoid when sober. In March, a man at a dance suddenly sat down next to his wife, who had for some time been watching him anxiously, and held her tightly, resting his head on her breast. She nestled his head comfortingly until he jumped up and tugged at her to dance, an invitation she strenuously resisted. Intoxication relaxes some men to the point where they become exuberantly silly. Girls seem to stay watchful and hence generally remain more decorous. At dances drunken men get up and dance solo to an irresistible rhythm or they hunt for partners among the girls, who warily evade and reject them. Girls fear that a drunken partner will subject them to humiliating exhibitionism on the floor.

Reports of anger and aggressive behaviour accompanying drunkenness mostly reached us by hearsay. When certain Eskimo men were intoxicated they damaged other people's property, apparently as an expression of anger; grew obstreperous, trying to force themselves into homes whose owners didn't want them, and quarrelled publicly and even struck their wives and accused them of sleeping with other men. Undoubtedly these incidents of drunken aggression are true. In one instance, a drunken man killed a child after seriously injuring its mother with a knife. . . .

For most Eskimos, no parts of life demand drinking in order suitably to express the meaning of certain occasions. With the exception of two or three sophisticated families, social affairs like baptism, marriage, and Christmas don't call for alcohol. While Euro-Canadians naturally drink while attending Saturday night events in the U.S. Air Force clubs, alcohol isn't appropriate at Saturday night dances for Eskimos; in fact, the Community Association prohibits drinking or drunkenness. Integration of drinking with many social affairs in Euro-Canadian culture denotes a major difference between that and the Eskimo style of drinking. Social segregation dividing Euro-Canadians and Eskimos effectively prevents Eskimos from learning and adopting ceremonial uses for alcohol, as well as the attendant meanings of alcohol that its ceremonial use would encourage. As a consequence, alcohol, instead of accumulating auxiliary, expressive meanings which would help to shape and control its use, remains primarily an intoxicant. Instead of additionally valuing it as an attribute of graciousness and symbolic of holiday pleasure, Eskimos regard it essentially as a medium for release.

Notes on the Cooperative Movement and Community Organization in the Canadian Arctic

FRANK G. VALLEE

There are two types of economic development programmes for the Canadian Arctic to which the federal government and the Quebec Provincial government have committed themselves. One involves the very long-term, large-scale exploitation of mining, timber, hydro-electric and other massive resources; the other is more of a short term, ameliorative, or even preventative, type of programme, the aim of which is to encourage people in Arctic communities to exploit whatever resources there are — such natural ones as fish, sea mammals, caribou, or human ones like artistic and handicraft skills. It is in the latter kind of programme that the Co-operatives, the subject of this paper, are playing an increasingly important part. The specific government agencies charged with carrying out these programmes are the Département des Richesses Naturelles of the Quebec government and the Department of Northern Affairs and National Resources of the federal government. It is the policy of both these departments to give or lend capital, technical assistance, and marketing services so as to maximize the efficiency and profitability of the exploitation of wildlife or of human resources. The aim of this policy is to promote economic self-sufficiency by organizing production, consumption and marketing in the hope of raising the standard of living, reducing dependency on direct government welfare, and helping the people achieve some measure of control over their economic fates.

If it is evident that the machinery of a co-operative will contribute to attaining these goals in a community, the people there are encouraged to apply for incorporation as a Co-operative Society. Since 1959, when the first Society at George River and

SOURCE: *Arctic Anthropology*, vol. 2 (1964), pp. 45-49. Reprinted by permission of the author and publisher.

at Port Burwell in Northern Quebec were created, no less than nineteen Societies have been incorporated in the Canadian Arctic, all but six in the Central and Eastern Arctic. Only one of these co-operatives, a new one at Fort Franklin, is an exclusively Indian one; in two others a small number of Indians share membership with an Eskimo majority; in one, a housing co-operative at Inuvik, Eskimo, White and Indian are represented on the membership. In all of the others, including the ones we are to concentrate on in this paper, the membership is exclusively Eskimo or virtually so. It is in tacit recognition of this fact that co-operatives in the Arctic are often referred to as Eskimo Co-ops, even though it is against co-operative principles to affix an ethnic or religious label to one of their societies.

When we consider that there are only about 12,000 Eskimos in the Canadian Arctic, the establishment of so many co-operatives among them represents a social movement of outstanding significance for community organization in the Arctic. Perhaps I should say of *potentially* outstanding significance, for some of the incorporated co-operatives are practically inactive, existing only on paper, while others are active in only a very limited area of activity, such as in housing or in the marketing of handicrafts. In such cases, where the tasks are confined to only marketing or cutting the costs of consumption, the organization is regarded simply as an alternative to agencies such as the Hudson's Bay Company and is of little cultural or social significance on the local scene.

All co-operatives in the Arctic have certain features in common. First, they are ultimately dependent on government support: it is doubtful that any of these co-operatives could survive without outside support, in the form of financing, technical assistance, and some supervision – even though the latter be concealed behind the scenes in order to foster the impression that people are pulling themselves up by their own *kamik* straps. The Eskimos simply cannot provide the capital on their own, nor can they borrow it through the normal channels we use in the south; they require special sources of capital. They do not yet have the know-how to increase productivity per capita significantly. They cannot, on their own, manipulate outside markets successfully.

Another feature that applies to all Arctic co-operatives is that in each case white persons initiated the venture and provide sustained impetus. In most places some government administrator was the initiator; in others Oblate missionaries or Royal Canadian Mounted Policemen played this role. The stance of the whites is that of *Eminences Blanches* if I may twist a well-known historical *mot*. Because of the democratic and adult educational accents in the co-operative movement, the approach of these whites – with a few exceptions – is more avuncular than paternalistic. They offer guidance in such technical aspects of the operations for which there are no traditional Eskimo precedents, such as accounting, pricing, and correspondence with outside dealers. Major policy decisions about production and consumption and credit are formally made by the various boards and committees corresponding to the various functions of the corporation. These bodies are at least 90 per cent Eskimo in membership, but such major decisions almost always follow the ideas of the white members and advisors, both within and without the community. The accepted rule, understood by white and Eskimo alike, is that whites have more say in matters whose significance transcends the local community or is of long-term significance, for instance, marketing and borrowing strategies. It is explicitly understood that the whites are the initiators of new ways of doing things in the local economy and that they are grooming the Eskimos to take over an ever-growing part in the decision-making and operations connected with the enterprise. In fact, the bulk of the *day to day* local operation of the producing and consuming apparatus is already under Eskimo control in at least five of these Co-operatives.

Thus there is a characteristic of the co-operative form of organization in the Arctic which is not found in other organizations, insofar as the relations between whites and Eskimos are concerned. That is the definition of the relationship as one of fellow-member and a denial of the asymmetrical shape into which almost all Eskimo-white relationships have been fashioned: missionary-catechist; Royal Canadian Mounted Police constable–special Eskimo constable; Hudson's Bay manager–post servant, etc. In the case of the co-operative, there is a self-conscious public denial that this ethnic imbalance exists or should exist and the Eskimo is defined as someone who has as much say as anyone else. All this goes on against a background of a real imbalance between white and Eskimo in relevant skills, power, and role.

In each arctic co-operative for which I have information there is a core of Eskimo people who espouse the ideology of the movement, who evidently understand its implications, and who join with the whites in seeking converts and maintaining support once this has been achieved. The size and local importance of this core varies from place to place, being rather large in, for instance, Povungnituk, and rather small in Cape Dorset. Originally, the co-operative societies in many places sought the support and offered at least nominal leadership to those who had power or influence in the traditional system: heads of camps, catechists (very often these offices coincided in the Eastern Arctic), and other older men of influence. The trend since 1962 or so has been towards the replacement by election of these people by younger adults who combine an ability to live the traditional life and an ability to handle life in the new settlements with a kind of poise lacking in the older generation. These new leaders are highly adaptive people: most of the ones I know in the Eastern Arctic speak only Eskimo and make much point of being Eskimo, but at the same time show an eagerness to try their hands at operations which have always been defined as white (trading, bookkeeping, store managing, acting as settlement spokesmen), and present the whites with a front in marked contrast to the deferential front of the older generation. Recent elections in two co-operatives known to the author have resulted in the replacement of older men with widespread kinship networks, whose way it was to deal with people "personally," by younger ones with fewer such connections who use a more "impersonal" approach. Such evidence is too flimsy to warrant a generalization about trends, but we think it worth mentioning as something to look for in future research. Whatever the nature of the leadership in the co-operatives, the main point I want to make here is that in each one there is a core of Eskimos who have been converted to the movement and who throw varying amounts of weight behind the white generators in their efforts to convert the bulk of the population, most of whom are indifferent and responsive more to demonstrated economic success (power) rather than to ideology.

While these are a new kind of leader, they frequently use arguments based on traditional cultural values in order to capture and maintain support. On many occasions I have witnessed attempts to legitimize the co-operative in terms of its similarity to the traditional camp or band organization where, it was pointed out, everyone worked together and shared. According to this view, the co-operative is the natural successor of the camp or band which, it is argued, virtually disintegrated under the regime of individualistic trapping and the decline of group hunting.

I now want to focus down on a limited picture: in this case one kind of Co-operative situation. For the purposes of this paper we divide the arctic Co-operatives into types based on the following criteria: range of activities; population inclusiveness; local economic significance. In the remaining part of this paper I will deal with those co-operatives which engage in a variety of activities having to do with production, consumption, marketing, and credit control; which include all or most people of the community in their membership; and which, when considered as enterprises, account for the single largest source of income in their communities. In the Eastern Arctic Povungnituk stands highest according to these criteria, along with George River, Port Burwell, and Cape Dorset. A number of other communities are high on one or more but low on one or more other of the criteria mentioned: Chimo, Grise Fjord, Cambridge Bay, and so on. These are places with Eskimo populations of between 100 and 500. The co-operatives with more limited membership and specific functions are found mostly in larger places, such as Frobisher Bay and Aklavik-Inuvik. It would be worthwhile to take all of these types into account and trace out the particular impacts on their settings, but we have time to consider only the one type – the wide-ranging, all-embracing (at least ideally) and economically very significant type. I select only a few from the many points that can be made about the impact of this kind of co-operative on its setting.

One consequence of the co-operative movement in those

places where it has come to dominate the economy by control of credit, marketing, and by organizing important production activities, is the legitimizing of a market or contractual kind of relationship among people who formerly were interlocked in exclusively kinship or "status" kinds of relationship. We are all familiar with the traditional band and camp sharing patterns among the Eskimos where the yield from the hunt was defined as a camp resource rather than as an individual or household one entirely. We have much documentation of how the yields from trapping or wage labour came to be defined as an individual or household fund, rather than one to which the whole camp had access. Balikci and others have documented how a group returning from a hunt were expected to allocate the proceeds of the hunt according to the traditional sharing patterns, or some modification of them, whereas those who remained in the settlement working for wages, earning cash from carving, or living from relief, while receiving a share of the hunt, were not expected to allocate *their* proceeds in the same way. In new settlements, the kinds in which most Eskimos now live, where both hunting and other forms of productive activity were carried on in roughly equal measure, there resulted an imbalance of exchange in terms of community goods. The hunters were impelled by tradition to spread beyond their own households the gains of their outputs of time and energy, while the carvers, janitors, store clerks, and so on, were not. The latter had a market orientation to their energies and payoffs while the former followed the tradition of group reciprocity.

In those communities where the co-operatives have a role in co-ordinating production and consumption for local needs, they have provided the hunters with a recognized right to put their yield on the market *within* the community, for in such communities the Co-op buys the meat and fish from the hunters and sells it for cash.

Eskimos are not totally unfamiliar with the notion of impersonal markets. As we know, for generations Eskimo groups have traded with one another – caribou skins for drift wood, soapstone for polar bear skins, and so on – across group boundaries. In more recent times they have had sporadic and very partial glimpses of remote outside markets through traders, but that trading process was little understood, being perceived as simply a face-to-face exchange with individual traders.

Now, in such communities as Povungnituk, George River and Dorset, they are exposed to the daily acting out of the market processes within their own households and stores and much of the socially and culturally induced fog of mystification surrounding the economy in which they are embedded is being dissipated. This is true especially for those on the various committees and the executive employed who take part in decision making about pricing, management of surplus, credit policies, and so on.

In three of the communities which I know best, the white and Eskimo managing élite use frequent meetings of the members to deliver sermons in economics, using the local scene as well as the marketing and credit experiences of the Co-op outside the community as concrete illustrations. I have attended co-operative meetings in Povungnituk where experience in local and outside dealings have been used to illustrate such notions as the division of labour, capital formation, the function of investment, the ways in which money can make money, and other abstract ideas normally transmitted to people in advanced societies at the university level if at all. Needless to say, the actual terminology of economic and sociological analysis was, mercifully, not used on these occasions, but the ideas came through. At least they came through to the core of believers who are to be found in every one of these Co-operative communities. It is perhaps this kind of insight into the workings of the big world which will in the end prove of most telling significance, for once having had these insights people cannot revert to the view of the world as a mysterious sphere of magically endowed personalities and ethnic groups, at least as far as economics and power are concerned.

In those communities where the co-operatives are multi-functional and strong, the co-operative is viewed not simply as an economic instrument but as the chief, all-inclusive unit of community organization. Echoes of the slogan, "What is good for General Motors is good for North America," are heard in Arctic communities in the slogan, "what is good for the Co-op is good for the community," or, indeed, for all Eskimos everywhere. As the co-operative grows in economic strength, its leaders assume for themselves the right to define what is and what is not good for the community as a whole, the right to publicly criticize those who do not support the enterprise.

Many co-operative meetings I have attended developed into sermons or discussions about problems which were only indirectly, if at all, connected with the terms of reference of the co-operative itself: questions about human relations in the community; about keeping dogs tied; about controlling deviance; about making payments on houses purchased from the government. To put it briefly and technically, in at least four places in the Eastern Arctic the tendency is for the co-operative to provide an integrative and co-ordinative machinery for the whole community, a machinery transcending the traditional familiar and camp groupings and one which usurps some of the functions of such bodies as community councils, originally set up under the auspices of government administrators as a first step towards local government.

While on the topic of levels of socio-cultural integration, let us look for a moment at the signs of emerging links among different Eastern Arctic communities in what could become mutually supportive and interdependent relationships, which in turn could provide a partial base for pan-Eskimo solidarity. As I have noted elsewhere, most communities in the Eastern Arctic simply duplicate one another. Settlements are linked in a network of radio communication in the national interest, exchanging and relaying messages about weather, flying conditions, flight programmes and so on. Each is also a link with others in an administrative chain serving various government departments, the Hudson Bay Company, Royal Canadian Mounted Police, etc. As far as the Eskimos are concerned there is a certain amount of migration among settlements and of interaction between settlements where kinship networks stretch across settlement boundaries. However, these settlements are not linked in any kind of *interdependent* network as far as the local Eskimos are concerned. Each settlement is more oriented to the south than it is to other settlements in the same district, looking to the south for many of its living needs, markets, and so on.

If the Arctic Co-operative movement develops in the day

its supporters hope it will, it would certainly serve as an inter-linking agency. Already there are a few such links and others are soon to be added: for instance, the Resolute and Grise Fjord Co-operatives trade with the Ikaluit Fishing Co-operative at Frobisher; canoes made at the new Great Whale River Co-oper-ative have been traded to several other Arctic settlements for cash and various articles of consumption. The Grise Fjord Co-operative hopes to trade its surplus of seal skins – a surplus resulting from co-operative hunting–to handicraft co-operatives in communities where seals are not in abundance. A common marketing agency for Arctic co-operatives has been set up and one of the understandings is that co-operatives which are closer to the markets should bear some of the extra costs of transporta-tion imposed on the ones farther away from the southern markets.

The examples I have just given are of economic links across community boundaries. However, the motivation which impels people to recommend and forge such links among Eskimo communities is not simply a matter of economic advantage, for implied in the arguments I have heard from many Eskimo and white advocates of such links is the view that the Co-operative movements should be a carrier of Pan-Eskimo sentiments of solidarity.

Certainly there is clear evidence from the Northern Quebec region of a view that the Co-operative movement is the ideal medium to carry links among Eskimo communities. Eskimo co-operative leaders in Povungnituk have assumed the respon-sibility for spreading the movement into other communities in New Quebec, in a quest for total Eskimo conversion to the movement in that area. Since the spring of 1963 several visits have been made by Eskimo leaders of the Povungnituk Society to Great Whale River, Port Harrison, Ivuyivek, Sugluk, Wake-ham Bay and Payne Bay. In most of these places the Povungni-tukers were greeted initially with some suspicion, for their visits were linked in many minds with the so-called "Quebec Take-over" (the Provincial government is a strong supporter of the Povungnituk Co-operative) and the Roman Catholic Church, for the Povungnituk Co-operative was initiated by a Roman Catholic missionary. However, that suspicion appears to have abated somewhat, for very recently Povungnituk co-operators have been asked by Eskimos in two of these communities to return to them and help the people there begin local co-operatives.

I do not want to give the impression that the co-operative movement is booming and can go nowhere but up in the Canadian Arctic. As I said earlier, any of the established ones could fold tomorrow if support were withdrawn. Furthermore, it is still really too early to make conclusive statements about trends and tendencies. I have said nothing specifically about the obstacles to co-operative development, how community factions in some cases prevent such development or are brought together by the development in others; how competition from traders can both hinder and propel forward co-operative development. I have tried to bring out in this paper the rather unique features of the co-operative form of social organization as compared with other forms of organization which have been introduced into the Arctic and in discussing the impact of the co-operative movement have mentioned only a few aspects, namely: the explicit definition of relationships in non-ethnic terms given co-operative societies, while in just about every other relationship the ethnic dimension is made to stand out; the attempt to legitimize the co-operatives by likening it to the traditional camp or band organization; the legitimizing of a market approach to exchange *within* Eskimo communities in matters which were formerly governed by the principle of reciprocity; the learning function of the co-operative, through experiences in which people get to know at first hand ideas normally transmitted to people in advanced societies at the university level; the tendency for co-operatives to outgrow their specific terms of reference and become the key unit of community organization with functions which have little if anything to do with production, consumption, marketing, credit control, etc.; and the possibility that the movement will take on increasing significance as a carrier of PanEskimo sentiments of solidarity.

Eskimo Art –
A Living Art Form

GEORGE SWINTON

It is evident by now that economic motivation has been a prime factor in the creation of Eskimo art during the past century and a half. This need not be defended or disguised. It is equally important to understand that in 1949 the primary intention in promoting Eskimo art and handicrafts was the economic well-being of the Eskimo. In this regard it was Houston's definite task "to find out whether the Eskimos on the east coast of the Bay could produce carvings in quantity and of a quality that would be saleable." Also, the government became interested in the project, mainly because of "the need for work in areas that were depressed" and for this reason "asked the [Canadian Handicraft] Guild to extend its search [for Eskimo handicrafts] even further north." The Guild, together with the Hudson's Bay Company and Houston, were delighted to comply. The intentions of this project were sincere and were not in conflict with the prevailing conditions of Eskimo art, as "traditional Eskimo culture" purists seem to think. This point cannot be emphasized strongly enough.

Similarly, it must be stressed that the truly great peaks of the contemporary art phase are the results of the new stimulation which Eskimo carvers received from the encouragement and understanding given them by a few sensitive people. Before discussing the nature of this stimulation, another, often neglected, point needs clearing up. For, in addition to recognizing the one-and-a-half-century-old tradition of economic motivation in Eskimo art production, we must also come to realize that it is this aspect of Eskimo art, more than any other, which resembles an important tradition of Western art.

Since the rise of Protestant capitalism in the seventeenth

SOURCE: *Eskimo Sculpture* (Toronto: McClelland and Stewart, 1965), pp. 52-72. Reprinted by permission of the author and publisher.

century, and, more noticeably, since the beginning of the Industrial Revolution, Western art — like Western civilization largely deprived of its religious motivations — has had an increasingly secular and commercial background. Yet when we discuss Western art as art, we either ignore secularization and commercialization, or take them for granted. We stress qualities and achievements of art in terms of aesthetics, stylistic relationships, individualities, iconography, and history; we might discuss, but we would seldom criticize socio-economic roots or roles. We recognize, for instance, that an early Italian Renaissance Madonna, a Dutch seventeenth-century genre painting, a nineteenth-century Impressionist landscape, and an American twentieth-century oversize abstraction not only reflect different and changing aesthetic attitudes, but also imply different and changing structures and motivations in societies. Yet when we discuss contemporary Eskimo art, some of us refuse to accept the changes in art and motivation which correspond to the changes in Eskimo life.

These changes can be expressed in several terms. For instance, the economy of the contemporary Eskimo has changed from a primary to a secondary one. Instead of being a hunter, he has become a trapper and wage earner; instead of directly providing his primary needs for livelihood, he is now earning money (by supplying the commodities of labour, furs, art, handicrafts, and services) with which to subsequently acquire the major share of his needs for food, clothing, fuel, transportation, housing, entertainment, and so on. Another way of describing this change is that the Eskimo economy has shifted from "subsistence production" to "commodity production," making it now largely a money economy.

This change in economy is neither recent nor sudden. It began with the initial trading activities when explorers, whalers, and traders arrived in the early nineteenth century. Changes in Eskimo art show a marked analogy to the changes in economy and, in fact, reflect accurately the changing phases of culture. The decisive shift to a money economy as opposed to the trading economy of the preceding one hundred and fifty years occurred after World War II, and correlates with the "commercial" phase of the new Eskimo art. Production of this art today is no longer for the artists' own gratification, but for the gratification of others, known or unknown. The strange and wondrous thing about contemporary Eskimo art is that its miracles occur both because, and in spite of, these economic motivations and primarily commercial objectives.

When Houston went north to explain the Guild's intentions, he reported that the Eskimos "went at this *new industry* excitedly" [italics mine G.S.]. While this was an inaccurate phrase at that time (1949-52), it was nevertheless prophetic. Today, in most areas of the Eastern Arctic, a large percentage of the population is involved in art activities of some kind or other. It is still difficult to establish just how it all happened.

There were many people and many factors contributing to the complex process of developing the new styles. I myself have often observed several styles going on side by side with many carvers hardly aware of the innovations of others. On the other hand, at Povungnituk in the mid-fifties, three, perhaps even four, different influences became noticeable at one and the same time. While it would be wrong to say that one single influence prevailed, it would be equally wrong to say that one did not. For the development of the conspicuous regional style towards representational realism may have been the result of the aesthetic ideas (and the corresponding payment policy) of the then resident Post manager, Peter Murdoch, or it may have been one aspect of a new, more general, carving tradition.

One of the patterns of this new tradition might well be a definable sequence of change in the general and individual styles of the contemporary carvers. Such a pattern has become noticeable in several areas over a period of years. However, because the evidence is still scanty and the time lapse short, a definitive theory concerning this pattern cannot be attempted at present. Nevertheless, its existence should be noted in a preliminary way.

In the usual sequence, the first carvings have simple and generally smooth forms. Also, regardless of size, they have an appearance of largeness and bulk. They reveal an elemental, primitive expression with little concern for details, or for anything which does not seem important to the carvers. At this stage the carvings show an intuitive understanding and respect for the beauty and intrinsic nature of the materials used. Then, gradually, this phase is followed by a growing concern for refinements and for detail, with a corresponding decline in respect for the material. Coinciding with this development, the interest shifts from expression to naturalistic representation, and then eventually to what may be called "literal communication," which usually takes the form of mannerism. This mannerism is not bad in itself but very often degenerates into empty stylishness.

This pattern of stylistic evolution can be readily observed in the carvings from the east coast of Hudson Bay, although some new, more vital carvings have started to re-emerge from Povungnituk and from Port Harrison. Quite recently, similar patterns have been observed in such remote areas as Repulse Bay and Arctic Bay, though there, because of the relative isolation of these communities, the changes are taking place much more slowly and inconspicuously. These sequences in themselves are nothing new in the history of art. Notable parallels would be the development of Greek sculpture from its archaic origins to Hellenistic mannerism and, in our own civilization, the general stylistic developments starting roughly with the highly primitive (that is, the unsophisticated) mediaeval art forms and developing gradually into the academic "isms" of the nineteenth and twentieth centuries. While these Western developments occurred over periods measured in terms of several centuries, the remarkable feature of the current Eskimo changes is the swiftness with which they are taking place, in periods of a mere decade or even less.

It would be easy to say that these stylistic developments and changes are due mostly to outside influences, which make their presence felt continuously. But these influences are not easy to pinpoint, and changes in style or attitude often occur, not because of them, but in opposition to them.

Another aspect of contemporary Eskimo art, which relates to the problem of outside influences, is the complete unpredictability of results, particularly if one makes some qualification as to what is meant by the term Eskimo art as opposed to, say, Eskimo carving, handicrafts, and so on.

*　　　　　*　　　　　*

An Eskimo artist wrote to a collector in late May, 1963:

. . . you wrote. I am answering a short letter. I read your letter. I do not recall your name. . . . I am thankful to you to be interested in my carvings. I will carve, please do not doubt my words, now I do not have good stone. It is still winter. In July I will have good stone. The stone used now by Eskimos here is not good. I do not enjoy working poor stone. *Do not get tired of waiting for my work.* The white people will soon refuse our carvings if we use poor stone. *I am not doing much carving now, also I am a slow worker.* I like to think of something that would please the buyer. . . . *Please answer me soon. I like to hear from you. Do not doubt my words I will do some carvings for you. My hands are slow. Let me know* if any carvings . . . were broken. *I have not been carving much now for two years.* . . .

[Emphasis mine]

In addition to the anxious and humble tone which makes it one of the most moving documents of contemporary Eskimo culture, this letter clearly states the artistic problems which confront all Eskimo carvers, especially those who are good artists. The emphasized passages speak for themselves; their concerns are with standards, with wanting to know what to create and how, and with wanting to do it well. Yet, thus far contemporary carvers have not established any general criteria for judging their own work. They are still uncertain of our preferences, and after all, they do create their works for our appreciation and not for their own use.

Unfortunately their occasional evaluations often depend on the standards of a single white man buying their work in a particular area at a particular time. Thus, not *the* white man, but an individual buyer has frequently exercised considerable influence on carving styles; his taste and aesthetic attitude are tangibly reflected in the varying prices he pays for individual works. The Eskimo carvers are very much aware of this evaluation and, unfortunately, have sometimes paid too much attention to it. However, not all influences were necessarily bad; some buyers did not let their personal feelings and preferences interfere with pricing policies. But a few did influence the Eskimo carvers a great deal, and it is mainly because of their actions that contemporary carving activities have developed their present general nature, good or bad.

It follows that these men were blamed for nearly everything that has gone wrong and were hardly ever praised for any achievements. While it might be difficult to prove, the opposite would probably have been more to the point.

Even though negative criticism frequently comes from respectable quarters. it is often not well-informed and causes a great deal of harm to the Eskimo artists. It also gives a distorted picture of the actual situation. In the final analysis, most of the bad influences that exist and the bad results that come from them are, in their origin, largely cultural and not personal. And even the most personal influences have wider cultural implications. For they come from men who hold what may be called general opinions; that is, opinions held generally by white men without special training; men who think in very general terms of white culture and popular taste. These cultural influences persist wherever white man goes. One of the many miracles of Eskimo art is the survival of any Eskimo traits at all.

Among these cultural influences, commerce and industry are the two most conspicuous. They are the favourite targets of the detractors of contemporary Eskimo carving. (By "industry" is meant the production of carvings in quantity with the object of sale.)

Statistically speaking, it is interesting to note that the quantity of carvings fluctuates in an inverse proportion to the cycle of the fox and to the value of seal pelts. This is not surprising, in view of the original and primary purpose of the "carving industry" which was to counteract the scarcity of other means of livelihood in depressed areas. What *is* surprising is that, in spite of increased production, so much good work was produced.

The judging of contemporary Eskimo carvings by their worst and most commercial examples stems from our failure to make distinctions between the various kinds of carvings produced today, and from our lumping them all into one category under one identifying symbol. This symbol, designed to avoid distinctions, establishes the ethnic origin of the carvings as the one gauge of value. This is, of course, absolutely absurd from the viewpoint of art, which is concerned with aesthetic and communicative qualities and not with exotic derivation. But from the viewpoint of the souvenir trade, for which most of the carvings are produced, the most important selling point is ethnic (that is, exotic) origin, and not quality. Futhermore, quantity production is a highly desirable asset in the souvenir trade, because it permits a lower price. This contrast strongly with art, where price has only little significance and where uniqueness and quality play an important role.

Thus, from the point of view of the souvenir trade, both industrial production and emphasis on exotic origin can be justified. And there is hardly a doubt in my mind that a great deal of Eskimo carving today fulfills this purpose well. To judge souvenir carvings by any other standard shows little understanding of art and even less of Eskimo culture. One might add that Eskimo carving as a souvenir industry has very high standards. And though, personally, one might not get very excited about souvenirs, they do have a definite cultural existence and definite economic values. Considering these, and speculating about the future in terms of the past, one might say that, once the current phase of Eskimo carving, together with the current phase of Eskimo culture, have ceased to exist, these souvenir carvings will acquire a special aura both cultural and economic.

Furthermore, closely related to souvenir art is a type which I would call fork art. It is possible to draw parallels between these two types of Eskimo carvings and various types of Western art and music. In visual art, there are the Currier and Ives prints, the Bartlett prints, the chromos of the nineteenth century, and most of the china figurines and groups of the last two hundred years from England, France, Germany, and Austria. All of these are popular art forms, ranging from extreme complexity and delicacy to simplicity and even crudeness. Many of them have become more or less valuable antiques, even though their intrinsic value as art is very limited.

In Eskimo art, complex examples of folk art are many of the carvings from the east coast of Hudson Bay (Great Whale River, Belcher Islands, Port Harrison, and Povungnituk), and, to a lesser extent, carvings from Northern Ungava up to Grise Fiord (except Cape Dorset). As far as simpler examples are

concerned, Repulse Bay would be the most prolific and conspicuous area of production, but simple carvings of birds, seals,
and bears can be found everywhere.

The folk art character of the Repulse Bay carvings, which
has attracted my personal attention for years, introduces another
analogy – the affinity of Eskimo carving to music, especially to
folk music, folk songs, and popular songs. The differences in
musical concept might help us clarify, in very general terms,
some of the differences between carvings.

Souvenir carvings are much like our popular tunes and
songs. In popular songs, triteness of content and sentimentality
of music are of primary concern. In fact, mere pleasantness of
tune is of greater significance than depth of feeling and verbal
meaning. By contrast, in authentic folk songs and spirituals,
depth of feeling and verbal meaning are all-important. The
Negro spiritual was originally improvised as the spirit moved
the singers. The same is true of Eskimo chants. Here, too, the
singers were moved by the spirit of the moment, singing thoughts
rather than words; repeating the words and ideas rhythmically to
the beat of the drum or to the rhythm of the language, like the
spoken poems of Dylan Thomas, delighting in cadence, music,
and image alike. Here is such an Eskimo song:

> Look up at the dome of the sky overhead
> As you do your song and dance,
> Spead wide your legs
> And bend your knees,
> Swaying in time with the song!

or a caribou hunting song:

> aii-aii-aii-a aii-a aii-aii-aii-a aii-a
> All unexpected I came and took by surprise
> The heedless dweller of the plains,
> aii-aii-aii-a, aii-aii-aii-a aii-a
> All unexpected I came and took by surprise
> The heedless dweller of the plains,
> aii-aii-aii-a aii-a
> And I scattered the herd
> In headlong flight.
> aii-aii-aii-a aii-a

In souvenir carvings – as in popular songs – the main object is to be pleasant. And, like the simple enjoyment derived from a tune, the easy, uninvolved enjoyment derived from such a carving is more important than expression of feelings or communication of ideas. The carving's success is determined by its ability to be pleasant; by its ability to establish an agreeable *sight* or *memory*, a *souvenir*, of things associated with Eskimo life. Although such a carving may have artistic or intellectual merits, these are merely incidental to its merit as a souvenir, whether it is produced in quantity or not.

The work of art, on the other hand, has very different attributes. Its purpose is not necessarily to be pleasant, but to give the kind of satisfaction that comes from participation in the content of the work. We have seen repeatedly that his deeper satisfaction comes from aesthetic sensations combined with feeling, thought, and expression, which transcend mere subject matter. This, indeed, is very akin to good folk songs, where ideas, words, rhythm, expression, feeling, and melody break free from pleasantry and platitude and evoke stirring (and often even unpleasant) experiences which command participation. In music, the most impressive form of this artistic expression is opera, which is a kind of folk art on a grand scale; but we can find the same drama in the much less complex songs, dances, and singing festivals of non-literate civilizations, and in the folk arts, both musical and visual, of all civilizations, past and present.

Eskimo art of nearly all periods has been able to achieve this kind of drama and power of expression. In prehistoric times, most of the carvings contained these transcendental qualities, because of the conditions under which they were produced. Today, however, with conditions changed, only the artists – and by no means all carvers – are able to achieve such results.

Culturally speaking, the Eskimo carver of today no longer produces an art that is directly related to his life; he produces for consumers whose strange fascination for his art he is only partially able to grasp. At the same time, he is most anxious to please these consumers, and he is, therefore, constantly trying to assess what might appeal to them. Here of course, lies the greatest danger to his new art.

Yet, Eskimo art could never have developed to its present heights without the understanding, the sensitive guidance, and the commercial incentives of the white man. This fact has been largely underestimated and often denied altogether. Yet, in varying degrees, people like the Houstons, Terry Ryan, Father Steinmann, Gabriel Gély, Claude Grenier, Bob Williamson, Bill Larmour, and Peter Murdoch, have guided and goaded the Eskimos in their artistic development. Without the influence of these people, the Eskimo might never have had the courage or the stimulus to produce their new carvings which belong among the most unusual and moving art expressions of our time.

Yes, the Eskimo were influenced by white men; but the true Eskimo artist created works that no white man could possibly have conceived. I have seen sketches for carvings made by white men for the Eskimo, but they were almost all bad, and the carvings that came from them never rose above souvenir quality. In all the areas that I visited, the true artists are unmistakably individuals with distinct, personal styles that bear little or no resemblance to any "white" ideas and concepts. It is good to know that some of the art-oriented anthropologists have had similar experiences in other parts of the world. In this respect, special attention should be drawn to the essay "Art and Value" by Melville J. Herskovits, which clears up many scientific and popular myths about the absence of individuality in primitive art. In contemporary Eskimo art, the major emphasis is certainly on individual artists and not on collective styles.

A SELECTIVE BIBLIOGRAPHY ON
THE CANADIAN ESKIMO

The student seeking more detailed or specialized reading materials is directed to the *Arctic Bibliography* compiled and kept up-to-date by the Arctic Institute of North America, with offices in Washington and Montreal. Regular English-language publications carrying a heavy content of articles on the Eskimo are *Anthropologica, Arctic Anthropology*, and *Anthropological Papers of the University of Alaska*. The National Museum of Canada also provides abundant documentation on the Eskimo.

Readers interested in less specialized but more popular treatment of Eskimo culture and affairs in Canada would do well to consult issues of *The Beaver*, published by the Hudson's Bay Company in Winnipeg, and *North*, published by the Department of Indian Affairs and Northern Development in Ottawa. Regular publications of the Anglican Church and of the Oblate Order in Canada also carry much useful and significant reading materials on the Canadian Eskimo.

Asen Balikci / *Relations inter-ethniques à la Grande Rivière de la Baleine* (Ottawa: National Museum of Canada, Bulletin 173, 1957).
Suicidal Behaviour Among the Netskilik Eskimos (Ottawa: Dept. N.A.N.R., NCRC, 1960).*

Kaj Birket-Smith / *The Eskimos* (London: Methuen & Co., 1959).

Franz Boas / *The Central Eskimo* (Washington: *Sixth Annual Report of the Bureau of American Ethnology*, 1888).

M. G. Brown, et al. / "Response to Cold of Eskimos of the Eastern Canadian Arctic," *Journal of Applied Physiology*, vol. 18, no. 5 (1963).

John M. Campbell (Ed.) / *Prehistoric Cultural Relations be-*

tween the Arctic and Temperate Zones of North America (Montreal: Arctic Institute of North America, Technical Paper 11, 1962).

E. S. Carpenter, R. Flaherty, and F. Varley / *Eskimo* (Toronto: University of Toronto Press, 1959).

B. Chown and M. Lewis / *Blood Groups in Anthropology: With Special Reference to Canadian Indians and Eskimos* (Ottawa: National Museum of Canada, Bulletin 167, 1958).

Donald H. T. Clairmont / *Deviance Among Indians and Eskimos at Aklavik* (Ottawa: Dept. N.A.N.R., NCRC, 1963).

Raymond de Coccolo and Paul King / *Ayorama* (Toronto: Oxford University Press, 1955).

Robert C. and Lois A. Dailey / *The Eskimos of Rankin Inlet* (Ottawa: Dept. N.A.N.R., NCRC, 1961).

David Damas / *Igluligmiut Kinship and Local Groupings: A Structural Approach* (Ottawa: National Museum of Canada, Bulletin 196, 1963).

R. W. Dunning / "An Aspect of Recent Eskimo Polygyny and Wife-Lending in the Eastern Arctic," *Human Organization,* vol. 21 (1962).

J. D. Ferguson / *The Human Ecology and Social Economic Change in the Community of Tuktoyaktuk, N.W.T.* (Ottawa: Dept. N.A.N.R., NCRC, 1961).

Jacob Fried / *A Survey of the Aboriginal Populations of Quebec and Labrador* (Montreal: Eastern Canadian Anthropological Series, McGill University, no. 1, 1955).

J. Louis Giddings / "Cultural Continuities of the Eskimos," *American Antiquity,* vol. 27, no. 2 (1961), pp. 155-73.

Nelson H. H. Graburn / *General Introduction to Lake Harbour, Baffin Island* (Ottawa: Dept. N.A.N.R., NCRC, 1963). *Taqaqmiut Eskimo Kinship Terminology* (Ottawa: Dept. N.A.N.R., NCRC, 1964).

---

* Several works listed here were sponsored and published by the Department of Northern Affairs and Natural Resources (now the Department of Indian Affairs and Northern Development) through its Northern Coordination and Research Centre. Throughout this bibliography the reference to this agency will be indicated by the abbreviation Dept. N.A.N.R., NCRC.

D. L. Guemple / *Inuit Spouse Exchange* (Chicago: University of Chicago, Department of Anthropology, M.S., 1961).

Elmer Harp / *The Archaeology of the Lower and Middle Thelon, Northwest Territories* (Montreal: Arctic Institute of North America, Technical Paper 8, 1961).

E. W. Hawkes / *The Labrador Eskimo* (Ottawa: Geological Survey of Canada, Memo 91, Anthropology Series 14, 1916).

John J. Honigmann / "The Great Whale River Eskimo: A Focussed Social System," *Anthropological Papers of the University of Alaska*, vol. 9, no. 1 (1960), pp. 11-16.
Community Organization and Patterns of Change Among North Canadian and Alaskan Indians and Eskimos, Anthropologica, n.s., vol. 5, no.1, 1963 (special issue).

John J. and Irma Honigmann / "Notes on the Great Whale River Ethos," *Anthropologica*, n.s., vol. 1, nos. 1 & 2 (1959), pp. 106-121.
Eskimo Townsmen (Ottawa: Canadian Research Centre for Anthropology, University of Ottawa, 1965).

Charles C. Hughes / "Under Four Flags: Recent Cultural Changes Among the Eskimos," *Current Anthropology* (February 1965), pp. 3-69.

Diamond Jenness / *The People of the Twilight* (Chicago: University of Chicago Press, Phoenix Books, 1961).
Eskimo Administration: Canada (Montreal: Arctic Institute of North America, Technical Paper 14, 1964).
Eskimo Administration: Labrador (Montreal: Arctic Institute of North America, Technical Paper 16, 1965).

Charles A. Martijn / "Canadian Eskimo Carving in Historical Perspective," *Anthropos*, vol. 59 (1965), pp. 546-596.

Richard S. Macneish / "A Speculative Framework of Northern North American Prehistory," *Anthropologica*, n.s., vol. 1, nos. 1 & 2 (1959), pp. 7-23.

Farley Mowat / *People of the Deer* (Boston and Toronto: Little Brown and University of Toronto Press, 1954).
The Desperate People (Boston and Toronto: Little Brown and University of Toronto Press, 1959).

L. Ochinsky / *The Most Ancient Eskimos* (Ottawa: Canadian

Research Centre for Anthropology, University of Ottawa, 1964).

R. E. Popham / "A Bibliography and Historical Review of Physical Anthropology in Canada: 1848-1949," in G. W. Lasker and J. L. Angel (editors), *Yearbook of Physical Anthropology, 1950* (New York: Wenner-Gren Foundation, 1951).

Report of the Fifth Thule Expedition, 1921-24. This report was published in ten volumes over the span of about ten years. The following titles and volumes are most relevant to anthropological study of the Canadian Eskimo. The publisher is Glyndalske Boghaindeln, Copenhagen.

Kaj Birket-Smith *The Caribou Eskimos* (vol. V, 1929).

Therkel Mathiassen *Material Culture of the Iglulik Eskimo* (vol. VI, no. 1, 1928).

Knud Rasmussen *Intellectual Culture of the Iglulik Eskimo* (vol. V, no. 2, 1929); *Intellectual Culture of the Caribou Eskimo* (vol. VII, no. 2, 1930); *Netsilik Eskimo: Social Life and Spiritual Culture* (vol. VIII, nos. 1 & 2, 1931); *Intellectual Culture of the Cooper Eskimo* (vol. IX, 1932).

Geert van den Steenhoven / *Legal Concepts Among the Netsilik Eskimos of Pelly Bay, N.W.T.* (Ottawa: Dept. N.A.N.R., NCRC, 1959).

George Swinton / *Eskimo Sculpture* (Toronto: McClelland and Stewart, 1965).

Frank G. Vallee / *Kabloona and Eskimo in the Central Keewatin* (Ottawa: Dept. N.A.N.R., NCRC, 1962; second edition published by Canadian Research Centre for Anthropology, University of Ottawa, 1967).

"Eskimo Theories of Mental Illness in the Hudson Bay Region," *Anthropologica*, n.s., vol. 8, no. 1 (1966), pp. 53-83.

James Van Stone / *The Caribou Eskimos of the Eskimo Point* (Ottawa: Dept. N.A.N.R., NCRC, 1959).

"Three Eskimo Communities" (*Anthropological Papers of the University of Alaska*, vol. 9, no. 1, 1960).

William E. Willmott / *The Eskimo Community at Port Harrison, P.Q.* (Ottawa: Dept. N.A.N.R., NCRC, 1961).

THE EDITORS

VICTOR F. VALENTINE, Associate Professor, Department of Sociology, Carleton University, Ottawa: B.A., M.A. in Anthropology, University of Toronto; formerly chief research officer, Northern Coordination and Research Centre, Department of Northern Affairs and National Resources, and Chief of the Economic Development Division, Indian Affairs Branch. Initiated a number of research projects in the Canadian arctic. Publications on the Métis, Community Development in the Caribbean, and anthropology in the North.

FRANK G. VALLEE, Professor and Chairman of Sociology, Carleton University, Ottawa: B.A., McGill, and PH.D., University of London, in Social Anthropology; formerly chief, research division, Department of Citizenship and Immigration, Ottawa; appointed member, Northwest Territories Legislative Council, 1964-1967. Research and publications on Hebrideans of Scotland, and ethnic group integration in Canada including the Eskimo and Indians.

THE CONTRIBUTORS

WILLIAM E. TAYLOR, Director, Human History Branch, National Museum of Canada, Ottawa.

DAVID R. HUGHES, Professor, Department of Anthropology, University of Toronto, Toronto.

RAYMOND C. GAGNÉ, Chief, Linguistics Section, Northern Administration Branch, Department of Indian Affairs and Northern Development, Ottawa.

EDMUND S. CARPENTER, Professor of Anthropology, San Fernando Valley State College, California.

RT. REV. ARSENE TURQUETIL, O.M.I. (1876-1955), Eskimologist. Formerly Roman Catholic missionary in the Canadian Arctic, and Vicar Apostolic.

SVEND FREDERIKSEN, Eskimologist, retired. Adelphi, Maryland.

CHARLES A. MARTIJN, Department of Anthropology, University of Wisconsin, Madison.

GEERT VAN DEN STEENHOVEN, Professor of Ethnology, University of Nijmigen, Netherlands.

DAVID DAMAS, Ethnology Section, National Museum of Canada, Ottawa.

DIAMOND JENNESS, formerly Director of the National Museum of Canada, Wakefield, Quebec.

WILLIAM WILLMOTT, Associate Professor, Department of Anthropology and Sociology, University of British Columbia, Vancouver.

ASEN BALIKCI, Professor, Department of Anthropology, University of Montreal, Montreal.

JOHN HONIGMANN, Professor of Anthropology, University of North Carolina, Chapel Hill.

IRMA HONIGMANN, Research Associate, Institute for Research in Social Science, University of North Carolina, Chapel Hill.

CHARLES S. BRANT, Professor of Anthropology, University of Alberta, Edmonton.

CHARLES W. HOBART, Professor of Sociology, University of Alberta, Edmonton.

GEORGE SWINTON, Professor of Art, University of Manitoba, Winnipeg.

THE CARLETON LIBRARY